RECOGNIZING AND ADDRESSING AUTISM SPECTRUM DISORDERS IN TODDLERS

RECOGNIZING AND ADDRESSING AUTISM SPECTRUM DISORDERS IN TODDLERS

A Comprehensive Guide for Teachers and Parents of Young Children with Sensory Processing Disorder (SPD) and Autism Spectrum Disorder (ASD)

Michelle A. Souviron-Kehoe

Copyright © 2019 by Michelle A. Souviron-Kehoe.

Library of Congress Control Number:		2019904051
ISBN:	Hardcover	978-1-7960-2562-0
	Softcover	978-1-7960-2561-3
	eBook	978-1-7960-2560-6

All rights reserved. No part of this book may be reproduced or transmitted in any form or by any means, electronic or mechanical, including photocopying, recording, or by any information storage and retrieval system, without permission in writing from the copyright owner.

Any people depicted in stock imagery provided by Getty Images are models, and such images are being used for illustrative purposes only.
Certain stock imagery © Getty Images.

Print information available on the last page.

Rev. date: 04/03/2019

To order additional copies of this book, contact:
Xlibris
1-888-795-4274
www.Xlibris.com
Orders@Xlibris.com
791416

CONTENTS

1

Introduction

MY CAREER AS a bilingual special education itinerant, home and community early intervention and preschool-level teacher, and behavioral therapist began in 2000. Yes, that is a mouthful! The job is as specific and specialized as it is rewarding and fulfilling. From 1996 until 2002, I had been in a bilingual special education classroom, and one year prior to that, I worked as a bilingual special education, early intervention, and preschool-level evaluator. On occasion, I will do an evaluation for one of the agencies I work for, but I mostly work with students who are at the early intervention level. Early intervention–level students are aged birth to three years (technically one day before their third birthday). Preschool-level students are from age three to five years and present with a vastly different set of developmental and logistical challenges than children age birth to three.

I prefer working with early intervention–level children. They are like little sponges cognitively, emotionally, and socially. Their overall developmental success/improvement can be more positively affected by therapeutic intervention at an age of less than twenty-four months. An individual's core cognitive and psychological frameworks are mostly set by age three. Many special education preschool-level students are graduates of an early intervention program, whether center-based or home-and-community-based services. I typically see more consistent overall growth and improvement with early intervention–level students. One would have to refer to a longitudinal study to know whether or not these students continue to see similar successes while in the preschool program. Likewise, I would think that preschool-level children who did go through an early intervention program would benefit from an even higher level of developmental improvement as opposed to those with no prior therapeutic early intervention.

Delivering services at the early intervention level as an itinerant home/community teacher means you have to go to day-care facilities, head starts, and most often to children's homes. Most head starts and facility-based day cares are very clean and with nurturing environments. There are many home-based situations that are glaringly less than appropriate settings for young children to learn and grow. This is the nature of the job. You must get used to it and resign yourself to knowing you cannot fix every child's situation or circumstance. It's an unrealistic expectation, and it will take a toll on you emotionally and professionally. I prefer going into the city to anywhere else. I generally feel very appreciated and comfortable there. Many early intervention and preschool-level itinerant teachers and therapists avoid some geographic locations. Those who choose to go into center city and highly populated urban areas should be prepared for a variety of circumstances that may not necessarily present to the same degree in suburban or rural areas.

That being said, after you've been offered a case by your agency, you will contact the child's family to make your first appointment. Families are initially contacted by phone most often. Occasionally, if phone contact can't be made, you'll have to drop in unannounced to establish initial contact. Then your next visit will be your first billable visit. A parent or legal caregiver must sign billable visits. A relationship needs to be established with the parents and the child, as well as other team members and the ongoing service coordinator. Finding a good service coordinator can be tough at best and finding a fabulous one is sometimes next to impossible. I have noticed that children with very effective ongoing service coordinators enjoy more overall growth and improvement than those whose service coordinators were less effective.

Ongoing service coordinators connect and organize the team so that the child's services are delivered consistently and effectively. After the service coordinator, the team is the next important component to realizing developmental growth and improvement. The team strives to deliver the most comprehensive and effective level of therapy to ensure developmental success for the child. After the team, the next important component to developmental success and growth is the parents. Overwhelmingly, children whose parents are involved and active with their progress enjoy far greater success than those parents who are not involved. Thankfully, most parents are dedicatedly involved in their child's growth and improvement. Some parents are incredibly involved, and only a few lack involvement skills entirely. This is unfortunate, especially for the child. Therefore, certain steps are taken to work with the parents to afford them more parent-child involvement skills. I can honestly say that the majority of my students over the past, for almost seventeen years, have enjoyed moderate to good success and improvement, which roughly represents 75 to 80 percent of all my students. This is good, of course, but it can be higher.

Once therapy has been in place for at least three months, the child's progress will be recorded and discussed quarterly. This document reports the child's overall progress in your specific area of developmental expertise. The child will either stay at the same level or could be increased or decreased if so requested.

Therapy generally lasts until the day before the child's third birthday unless he or she has had transition testing by the child's particular school district and has a meeting before their third birthday. At this time, the child will either continue to qualify for special instruction services at the preschool level or will be dismissed. If the child does continue to qualify, he or she may stay in the early intervention program until the next cut-off date, if the parent so chooses. For children who are born from January 1 until August 31, cut-off date is August 31; for children born from September 1 until December 31, the cut-off date is December 31.

Every three months, children are reassessed via quarterly reports. They either continue to qualify at the same frequency, or they may be increased or decreased depending on assessment outcomes. When a therapist feels a child needs another service or a change in an existing service, the therapist must complete what is known as a part 2. I have included a blank copy of a sample quarterly report and a part

2 fully explaining their purpose in the forms and reports section of this guidebook. The majority of this guidebook consists of blank charts, checklists, forms, and reports. There will be a blank that can be reproduced if needed and another filled in with donations, which can also be reproduced. Many checklists will also impart information regarding the following topics: sensory integration, developmental milestones, behavioral issues, diagnostic criteria for autism spectrum disorder (ASD) and sensory processing disorder (SPD), therapy and teaching techniques, document and record keeping, paperwork issues and deadlines, team communication tips and checklists, protocol for approaching families regarding ASD, person list of typical versus ASD two-year-old development, lists of diverse and varied therapies, diet, lists of assessment tools, lists of useful acronyms and phrases, ICD-9 codes, parent involvement checklists, and many more.

I am putting the bulk of the information contained in this guidebook in checklist, chart, and reproducible fill-in-the-blank form so that they can be copied and consumed as needed. Many other informational pamphlets are written in narrative form, such as chapters and paragraphs, which is not conducive to being able to use and consume information in daily life situations. I had always wanted a comprehensive handy guidebook of reference-type information and consumable charts and forms but was never able to find one. So I have taken the opportunity to compile such a guidebook. This handbook will give you assistance and general information regarding itinerant home and community special education at the early intervention level. I've included a section of common occurrences and situations and lists of community services, resources, related programs, and phone/contact information. Anyone who is involved with a child with ASD, whether as teacher, therapist, parent, or other family member, can benefit from this guide. You are welcome to copy and use all templates provided as needed.

2

Note to Parents

I F YOUR CHILD has recently qualified for early intervention services due to a concern of a delay in a developmental area, I have written this guidebook for you, too, as you are your child's strongest advocate and supporter. It must be confusing and even scary that your child may not be meeting his or her developmental milestones on time. I am a parent of two daughters, and when they were little, they were my first priority. As parents, we want the best for our children, and when there is something wrong, all we want is to make it right. I have seen amazing success stories in my years of teaching and working with families. I've also seen situations where children sadly fall through the cracks due to a myriad of reasons: lost paperwork, paperwork filed too late, or paperwork that was never sent. But when all things go well, most children have an excellent chance of making great gains with their overall development and success in the early intervention program.

The EI program can be rather demanding, especially if your child receives more than one therapy. Sometimes children may receive as many as several therapeutic visits per week, and it may seem like a constant parade of teachers and therapists. Your home will also be open to service coordinators, county representatives, evaluators, and supervisors from time to time. It is encouraging when parents act as their child's main advocate by observing sessions, taking notes, asking questions, and following through with carry-over activities. This is because children benefit most when parents play an involved and active role in their education and developmental progress. Early intervention can be a wonderfully useful program when all pieces of the program are implemented properly and consistently. I hope that all parents reading this will give you all the advice, support and helpful hints, as you need to have a positive and rewarding experience with the early intervention program.

3

Note to Fellow Colleagues

WORKING AS AN itinerant special education teacher and going from home to home and day care to day care to deliver services to EI level students have been as challenging as they have been rewarding. And because of the wide variety of challenges, I had always wished I had some kind of manual or guidebook. I felt that I needed some words of advice and experiences to help me threw some daunting experiences and tricky situations. Even though many aspects of the job are "learn as you go," it's always helpful to have some form of practical references written by someone who has experienced similar circumstances. In fact, there have been many times over the past two decades when I thought that I should just write one myself, but who has time to do that? As an EI teacher, I can take on as many or as few students as I want, and I can work full-time for one agency or part-time for more than one and make my own schedule. Since I have a tough time saying no to new cases, I am usually rather busy. When my caseload is a bit too full, I feel frazzled, so I try to maintain a more manageable level. This is important to provide students with a fully focused teacher.

I had this need for a guidebook, though never wanted, so after many years of nagging myself to write one, I decided to just do it. I thought it would be a fairly simple undertaking; I'd just put to paper all my knowledge and experiences of the past twenty years working in early childhood special education. However, it was not the case. The more I wrote, the more topics I found about which to write. There were so many issues, subjects, and circumstances that needed to be defined and explained. There are many aspects of the job that no one explains to new EI teachers/therapists. One must learn the ropes little by little, day by day with each new child and each new case. So if you are new to the profession, I hope that the pieces of information, the personal anecdotes, and words of advice and experience will help fellow EI-level teachers and related-service therapists in gaining some measure of understanding, professional growth, insight, and success in working with children with EI-level special needs and their families.

4

List of Acronyms and Common Terms

ABA (applied behavior analysis): This is a type of behavior analysis that is based on the traditional theory of *behaviorism* and seeks to modify human behaviors as part of an educational and/or treatment plan. ABA is often used to help children with autism to learn a variety of skills. It is the most commonly used and one of the most evidenced-based methods of teaching individuals with a pervasive developmental disorder or social, motor, verbal, reasoning, and problem-solving skills delays. ABA can also be an effective method for managing problem behaviors with nearly anyone.

A-DOS (autism diagnostic observation schedule): This is an instrument for assessing and diagnosing autism. The protocol consists of a series of structured and semistructured tasks that involve social interaction between the examiner and the subject. Segments of the subject's behaviors are observed and identified and then are assigned to predetermined observational categories. Cutoffs have been determined by research to identify the potential diagnosis of autism or a related ASD.

ADD (attention-deficit disorder): This is one of the three subtypes of attention-deficit / hyperactivity disorder or ADHD. It is characterized primarily by inattention, easy distractibility, disorganization, procrastination, and forgetfulness. Different countries have different ways of diagnosing ADD. For example, in the UK, diagnosis is based on a narrow set of symptoms and about

0.5–1 percent of children are thought to have ADD. In the US, approximately 10 percent of children are described as having ADD. About five times more boys than girls are diagnosed with ADD.

ADHD (attention-deficit / hyperactivity disorder): This is a neurobehavioral disorder characterized by either significant difficulties of attention or hyperactivity and impulsiveness or a combination of the two. ADHD affects school-aged children and results in restlessness, acting impulsively and lack of focus, which impair their ability to learn.

ASQ (ages and stages questionnaires): These are parent-completed developmental and social-emotional screening tools that educators have trusted and valued for almost twenty years. These screening instruments help parents and educators catch early childhood delays and disabilities as soon as possible so that children may receive crucial support and services necessary for developmental health and well-being. ASQ is highly valid, accurate, and reliable. It was researched and tested with a wide, diverse sample of children. There are two ASQ screeners: (1) *ages and stages questionnaires third edition* is for developmental screening and (2) *ages and stages questionnaires social-emotional* is for social and emotional screening purposes.

ASD (autism spectrum disorder): This describes a range of conditions classified as pervasive developmental disorders in the *Diagnostic and Statistical Manual of Mental Disorders (DSM)*. The range of pervasive developmental disorders include autism, Asperger's syndrome, pervasive developmental disorder not otherwise specified (PDD-NOS), childhood disintegrative disorder, and Rett syndrome. However, only the first three are typically considered part of the autism spectrum. These disorders are characterized by social deficits, communication difficulties, stereotyped behaviors and interests, and in some cases, cognitive and learning delays. In May 2013, the *DSM-V* revised the diagnostic criteria for autism. There is now one category referred to as autism spectrum disorder, and it includes autism, Asperger's syndrome, childhood disintegrative disorder, and PDD-NOS.

AEPS (assessment evaluation and programming system for infants and children): This is an assessment tool that covers the developmental progress of children's functional skills in six principal domains: fine motor, gross motor, adaptive, cognitive, social-communication, and social development. The AEPS measurement tool is designed to help early interventionists improve the overall assessments of the abilities and needs of children ages birth to three who may have a disability or may be at risk for developmental delays.

Auditory association: This is the ability to connect two or more things using one's auditory sense, for example, hearing the first few words of a song and being able to recall the rest of the lyrics.

Auditory discrimination: This is the brain's ability to organize and make sense of language sounds. Some individuals who have had difficulty with this might have trouble understanding and developing language skills because their brains either misinterpret language sounds or process them too slowly.

Bell curve: It gets its name from the shape it commonly takes, which is a bell. It is also referred to as the normal probability distribution because under normal or typical circumstances, most subjects will fall at or be clustered around the center of the curve, the top of the bell. The center represents the general *mean* or average. The *standard deviation* represents how spread out the bell curve actually is or how many subjects fall on either side of the bell. Higher-standard deviations produce short, wide bells with more subjects on either side, and lower-standard deviations yield taller, narrower bells with fewer subjects on either side.

Bilateral coordination: This is the ability to use both sides of one's body at the same time. This can mean using both sides while doing the same activity (clapping), while using alternating movements (stacking blocks), or while using each side for a different action (picking up a toy with one hand while drinking from a cup with the other). Bilateral coordination is also referred to as *crossing midline.*

Bilingual language proficiency questionnaire: This is a parent-interview communication profile that is designed for use in the speech and language assessment of children ages birth to eight who speak either English or Vietnamese. Items examined are articulation, language, voice, fluency, and pragmatics. Items are listed in English and Spanish or in English and Vietnamese, which will be helpful in determining which language is most appropriate for the child's instructional program.

BBCS—R (Bracken basic concept scale—revised): This is an assessment tool that used to measure basic concept development in children ages two years, six months and seven years, eleven months. It is used to assess comprehension of 308 basic and functionally relevant educational concepts in eleven subconcept categories: colors, comparisons, shapes, direction/position, self/ social awareness, texture/material, quantity, and time/sequence.

BITSEA (brief infant toddler social emotional assessment): This is a social-emotional screening tool designed to assess children ages twelve to thirty-six months in the developmental areas of social and emotional skills and behaviors. It is a shorter and more condensed version of the ITSEA. (See separate reference in this section.) This test also is available in Spanish. It was developed by Margaret Briggs-Gowan, PhD, and Alice S. Carter, PhD.

CDD (childhood disintegrative disorder): This is also known as Heller's syndrome and regressive autism. Development appears to be normal for at least the first two years of life. The child then develops autistic symptoms and characteristics much later than is expected of "typical" autism. CDD is sometimes considered a low-functioning form of autism.

CNS (central nervous system): This is the part of the nervous system that integrates the information that it receives and coordinates all parts of the bodies of *bilateral* (both sides equally) animals. It comprises the brain, the brain stem, and the spinal cord. It is the processing center for the nervous system.

CSBS (communication and symbolic behavior scale): This is a standardized, norm-referenced evaluation instrument that examines communication, social, emotional, and symbolic abilities of children whose chronological age ranges from nine months through six years with a functional communication age of eight months to twenty-four months. This evaluation tool has two purposes: to early identify children who have or are at risk of developing a communication difficulty and to establish a profile of communication, symbolic, and social-emotional functioning to assist in future assessment, intervention, and monitoring of behavioral changes.

CPSE (Committee on Preschool Special Education): This services children from ages three to five with special learning or developmental needs. These children are usually coming from the early intervention program (EIP), or a pediatrician or educational professional may have more recently referred them.

CSE (Committee on Special Education): This services children and youth ages five through twenty-one. This can include programs that will help the child transition from school to work or school to college.

DAS (differential ability scales): This is a comprehensive, individually administered clinical instrument for the assessment of the cognitive abilities that are necessary for learning, such as visual and verbal memory recall, visual recognition and matching, visual and auditory processing, and basic number concepts.

DD (developmental delay): It is when a child presents a delay or deficit in one or more of the following five developmental areas:

- Cognitive
- Physical
- Communication
- Social/emotional
- Adaptive / self-help

DIAL-3 (developmental indicators for the assessment of learning): This is a norm-referenced screening instrument that seeks to identify young children ages three years to six years, eleven months at risk of or with delays in one or more of the following five developmental areas: cognitive and basic concepts, language, motor, self-help, and social-emotional. This tool is available in English and Spanish.

DECA (Devereux early childhood assessment program): This is a standardized, norm-referenced behavior rating scale that measures resilience or flexibility in preschool children. This assessment tool measures the ability of young children to bounce back from misfortune or extreme change. Test forms are available in English and Spanish.

DIR model (developmental, individual differences, relationship-based model): This model was developed by Dr. Stanley Greenspan in 1979. This model is used to assess the strengths and weaknesses of any individual but is especially useful with children and individuals who are on the autism spectrum. The DIR model challenges and encourages children to move up a hierarchical ladder of emotionally developmental *stages* or milestones. These are typically difficult for many on the spectrum to master. The goals of Dr. Greenspan's Floortime model relate to and correspond with these stages/

milestones to offer the child a comprehensive developmental intervention that seeks to meet the child at her current development. (Please refer to DIR/Floortime entry.)

DSM (*Diagnostic Statistical Manual of Mental Disorders*): This is a guide published by the American Psychiatric Association, which provides a common language and standard criteria for the classification of mental disorder. The current edition is the *DSM-V*, which replaced the *DSM-IV* in May 2013.

Dysrhythmia: In linguistics, it refers to a disturbance in the rhythm of speech. It is an abnormality in an otherwise normal rhythmic pattern of speech production. Sometimes this type of speech sounds choppy or halted, with too many or not enough pauses in between individual words or short phrases. Many individuals on the autism spectrum have evidence of *dysrhythmia* in their manner of speech.

E-LAP (early learning accomplishment profile): This is a criterion-referenced assessment tool that examines six different developmental areas: cognitive, language, gross motor, fine motor, self-help, and social-emotional in children from birth to thirty-six months. It is available in English and Spanish. This tool can be used with any infant or toddler and children with disabilities.

ESI—R (early screening inventory—revised): This is a brief developmental screening instrument that is individually administered to children ages three to six. This tool is designed to identify children who may need special or enhanced services in order to perform successfully in school. Since three- to four-and-a-half-year-olds and four-and-a-half- to six-year-olds differ greatly in several critical developmental areas, there are separate forms that are reflective of these differences.

EIP (early intervention program): This services children ages birth to three. These children have been identified with special needs in that they have some delay or difficulty in a developmental area such as cognitive, communication, motor, social, or behavioral. These children receive therapy as their specific needs on a weekly or monthly basis. Their parents are encouraged to participate in the sessions. They are given tips by the therapists regarding how they, too, can facilitate their children's development and overall progress (see PAPI).

Expressive language skills: These are used when speaking, including the level and degree of skills and the speaker's ability to use their spoken language skills to express their needs, feelings, etc.

FBA (functional behavioral assessment): This is a problem-solving process for assessing challenging behaviors in children. These behaviors are seen as being the result of real incidents or situations in the child's life. An FBA looks at the reasons and triggers for the behaviors and then helps the child's team to select a variety of interventions to directly address the behaviors.

GARS-2 (Gilliam autism rating scale-2): This assessment tool is a forty-two-item, norm-referenced screening instrument used for the assessment of individuals ages three to twenty-two who have severe behavioral problems that may be indicative of autism. Its purpose is to help professionals identify ASD, but in the school setting, it is used to help educational teams determine whether a child may meet state educational criteria for receiving special education services under the autism spectrum disorder category. It is important to stress here that this is *not* a medical diagnosis. Rather, it is a way to determine a category for receiving special education services. The GARS-2 seeks to gather information regarding specific characteristics typically seen in children with ASD in three main areas: stereotyped behaviors, communication skills, and social interaction skills. This assessment tool was normed entirely of individuals with autism diagnoses. The tool provides standard scores and percentiles by which the *likelihood* of the presence or autism can be determined.

Greenspan social-emotional growth chart: This is a social-emotional developmental milestones growth chart developed by Dr. Stanley Greenspan to measure and assess social-emotional milestones in young children ages birth to forty-two months. Early detection of social-emotional delays leads to more fruitful interventions and therapies. This tool offers a brief and dependable tool to meet your and your child's needs in several crucial social and emotional areas of concern. These include determining mastery of early social-emotional abilities, monitoring healthy social-emotional functioning, establishing goals and objectives for early intervention planning, monitoring growth in early intervention programs, and detecting delays or concerns with developmental social-emotional abilities. This tool is designed to be completed by the child's parent, educator, or other close caregiver to understand how the child uses all their abilities to meet their needs, deal with their feelings, think, problem-solve and communicate.

Hawaii early learning profile (birth to three years): HELP is widely recognized as a comprehensive, family-centered, curriculum-based assessment tool for the instructors and families of infants and toddlers. This tool assists in identifying 685 developmental skills and behaviors that are present from birth to three years. Developmental domains include: cognitive, language, gross motor, fine motor, social-emotional, and adaptive/self-help skills. This tool provides an excellent comprehensive framework for ongoing assessment, curriculum planning, and tracking progress.

IDEA (Individuals with Disabilities Education Act): IDEA was enacted by Congress in 1975 to ensure that all children up to age twenty-one have the opportunity to receive a free and appropriate public education. Its two recent amendments are Part B in 2006, and Part C in 2011. Part B concerns preschool and school aged children and Part C concerns children ages birth to three (babies and toddlers). IDEA Part C allows individual states to define "developmental delay" and how children qualify for services. This will vary widely from state to state. For example, in New York State, a child must have a 33 percent delay in at least one developmental area or a 25 percent delay in two areas. Other states may be more or less particular with their qualification guidelines.

IEP (individualized education program): This is mandated by the Individuals with Disabilities Education Act (IDEA). It defines the individualized short-term objectives and long-term goals for the child. The IEP is designed to help children meet their educational goals more easily than without the benefit of having an IEP.

IFSP (individual family service plan): This is very similar to the IEP but at the early intervention level for children ages birth to three. The IFSP is designed to address the child's needs within the context of the home and community and strives to involve the child's family in the therapy by infusing therapy techniques and strategies into the everyday activities experienced by the child. The IFSP contains information regarding how often the therapy is to take place—frequency and the length of the session or the duration. Both of these variables depend upon the child's specific needs. The majority of children start out at one time per week for thirty minutes and can be increased or decreased accordingly via the amendment process.

IFTI (infant-toddler and family instrument): This is an assessment tool developed to provide easy-to-use, clinically sensitive instrument to assist families and their workers in determining how well a young child from six to thirty-six months is developing and how well the family is managing parenting tasks and responsibilities. The IFTI offers clear, simple ways to question parents and other caregivers regarding children's characteristics, daily activities, health, overall development, and family life.

ISC (initial service coordinator): This is a county representative who guides the family through the core evaluation process. Once the child has been evaluated and qualifies for services, the ISC helps the family to choose an agency that will provide a therapist who specializes in the child's area of need. At this point, most families will receive an ongoing service coordinator (see OSC) who will typically provide coordination services until the child transitions out of the EIP.

Joint attention: This is when one person draws attention to an object by gazing at another person in order to share a common interest and, thereby, a common visual acknowledgment of that object. Engaging in joint attention is a skill that can be difficult for children on the autism spectrum. Researchers found that nearly all typically developing eight- to fourteen-month-old children engage in varying levels of joint attention.

Landmarks of normal psychosocial development: This is an assessment tool that is organized on the basis of social behaviors at different stages. It can be used to assess children ages birth to five. This tool provides a quick checklist for caregivers seeking to obtain a child's psychosocial developmental level through her social interactions with the environment.

Lateralization: This shows how each hemisphere of the brain works, either separately or together and with varying levels of dominance and contribution to produce cognitive functioning.

M-CHAT—R (modified checklist of autism in toddlers—revised): This is a scientifically validated tool for screening children between sixteen and thirty months of age to assess whether they are at risk for ASD. The American Academy of Pediatrics (AAP) recommends that all children receive autism screening between eighteen and twenty-four months and the M-CHAT-R is one of the preferred tools. To improve the accuracy of this tool, the authors have developed a follow-up interview for parents and other primary caregivers.

MMR (measles, mumps, rubella vaccine): This is the vaccine that children typically receive at around eighteen months of age.

Motor planning: This is the ability to conceive/think of, plan, and carry out a skilled, nonhabitual motor act in the correct sequence from start to finish while maintaining sufficient balance.

Negative reinforcement: This is a strong deterrent or consequence administered in response to an undesirable behavior so that its occurrence is diminished or eliminated.

NLD (nonverbal learning disorder): This is a condition characterized by a significant discrepancy between higher verbal skills and lower motor, visual-spatial and social skills on an intelligence test. NLD involves difficulties in perception, coordination, socialization, nonverbal problem-solving skills, and the understanding of humor in addition to a well-developed rote memory. It is also a common coexciting disorder with ADHD. There are striking similarities between Asperger's syndrome and NLD. Both exist on a spectrum and most people with Asperger's syndrome fit the criteria for NLD.

Norm-referenced test: This is a test, evaluation, or assessment measure that will yield an estimate of the individual being tested in a predefined population with respect to the trait being measured. The estimate is derived from the analysis of test scores and other relevant information from a *sample* drawn from the predefined population. If the test seeks to derive information regarding a particular age group or other specific demographic, then the sample needs to reflect that by drawing from a population that is of equal quality. For example, the PLS-3 seeks to obtain information regarding the receptive and expressive language skills of children ages two weeks to six years, eleven months. Therefore, the *sample population* for this assessment reflects that by using 1,200 children is this exact age group. Other important considerations in choosing a sample population for the PLS-3 are gender, race, socioeconomic background, parents' education levels, geographic region so that a good cross reference of the US population is obtained, thereby ensuring that the test and its results are reliable.

Object permanence: This is when a child will look for an item when placed out of sight, she understands that it still exists even though it was hidden. The child will attempt to look for it and will expect to see it again in the same spot that it disappeared. Children on the spectrum often develop this ability later than typically developing children. Therefore, games like Guess Which Hand may not come easily at first, but with some persistence it can be an excellent teaching technique to facilitate this skill.

OSC (ongoing service coordinator): This is the person who is responsible for coordinating all the child's services at the EI level. It is very important to have an experienced, proactive OSC especially when working with a sensitive or involved case (see the section-The Importance of Having a Fabulous OSC)

PLS-3 (preschool language scale-3): This standardized and norm-referenced evaluation tool is used to assess receptive language skills in infants and young children ages two weeks to six years, 11 months. The tool assesses behaviors that are considered to be language precursors. The tool directly screens children and interviews caregivers and is available in Spanish and English.

PAPI (parents as primary interventionists): This is a fairly recent EI program that has been implemented to provide families with the information and support necessary to make informed decisions about their child. This program promotes family-guided, routine-based intervention and intervention techniques. Family members are invited to watch and participate. Parents are encouraged to engage in frequent and on-going communication with their child's team members and are invited to all meetings. Ultimately, it is hoped that parents will be able to engage in similar therapeutic activities with their child in between sessions, as they, too, are considered to be their child's interventionists.

PDD (pervasive developmental disorder): This is a diagnostic category refers to a group of five disorders characterized by delays in the development of multiple basic functions including socialization and communication. The five disorders are the following:

1. PDD-NOS
2. Autism
3. Asperger's syndrome
4. Rett syndrome
5. CDD (childhood disintegrative disorder)

The first *three* of these disorders are often referred to as the *autism spectrum disorders*; the last two disorders are very rare and are not always included in the spectrum. PDD is *not* itself a diagnosis, while PDD-NOS is. Rather, PDD is a broader category of disorders in which the diagnostic subcategory of PDD-NOS is included. Many individuals diagnosed with PDD-NOS have many of the characteristics of classic autism but not all. They may also have many but not all the characteristics of Asperger's syndrome. There continues to be a lot of confusion around the use of and definition of PDD-NOS compared with autism and Asperger's syndrome.

PDD-NOS (pervasive developmental disorder-not otherwise specified): This is one of the five autism spectrum disorders (ASD) and is also one of the five disorders classified as a pervasive developmental disorder (PDD). Children with PDD-NOS typically have higher verbal and nonverbal IQ scores than those with classic autism. They display *perseverative* (repetitive and continual) behaviors, and their speech is marked with strange features and prosody (i.e., stress and intonation of utterances is odd or somehow "off"). Children with PDD-NOS are usually very social but are often seen as odd or different by others. Essentially, a child diagnosed with PDD-NOS is on the spectrum somewhere but doesn't fit neatly into any one category. However, he has marked characteristics of classic autism and Asperger's, as well as CDD.

Pragmatic language impairment: This is an impairment in understanding the pragmatic areas of speech. Pragmatic language refers to several social language skills including three major language/communication skills:

1) Language use—greeting, informing, demanding, promising, requesting.
2) Changing language—according to the listener's needs or the situation.
3) Following rules—taking turns in conversation, staying on topic, rephrasing when misunderstood, using verbal and nonverbal signals, using facial expressions and body language and how close to stand to someone when speaking.

Many individuals on the autism spectrum have difficulty using pragmatic language skills. They may say inappropriate or unrelated things in conversations with others. They may tell stories in a disorganized way. They may have little variety in language or vocabulary use.

Perseveration: The tendency of many individuals with an autism spectrum disorder to repeat something insistently or redundantly. Often times, the actions that are repeated are nonproductive or nonfunctional and can also include self-stimulating behaviors that primarily serve to calm the individual.

PDAS (preschool developmental assessment scale): This is a tool used to assess preschool-aged children's skills in a variety of areas including cognition, social-emotional, communication/language, fine and gross motor, and adaptive/daily living.

Positive reinforcement: It is rewarding an individual with a desirable outcome in response to some behavior or activity. Anything can be positively reinforced—good behavior as well as bad. When a child is engaging in an appropriate behavior or task, we want to reward them so that they know we notice their efforts and so that the behavior continues. However, many times, we also reward negative behaviors, such as giving into a child's tantrum because it's easier than dealing with it. I was guilty of this when my own daughters were little at times, so I fully understand how it can happen. When any behavior is rewarded with a desirable payoff, it is almost always guaranteed to continue. Regardless of the particular behavior, it continues because it is human nature to strive for things that we need or want, and when we're rewarded, we continue to engage in the same behavior in anticipation of the desired outcome.

Receptive language skills: The skills that are necessary for one to understand what is being said. These skills vary depending on the age of the individual. For example, between the ages of twenty-four to thirty-six months, children should understand words with different meanings such as up/down and concepts such as "happy" or "sad." How children respond to what is being said is often an indicator of how well they process and comprehend spoken language.

Rigid persistence: It is when the child displays a strong determination to engage in or complete a task in his or her own way even with equally persistent redirection from the teacher/therapist or parent. They do this with an intense resolve while attempting to prevent the adult from redirecting them to something else. Therefore, you must match their determination in your efforts to teach them how to complete the task more functionally or productively. After almost twenty years in EI, I believe that the child is actually engaging in some form of stereotypical behavior (stimming), and they are being stimulated by the manner in which they are performing the task.

And since it is sensorily pleasing, they will persist in performing the task their way until redirected and taught another way that will better facilitate learning new skills.

Routine: It is any activity that is performed with regularity and meaning. For example, we make a routine out of brushing our teeth. We do this at a particular time for the specific purpose of having good oral hygiene. Routines are extremely important for children to have so that they may learn healthy behaviors and responsibilities. (See appx. no.)

Self-stimulating behaviors: It is also called stereotypical behaviors, in that they have a fixed or set form. These behaviors are usually manifested as repetitive body movements such as rocking or hand-flapping. However, these ritualistic movements can also present in many forms, with some not easily detected. Since *stimming* seems to perk one or more of the senses, an individual can engage in most any kind of stim-type behavior. Parents and teachers/therapists must be consistently vigilant when with their child/student in noticing what they're doing and why because there is always a reason for any behavior. For example, *visual stimming* is common in young children on the spectrum. They may look at an item with an intense, lingering gaze, moving their eyes repetitively up and down or side to side. *Vocal stimming* is when the child produces repetitive vocalizations such as word parts, word approximations, and unintelligible jargon. *Auditory stimming* is not easily noticeable, but it may happen when the child fixates on sounds, voices, or music almost to the exclusion of everything else going on around them. *Tactile stimming* is what is most frequently seen with individuals on the autism spectrum. It can include touching things, picking them up, or carrying them around constantly, routinely, or even obsessively. Tactile contact can range from tapping to pounding and everything in between. Tactile contact can also be made by any part of the body, including lips and tongues (e.g., licking surfaces or putting objects to or into the mouth). This kind of tactile stimming is a bit more challenging to redirect at times, but it is important to be extra vigilant due to gagging and choking risks. *Proprioceptive stimming* can include tightening or loosening muscles to achieve different levels of muscle intensity—for example, clenching and unclenching fists or grinding teeth are fairly common. *Vestibular stimming* tends to be rare but may include movements that continually seek to promote different levels of or intensity in balance and how the body feels in space, if it's balanced and aligned comfortably. Redirection can help to reduce the frequency and intensity of the stim behavior and can facilitate engaging in more functional behaviors.

SBMD (sensory-based motor disorder): It is a motor disability that has several characteristics that are seen in many common sensory disorders. This disorder can present itself as either a postural disorder or as dyspraxia.

SMD (sensory modulation disorder): It is when the child has difficulty regulating the amount of sensory information that he is experiencing. This disorder can present itself as either sensory over-responsivity (SOR), sensory under-responsivity (SUR), or sensory seeking/craving (SS).

Speech: It is the vocalization form of human communication. Everyone capable of speech does so using words that are specific to and characteristic of their dominant language(s). An example of a nonvocal type of speech would be sign language, which is globally recognized as a language just as is Spanish or English.

Speech and language screening measure: This two-page checklist provides caregivers with a quick screening to obtain a child's speech and language activities and developmental level by answering simple "yes/no" questions. It can be used with children ages three to five. The tasks measure expressive language, receptive language, articulation, fluency, and voice quality. If more information needs to be obtained, there are some open-ended questions provided. This tool is available in Chinese and English.

SPD (sensory processing disorder): This is an atypical reaction in the central nervous system to ordinary sensory experiences, which causes an atypical response in areas such as work, play, and interpersonal relationships.

SID (sensory integration disorder): This is another way of labeling SPD. When we *process* sensory experiences, our brains work to *comprehend* the information so that we can integrate it into our daily lives as functionally as possible and in a variety of settings. If sensory information is misunderstood it is difficult to respond to it and then apply it usefully in daily activities.

SDD (sensory discrimination disorder): It is when the child has difficulty differentiating the sensory information that he is experiencing. These difficulties can be either visual, auditory, tactile, gustatory, or position/movement related.

SOR (sensory over-responsivity): It is when the child tries to avoid sensory information. She may be fearful or cautious. He may be negative and defiant. The fight or flight response is hypersensitive and may be in response to harmless situations. It is typically seen as being defensive.

SUR (sensory under-responsivity): It is when the child seeks out or craves an abundance of sensory input to get into gear. The child may have a limited perception of pain, poor self-protection, or may be injurious to self or others. She may be slow or sluggish in response to ordinary sensations. He may be excessively loose or floppy. Behaviorally, these children may be seen as being self-absorbed, disengaged, or inattentive.

Standardization: It is when the instructions of a test must be followed *exactly* the same way each time it is administered with no deviations whatsoever. This is so that the results of the test will be clinically reliable, as many of them will yield a diagnosis. The opposite of a standardized test is a *nonstandardized test*. This type of testing gives different testing tools to different test takers or they give the same test under significantly different conditions or test takers are evaluated differently. It is, therefore, recognized that standardized test are fairer and yield more reliable information.

TOM (theory of mind): This is the ability to understand the thoughts, reasonings, and different perspectives of others. Children on the autism spectrum often have difficulty connecting with others on that level and in understanding that others have beliefs, desires, and intentions that differ from their own.

Vineland social-emotional early childhood scales (SEEC): This testing tool was developed from the Vineland adaptive behavior scale. It is a standardized, norm-referenced evaluation tool for children ages birth to six. This instrument seeks to assess the young child's level of social and emotional functioning via an interview with a caregiver who is most familiar with the child's social and emotional behaviors.

Visual discrimination: This is a term that describes how our visual abilities detect specific features of an object to process it in a number of ways, such as recognizing it, matching it, duplicating it, and categorizing it in order to gain knowledge about the object.

Visual motor integration: This is the ability to coordinate vision with the movements of the body or parts of the body with sufficient balance in order to accomplish tasks.

Visual tracking: This is when one follows an object with their eyes without looking away or breaking their gaze with the object (e.g., watching a ball as it rolls out of sight or credits on television as they go from top to bottom or the reverse). It is a common form of visual type of stim for many children on the spectrum.

5

Recognizing and Identifying ASD (Autism Spectrum Disorder)

MANY TEACHERS AND therapists of children with special needs have been blessed with or have developed keen sensitivities in recognizing when a young child (eighteen months to three or four years) may be on the autism spectrum. I, too, am able to recognize many of the more common characteristics that typically present in children in this age group. This is partly due to required college courses and student teaching I completed. But it is mostly because of the knowledge and sensitivity I developed over the years as an EI teacher.

For the first several years, however, I was hesitant to even suspect that a student might be autistic. And the thought of the child's parents being told this was just heartbreaking! As a parent myself, I know that I would be devastated to find this out. I didn't want to draw incorrect assumptions or conclusions, so I strove to educate myself about "all things autism." I read books and research articles and attended workshops, in-services, seminars, and conferences to increase my knowledge. The numbers of children being identified and eventually diagnosed were steadily and rapidly increasing from just a few years prior. I felt it was my professional duty and responsibility to find out more about this neurological condition and how to better assist my students.

The following characteristic signs may be noticeable in the first few sessions. If a child presents with any three or more in any subgroup, it is suggested that the ongoing service coordinator be notified and a team meeting arranged to discuss the team's plan of action.

Ten Early Signs of Autism

1. Disconnection to others
2. Apparent lack of empathy
3. Indifferent to human interaction
4. Emotional outbursts
5. Delayed language development
6. Prone to nonverbal communication
7. Difficulty understanding figurative expressions
8. Repetitive behaviors
9. Pica (chewing or consuming nonfood items)
10. Sensitivity to external stimuli (sensory processing disorder)

Characteristic Signs of an Autism Spectrum Disorder (ASD)

1. **Social impairment:**
   - vague, limited eye contact
   - lack of joint attention to others
   - lack of awareness to others, acts as if deaf
   - abnormal greeting behaviors
   - abnormalities seeking/giving comfort or affection
   - impairment of social imitation
   - impaired ability to make friends
   - impairment of pretend/imaginative play
   - lack of awareness of social rules

2. **Communication impairment:**
   - abnormalities in pragmatics
   - impaired comprehension
   - bizarre speech patterns
   - impaired pitch, stress, rate, or volume
   - impaired ability to express abstract symbolism

3. **Ritual/repetitive activities:**
   - stereotypical motor behaviors (e.g., hand flapping)
   - abnormal sensory characteristics
   - preoccupation with objects
   - need to maintain sameness in environment
   - fixed routines
   - restrictive and/or perseverative interests

- absence of spontaneous interests and activities (see *self-stimulating behaviors* in "List of Common Terms")

Summary:

The above list of typically seen characteristic signs of autism spectrum disorders is meant to be used as a reference for anyone who cares for or works with children, whether they be typically developing or have special needs. When a few to several of these traits are present for any length of time, parents need to be notified so that their children can begin the early intervention process.

7

Frequently Observed ASD Behaviors

*G*ILLIAM AUTISM RATING Scale-2 (GARS-2) list of assessment items that were rated by parents and educators as *frequently observed* in each of the following categories:

Stereotyped Behaviors
- Avoids establishing eye contact, looks away when eye contact is made
- Stares at hands, objects, or items in her surroundings for at least five seconds
- Rapidly shakes fingers or hands in front of face and sometimes up to light for at least five or so seconds
- Eats only specific foods and refuses to eat what most people will eat
- Licks, tastes, or attempts to eat inedible items
- Smells or sniffs objects
- Whirls or spins self in circles
- Spins objects not designed to be spun
- Rocks back and forth or sometimes side to side while seated or standing
- Makes quick darting or lunging movements when moving from one place to the next.
- Walks on tiptoes
- Flaps fingers or hands in front of face or to the side
- Makes high-pitched sounds or other odd-sounding vocalizations for self-stimulation

- Slaps, hits, or bites self or attempts to injure self in other ways

Communication Behaviors
- Repeats or echoes words vocally or uses signs
- Repeats words out of context
- Repeats words or phrases over and over again
- Speaks or signs with a flat tone or effect
- Responds inappropriately to simple commands
- Looks away or avoids looking at the speaker
- Does not ask for things she wants
- Does not initiate conversations with peers or adults
- Uses "yes" and "no" inappropriately
- Uses pronouns inappropriately
- Uses "I" inappropriately
- Repeats unintelligible sounds over and over again
- Uses gestures instead of speech or signs to obtain items
- Inappropriately answers questions about a statement or short story

Social Interaction Behaviors
- Avoids eye contact or looks away when being spoken to
- Stares or looks sad or distant when being entertained or praised
- Resists physical contact from others
- Does not imitate others when imitation is encouraged as in games or other educational activities
- Withdraws or is standoffish in group situations
- Behaves in an unreasonably fearful or frightened manner
- Is unaffectionate or does not offer affectionate responses
- Shows no recognition of someone being present or looks through people
- Laughs, giggles, or cries at inappropriate times
- Uses toys or other items inappropriately
- Does certain everyday type things repeatedly or ritualistically
- Becomes highly agitated when routines are changed

- Responds negatively or with tantrums when given even familiar commands or requests
- Lines up items in orderly, precise manner and gets upset when it's disturbed

Note: The following *developmental delays* in the first three years were reported via the parent interview portion of the GARS-2

Social Interactions
- Did not reach out to be picked up by when parent tried to do so
- Did not cry or become upset when left unattended in playpen or crib
- Did not become upset when picked up or held; emotionally detached
- Did not cry or fuss when handed from one adult to another
- Did not try to join family members at a gathering

Language Used During Social Interactions
- Did not use single words by sixteen months
- Did not use meaningful phrases by the age two
- Did not develop normally in terms of language skills (i.e., babbling, cooing, and using simple words without regression or interruption)
- Did not follow familiar directions
- Did not appear to have normal hearing abilities

Note: The following observations of *abnormal functioning* during the first three years were reported via the parent interview portion of the GARS-2

Social Interactions
- Did not smile at parents or siblings when smiled at or played with
- Did not cry when approached by unfamiliar people during the first year

MICHELLE A. SOUVIRON-KEHOE

- Did not engage in pretend play before the age of three
- Seemed to tune people out and be in his own world
- Spent a good deal of time alone when she could have been with others

Language Used in Social Communication
- Did not respond to his name when called
- Did not ask for things or use gestures/signs to communicate what was desired
- Did not follow simple directions
- Did not appear to understand what to do when told to do something
- Did not indicate (by showing facial concern) when a parent or sibling was upset

Symbolic/Imaginative Play
- Did not engage in pretend play
- Did not pretend she was someone else
- Did not pretend an object was something else
- Did not pretend that he had an imaginary friend or animal
- Did not play with dolls pretending they were real people

8

What Exactly Is Stimming?

I N THE FIRST place, *stimming* is a very shortened form of *self-stimulating behavior.* When children engage in stimming, they are trying to self-sooth and self-calm. Quite often, stim behaviors are repetitive and can go on for several minutes to even hours if allowed. Also, I believe that children can engage in any form of stim imaginable. I've seen children stim while looking at something such as a spinning object or even one at rest. So making eye contact isn't always something that is engaged in with a functional or productive outcome. Sometimes kids can gaze for long periods of time, seemingly entranced by something most people would regard for only a few seconds.

Children who engage in a stim behavior typically do so without regard to what is going on around them or who may be present. In fact, much stim behavior is engaged in specifically for the purpose of distancing oneself from nearby activity, especially if that activity is too much sensory. This is most likely a defense mechanism against the outside world, or perhaps they're just mort interested in themselves more at that moment. Stim behaviors are also engaged in to self-stimulate or increase sensory excitement: visually, auditorily, and tactilely.

Sometimes children stim while engaged in a task or chore. For example, I have seen kiddos visually stim while putting items away into bags, boxes, or other containers. They are visually stimming while watching the object descend into the bag to the point where it can no longer be seen. I began to notice kids doing this with more and more students and figured it was a stim phenomenon specific to kiddos on the spectrum. One of the most popular activities that my students use is a game called Barnyard Bingo. With this game, children insert quarter-sized plastic coins into a slot at the top of a flat plastic barn. Then they must open a plastic flap at the bottom of the barn. The flap at the bottom, when opened and closed, makes a *boing-boing* sound, which the children seem to delight in opening and closing this flap without end, much to the chagrin of the adult trying to play the game with the child. Once a coin is retrieved, its color and animal is matched to one of four different colored plastic cards with pictures of four different farm animals.

Without fail, my students on the spectrum would rather watch mesmerizingly as they insert the coins and then *boing-boing* away than match colors/animals to receive bingo for correct matches. I try to get the kids past their desire to engage in this activity only for its auditory and visual stim qualities and emphasize how much fun it is to play the game productively. This is always a bit of a challenge. These kinds of stims are appealing to children for many reasons. They're visually, auditorily, and/or tactilely satisfying. One must be creative in trying to compete with that and get them to engage in functional play skills rather than engaging in stims.

My main point in writing this section is to urge therapists and parents to be aware of these kinds of stimming behaviors and that children can engage in just any kind of stim imaginable and under a wide variety of conditions and circumstances. When you recognize a behavior as a stim, rather than a functional, productive behavior, try to redirect the child toward engaging in more meaningful and appropriate activities. The more children are allowed to continuously engage in stims the less likely they are to develop age and socially appropriate interaction skills.

9

Conditions That May
Mimic an ASD

THERE ARE A few conditions that may mimic autism-like disorders. This is another reason that one must be nearly certain that the child does *not* fall into that category before alerting parents to a possible ASD. For example, a child may have an SPD and a legitimate hearing impairment or high lead levels, prenatal chemical, or substance exposure or any combination of these conditions. More often than not, I have students with an SPD and a hearing impairment. Children with high lead levels often present with ASD-like characteristics as do children who have been exposed to chemicals or harmful substances in utero. A list of possible mimicking conditions are as follows:

1. Sensory processing disorder
2. Hearing impairment
3. High lead levels
4. Fetal alcohol or any prenatal chemical or substance exposure
5. Attention-deficit disorder
6. Attention-deficit / hyperactivity disorder

It is, therefore, of the *utmost importance* that service coordinators, teachers, and therapists assist the family in having the child properly evaluated by a medical professional. This is the only way the child can receive a therapeutic program that is individually tailored to his or her specific needs.

10

The Sensory Disorders

1. **SID** (sensory integration disorder)—sometimes used synonymously with SPD, I see some difference between them. To integrate sensory information, one must find ways to use or put together that information in their everyday activities so that the individual may function productively in *all* aspects of daily life.

2. **SPD** (sensory processing disorder)—an atypical reaction in the central nervous system to ordinary sensory experiences and situations. Sensory information is not processed properly resulting in an atypical response in all aspects of one's daily life. When sensory information is processed improperly due to a neurological wiring or firing difficulty, the individual experiences reactions that are *atypical* or out of the ordinary compared to reactions to sensory information that the majority of people experience in similar situations.

3. **SDD** (sensory discrimination disorder)—when the child cannot discern among or between sensations, stimuli is typically visual and/or auditory. It may or may not coexist with SMD.

4. **SMD** (sensory modulation disorder)—how sensory information is regulated and fine-tuned can be hyper/over sensitive, hypo/under sensitive or a sensory seeker/craver.

*The three main hallmarks of SPD:

1. Avoids ordinary touch and movement

2. Seeks excessive touch and movement
3. Difficulty in making one's body cooperate

Summary:

Put quite simply, a child may have an SPD but *not* necessarily be on the autism spectrum. On the contrary, the vast majority of children with an ASD also have an SPD. There are three main or outstanding traits that often point to the child having a significant sensory disorder. When the child processes sensory information atypically, their responses will also present as atypical or different, even problematic for the child and their families. It is, therefore, essential that children with sensory processing difficulties receive therapy so they may develop and grow while learning how to manage and regulate their behaviors.

MICHELLE A. SOUVIRON-KEHOE

11

Sensory Issues and Concerns

A LL THE INFORMATION that we receive from the outside world is sensory data or information that we process, understand, and respond to depending on which specific sense has been aroused. Any of this information can, however, be registered, interpreted, and understood differently when someone has a *sensory processing disorder*— an SPD. What we see, what we hear, what we taste, what we touch, what we smell, and what we feel (physically not emotionally) is all information that we must process and then integrate into our daily lives.

The Senses:

Near Senses—close to or within you
Far Senses—external / on surface of body

Near:

vestibular/equilibrioception—inner ear, balance
interception—internal organs
proprioception—muscles, joints, body/limbs

Far:

smell/olfactory
taste/gustatory
touch/tactile
sight/vision
hearing/auditory

* The *far senses* are the ones that most commonly come to mind when thinking of the senses, and they are fairly self-explanatory.

* The function of the three *near senses* working together leads to overall coordination and balance in the child's body. They require some explanation:

1. The **vestibular system** includes the inner ear, which contributes to balance and spatial orientation and is the sensory system that provides the leading contribution regarding movement and sense of balance. This sense receives its name from the *vestibulum,* which is part of the *labyrinth of the inner ear.* The brain uses information from the vestibular system in the head and from the proprioception throughout the body to understand the body's position and acceleration from moment to moment.

2. **Interoception** is any sense that is normally stimulated from within the body. This internal sense helps to maintain a link neurologically from our internal organs to our brains via sensory receptors.

3. **Proprioception** also includes *kinesthesia*, which is the sense or awareness of one's limbs (arms, legs) and whole body in space and in relation to the surrounding environment. For example, when walking through a crowded or cluttered room, one must be aware of the surrounding objects and proceed with the appropriate amount of caution given the environment. Individuals with sensory concerns in the area of proprioception may have more difficulty negotiating such environments.

Summary:

Most everyone can name their five senses: sight, taste, smell, touch, and hearing. However, the three other lesser-known senses are equally as important to our sensory development—how we understand information from the world around us and how we *react* to this information. For the vast majority of individuals on the autism spectrum, any and all senses may be affected negatively when the neural pathways of the brain misdirect incoming sensory information. When sensory information is misdirected in the brain, the child has trouble responding to that information in a normal or typical way. The child on the spectrum experiences sights, tastes, smells, sounds, and touches in an atypical way that is often times overwhelming for his overly acute sensory systems. Individuals with autism can also present with underactive sensory systems. They often need considerable prompting, encouragement, and assistance to alert and engage their bodies so they can learn and grow.

In their extraordinary book *1001 Great Ideas for Teaching and Raising Children with Autism or Asperger's*, Ellen Notbohm and Veronica Zysk emphasize the simple but crucial fact that "sensory integration dysfunction is at the root of many of the core difficulties of autism spectrum disorders." I, too, have found this to be true in my own educational practice and interactions with individuals on the spectrum. Also, they state "addressing and treating sensory dysfunction should always be near the top of the what-to-do-first list." Again, I concur completely. Sensory integration affects behavior, learning, communication, daily living, and adaptive skills, which all in turn dictate how the child develops and grows.

Signs of Sensory Integration Dysfunction

1. Oversensitivity to touch, movement, sights, or sounds
2. Under-reactivity to sensory stimulation may whirl around or crash body
3. Activity level that is unusually high or unusually low
4. Coordination problems, poor balance, or motor coordination
5. Delays in speech/communication, motor skills, or academic achievement
6. Poor organization of behavior, may be impulsive, distractible, or aggressive
7. Poor self-concept, may seem lazy or unmotivated

* Usually, a child with a sensory integration disorder will present with at least two of the above signs.

Ten Common Signs of Sensory Processing Disorder

1. **Extra sensitive to touch**—don't like to be touched or cannot be touched enough.
2. **Sensitivity to sound**—may cover ears when others are not bothered by the same noises.
3. **Picky eater**—will only eat one or two familiar foods.
4. **Avoidance of sensory stimulation**—will not put hands in anything messy, such as glue, playdough, or mud and will wear only certain clothes.
5. **Uneasiness with movement**—fear of playground equipment, amusement park rides, and being turned upside down or picked up.
6. **Hyperactivity**—cannot be still during the day or get to sleep at night.
7. **Fear of crowds**—bothered by crowded areas and upset to the point of public meltdowns.
8. **Poor fine or gross motor skills**—trouble with hand/finger specific tasks or walking, running, or jumping.
9. **Excessive risk-taking**—may be unaware of touch/pain, which might be seen as aggressive behavior.
10. **Trouble with balance**—may be accident prone or may fall more often than peers and may prefer activities that require little or no physical action.

Levels of Sensory Processing

Level 1 (birth to twenty-four months)—primary sensory systems, such as touch, balance and movement, body position, visual and auditory senses.

Level 2 (twenty-four to thirty-six months)—perceptual motor foundations, such as body awareness, bilateral coordination, lateralization, motor planning.

Level 3 (thirty-six to forty-eight months)—perceptual motor skills, such as auditory and visual discrimination, hand/eye coordination, visual motor integration.

Level 4 (forty-eight to fifty-two months)—academic and social readiness, such as academic skills, complex motor regulation and attention, organized behavior, self-esteem, self-control, self-confidence.

Summary:

At each of the above developmental sensory levels, the child acquires the corresponding skills. When the child has difficulties with any of these skills or achieving developmental levels, early intervention therapy can help children reach these milestones. This is achieved through a variety of therapeutic, tested and evidence-based methods, such as cognitive, speech/language, play-drama, behavioral, fine/gross motor, and vision therapy. These therapies can help the child manage and control their sensory difficulties and help them to grow and develop and live happier, more productive lives.

Sensory-Focused Therapy

I N A RECENT article published in *HealthDay News*, a new and innovative therapy referred to as sensory-focused autism therapy shows early promise. This is a very exciting and encouraging news for any teacher, therapist, or parent/caregiver of children with autism.

Walking across textured surfaces, smelling essential oils, and dipping hands into warm water are some of the therapeutic experiences that boys, specifically, with autism engaged in in this small new study.

The researchers wanted to discover how *sensory-motor therapy* can be compared to traditional behavioral therapy methods in boys with autism.

In this study, twenty-eight boys aged three to twelve and their parents were chosen to participate in the six-month-long study, which was published online on May 20, 2014, in the journal *Behavioral Neuroscience*. The boys were split into two groups. Both groups of boys participated in daily behavioral therapy, but thirteen of the boys also received sensory environmental enrichment, which is another term for *sensory-motor therapy*.

The study's conclusion was that the environmental enrichment therapy had a significant positive effect on these children with autism, according to the authors of the study.

Michael Leon, the study's author stated, "What we've done here for the first time is to give humans a sensory-enriched environment and found that a neurological disorder autism responds favorably. We saw a 600 percent greater likelihood of having a positive clinical outcome in individuals who had enriched environments compared to those receiving the standard care that children have been receiving for autism up to this point." Dr. Leon is a professor of neurobiology and behavior at Center for Autism Research and Treatment at the University of California, Irvine.

However, other autism researchers who were not part of this particular study cautioned that other sensory-based therapies that also showed early promise have not proven effective so far.

For the new study, parents of the children in the sensory enrichment group were given a kit that contained a broad range of materials aimed at stimulating their child's senses of smell, touch, temperature, texture, sight, and movement. Vials of oils scented of apple, lavender, sweet orange, and vanilla were among the items. Squares of different textured materials include smooth foam, hardwood flooring, sponges, and felt and sand paper were also used.

The children were also allowed to play with Play-Doh, beads, a piggy bank with plastic coins, a bowl with warm or cool water, and pictures of famous art among other items.

The parents were asked to conduct two therapy sessions a day with their child. The sessions ranged from fifteen to twenty minutes and consisted of four to seven different exercises that involved different items from the kit. The children also listened to classical music once a day for the study.

As the six-month period progressed, parents were asked to offer their children more challenging enrichment exercises. For example, a child at first would be offered a textured square, and then at a later date, he might be asked to match it to a square of the same material.

By the conclusion of the six-month period, Leon said that the children in the enriched group had significantly improved compared to the groups of child who received only the standard behavioral therapy. He said that 42 percent of the boys in the enrichment group improved in their ability to relate to other people and to sights and sounds as compared to 7 percent in the standard behavior therapy group.

The boys in the enrichment group improved as well on scores for cognitive functioning skills, which include thinking, reasoning, and problem-solving skills. The boys in the standard care group experienced a decrease in their average scores. Also of note, two-thirds of parents with children in the enrichment group reported improvement in overall autism-related symptoms, while parents in the standard care groups represented only one-third reporting improved symptoms.

An additional positive conclusion to this study was that traditional standard behavioral therapy is generally more effective the earlier it is received; the sensory-focused therapy appeared to be effective in older students as well.

Choosing an effective therapy that is affordable is a daunting task for families. When therapies begin as early as a diagnosis is obtained, the resulting benefits to children and their families are more noticeable than when therapies are introduced later. While more research into sensory-focused therapy is needed, it is a low-cost, at-home therapy option that makes it possible for families to significantly increase the probability of improving autism-related symptoms in their children.

16

Theory of Mind

THE CLASSIC DEFINITION of theory of mind is the ability to attribute mental states such as beliefs, intentions, desires, knowledge, doubt, fear, pretense, etc. to oneself and others *and* to understand that others have mental states that are different from their own mental states. This ability is something that comes naturally and without explanation for neurotypically developing individuals. In other words, people not on the spectrum naturally know and understand that other people have thoughts, feelings, and intentions that differ from their own. We can grasp this as very young children typically. Children on the spectrum, however, have a difficult time understanding this concept. Quite simply, they just do not get that what's going on in their head is different than what's going on in someone else's head.

There are different degrees and levels of theory of mind:
1. **Cognitive theory of mind** states that we think and process information differently than do others.
2. **Affective theory of mind** states that we feel and process emotions differently than do others.

Within the *affective theory of mind* are two further abilities:
1. **Affective cognitive theory of mind** is the ability to understand the feelings of others *cognitively*.
2. **Affective empathy** is the ability to respond *appropriately* to others' emotions.

There are two classic assessments or tests of cognitive theory of mind. One is the *false-belief test*. This test is based on the understanding that an individual's belief about the world may contrast with reality and with that of others. The false-belief task is a frequently used methodology to examine theory of mind (i.e., the child's ability to construct people in terms of internal mental states, such as their beliefs, feelings, and intentions). With this test, it is possible for evaluators to distinguish between the child's belief (true) and the child's awareness of another person's belief (false). From false-belief test, we then have *first-order false-belief task*, which involve the child's ability to understand that others also experience. *Second-order false-belief task*, on the other hand, requires that the child infer the false-beliefs of one person based upon the thoughts of another person.

The other cognitive theory of mind assessment is the *Sally-Anne test*. In this test, Sally takes a marble and hides it in her basket. She then "leaves" the room and goes for a walk. While she is away, Anne takes the marble out of Sally's basket and puts it in her own basket. Sally then comes back and the key question is asked of the child, "Where does Sally think her marble is?" Well, neurotypical children at about six or seven years of age will answer, "She thinks it's in her own basket." However, children on the spectrum will invariably answer that they believe that Sally will look for her marble in Anne's basket because they *just saw* Anne put the marble into her own basket. They are unable to understand that Sally, who left and did *not* see the same thing, will not come to the same conclusion. They have extreme difficulty understanding that Sally cannot possibly *know* that her marble has been moved because she was absent even though the child saw the whole thing.

Testing affective theory of mind is a bit more difficult. *Affective theory of mind* states that what we feel and how we *each* process emotions varies from the feelings of others. Each person processes emotions differently than every other person. Neurotypical children and adults understand this. We also understand that some people may share how we feel, but others may not. Children on the spectrum have a difficult time understanding this concept. They have trouble understanding that concept.

From the affective theory of mind, we have the *affective cognitive theory of mind*, which is the awareness of and reflection on one's own emotions. It is the ability to recognize or infer what others are feeling (understanding the emotions of others *cognitively*). Then there is what is referred to as *affective empathy*. This is the drive to respond appropriately to others' emotions. A common test of affective theory of mind is the affective false-belief test. This states that others are capable of "hiding" or feigning their *true* emotions for a variety of reasons. That other people may act one way but feel the opposite. For example, when receiving a gift that you do not like or is disappointing in some way, you know not to actually tell the gift giver that you're not pleased with the gift because you'll hurt their feelings. So you *act* like you like it and thank them sincerely. This example is just one of myriad reasons why we might act one way but feel quite differently. We understand how to act and what to say and not to say. Neurotypical individuals get this, while those on the spectrum have immense difficulty with this concept. For example, there is an old saying "You don't know what it is like to be bird on a wire until you're on that wire" or "Walk a mile in my/his/her shoes." We who are neurotypical understand what these sayings mean; we can relate, so to speak. Children on the spectrum cannot "understand" how others feel or even why they feel that way. They are not being unsympathetic on purpose; they simply do not have neurological capabilities as do typically developing individuals.

Also, there are additional theories of mind that need to be considered when trying to understand how individuals on the spectrum process social, emotional, and cognitive information.

Cognitive Theory of Mind	Affective Theory of Mind
1. *Interpersonal cognitive theory of mind.* This is the social aspect of cognitive theory of mind—how we *inter*act with others. It is the ability to recognize the thoughts and emotions of others.	1. *Interpersonal affective theory of mind.* This is the emotional aspect of affective theory of mind—how we relate to and connect emotionally with others. It is the ability to make inferences about the behaviors and emotions of others.
2. *Intrapersonal cognitive theory of mind.* This is the introspective aspect of cognitive theory of mind. It is how we come to a conclusion in our own mind about a situation. It is how we make sense of what is going on around us and how it involves us or not.	2. *Intrapersonal affective theory of mind.* This is the introspective aspect of affective theory of mind. It is how we understand in our own mind how we feel about a situation and how to regulate, control, or evaluate our process those feelings and our feelings.

All of the above information may be overwhelming, confusing and difficult to understand. But imagine how children on the spectrum, children with language and communication disorders and brain injuries, feel. There are endless, countless social, emotional, and interpersonal situations that occur daily through which our children have trouble navigating. There are also a number of interventions that are designed to help our children develop their theory of mind. Following are a few that jumped out at me:

1. Engage children in *pretend play* where they take on the roles and perspectives of others, using materials such as toy animals, dolls, etc. The Little People play sets are excellent for pretend play.

2. Use verbs such as *feel, think, hope, believe, want, need,* and *like* when talking about your own thoughts during play sessions. (I *hope* I get a new bike for my birthday.)

3. *Play games and talk* about situations where the child gets to predict the outcome of an event. Then compare their predictions with what actually happens. (I thought I would get a new bike for my birthday, but I got a new doll instead.) Then talk about how you would *feel* in this situation and talk about how the child would *feel* too in that situation.

4. Help the child to recognize, describe, and manage his own emotions. Do this by continually talking to about feelings and emotions during play sessions. Talk about your own and then ask them about their own. They may not always be able to verbalize how they're feeling, but with constant conversations of this type, they will eventually *develop and cultivate* the beginnings of a theory of mind.

5. Help the child understand the *feeling of others* and what types of things might cause those feelings.

6. Discuss the inner reactions, thoughts, and emotions of the characters in books that you read to them. There are a vast multitude of *preschool level storybooks* that are wonderful for this. For example, *The Little Red Hen* is a story about a hen who lives with three very lazy friends: a cat, a dog, and a goose. They do not help out with daily household chores, including cleaning, shopping, and cooking. When the hen finishes baking a loaf of delicious bread, her friends want some but the hen says, "No, I did all the work, so I am eating all the bread." Ask the child how each of these characters feel at different times in the story. Ask the child, "How would you feel if you were the hen having to do all of the work, or how would you feel if you were one of the three lazy friends after having smelled the fresh loaf of bread but not being allowed to eat any of it?"

MICHELLE A. SOUVIRON-KEHOE

7. Lastly, teach your child that others have different thoughts and feeling than they do. Do this daily and frequently throughout the day. Have them predict what another person might be thinking or feeling in different situations and *why*.

Twelve Warning Signs of Impending Overstimulation

1. Child experiences loss of balance or orientation.
2. Child's skin flushes or suddenly goes pale.
3. Child is verbalizing, "Stop!"
4. Child persistently refuses activity.
5. Child experiences racing heartbeat or sudden drop in pulse rate.
6. Child experiences hysteria, crying.
7. Child experiences stomach-distress cramps, nausea, vomiting.
8. Child experiences profuse sweating.
9. Child becomes agitated or angry.
10. Child begins repeating echolalic phrases or a familiar phrase over and over (a form of self-calming).
11. Child begins to engage in stimming or other self-calming behaviors.
12. Child begins to lash out, hit, or bite.

WHEN ANY OF these happen, it is time to stop the activity. These behaviors are your child's way of telling you that the activity is just too much for her to handle at the time. It is okay and advisable to even offer her a break so that she can cool down, calm down, and be able to transition to another activity and complete it appropriately and productively.

* The above information was taken in part from *1001 Great Ideas for Teaching and Raising Children with Autism or Asperger's* by Ellen Notbohm and Veronica Zysk, p. 6.

Tips for Organizing Home Activities for Children with Sensory Issues

1. Be consistent with routines, rules, and consequences.
2. Keep child's belongings as organized and structured as possible, as this creates predictability and promotes greater success.
3. Keep a visual schedule posted for the child to see; use stickers and other attractive decoration.
4. Create special routines for challenging times of the day: naptime, bedtime, bath time, toileting, and mealtime.
5. Make a picture board for events such as transitioning from one activity to the next, running errands, or visiting friends and relatives.

Chromosomal Abnormalities

C HROMOSOMES ARE THE forty-six rod-shaped structures seen during cell division in the nucleus of most human cells. They are specifically organized and consist of proteins and DNA (deoxyribonucleic acid), which carry most or all of an organism's genetic information. Humans typically have forty-six chromosomes, which come in twenty-three pairs. Each chromosome has a p and a q arm. The p arm is the shorter of the two, and the q is the longer. These two arms are separated by a pinched area known as the centromere. We inherit one chromosome per pair from each parent. The first twenty-two pairs are called *autosomes* and the twenty-third pair are the sex chromosomes, xx-female and xy-male. The biological father determines the gender of the baby. The mother's egg contains twenty-three chromosomes as does the father's sperm. An egg or sperm cell may divide incorrectly, resulting in an egg or a sperm cell that has too fee or too many chromosomes. Sadly, approximately 1 in 150 children are born with a chromosomal defect in the US. These defects are caused when errors occur in the number or structure of the chromosomes. Many babies born with a chromosomal abnormality have mental and/or physical defects. Some chromosomal defects lead to miscarriage or stillbirth. More than 50 percent of first trimester miscarriages are caused by chromosomal abnormalities in the embryo. Chromosomal abnormalities can be either numerical or structural. A numerical chromosome abnormality can result when an individual is either missing a chromosome from a pair (monosomy) or has an extra chromosome in a pair (trisomy). Someone with Down syndrome has three copies of chromosome number 21 rather than the typical two copies. A common type of chromosomal abnormality is a trisomy. A trisomy results when one of the twenty-three chromosomal pairs contains a third chromosome or part of one. Structural chromosomal abnormalities can present in many ways, including the following:

Deletion: a portion of the chromosome is deleted or missing.

Duplication: a portion of the chromosome is duplicated resulting in extra genetic material.

Translocation: a portion of one chromosome is transferred to another chromosome.

Inversion: a portion of the chromosome has broken off, turned upside down, and reattached resulting in genetic material that is inverted.

Ring: a portion of a chromosome has broken off and formed a ring or circle. Genetic material may or may not be lost as a result.

Summary:
I felt it was important to include a brief overview of Down syndrome and the basics of chromosomal abnormalities because a fairly large percentage of my students have had Down syndrome or some other type of chromosomal abnormality. Children with a chromosomal abnormality typically display various characteristic physical traits, in addition to having behavioral difficulties. Children with Down syndrome can sometimes engage in difficult behaviors such as stubbornness, deviance, and opposition to being redirected toward more appropriate activities. I have included Down syndrome–related information sites in the website section of the guidebook (appendix 20).

20

Sorting Out the Differences Between the DSM-IV and the DSM-V

E VERY MEDICAL DISEASE or disorder, whether physical or mental in nature, receives a numeric code, which is referred to as an ICD-10. ICD-10 means international classification of diseases-tenth revision. The *Diagnostic Statistical Manual (DSM)* categorizes all diseases and disorders under an ICD-10 code. For example, ICD-10 codes from F80 to F88 as well as F93.9 list all mental disorders, including neurological and developmental disorders. (Please see the ICD-9 to ICD-10 conversion chart for more information.) Autism and other related disorders including Asperger's syndrome and PDD-NOS are considered to be neurological and developmental in nature rather than physical. The *DSM* lists and describes the characteristic symptoms that a person must exhibit in order to be diagnosed with a particular disease or disorder. For example, in the *DSM-IV* both Asperger's syndrome and PDD-NOS have their own list of diagnostic characteristics and are *separated* from those of autism. In the *DSM-V,* they are now *merged* with the autism dx (diagnosis) as one large combined dx of ASD (autism spectrum disorder).

To get a clearer idea of the diagnostic and descriptive differences between the *DSM-IV* and *V,* the following charts may help:

The *first* chart lists the diagnostic criteria for the five separate pervasive developmental disorders as listed and described in the *DSM-IV*: (Therefore, the old ICD-9 codes are listed.)

Pervasive Developmental Disorders
1. Autism—299.00

A. A total of *six or more* items from 1, 2, and 3, with *at least two* from 1 and *at least one* from 2 and 3:

1. A qualitative impairment in social interaction as manifested by *at least two* of the following:

   a.) marked impairment in the use of multiple nonverbal behaviors such as eye-to-eye gaze, facial expression, body postures, and gestures to regulate social interactions.

   b.) failure to develop peer relationships appropriate to developmental level

   c.) lack of spontaneous seeking to share enjoyment, interests, or achievements with others

   d.) lack of social or emotional reciprocity

2. A qualitative impairment in communication as manifested by *at least one* of the following:

   a.) delay in, or total lack of, the development of spoken language (but *not* accompanied by an attempt to compensate through alternative modes of communication such as gestures or sign language

   b.) in individuals with adequate speech, a marked impairment in the ability to initiate or sustain a conversation with others

   c.) stereotyped and repetitive use of language or idiosyncratic language

   d.) lack of varied, spontaneous, make-believe play or imitative play appropriate to developmental level

3. Restrictive, repetitive, and stereotyped patterns of behavior, interests, and activities as manifested by *at least one* of the following:
    a.) encompassing preoccupation with one or more stereotyped and restrictive patterns of interest that is abnormal either in its intensity or focus
    b.) apparently inflexible adherence to specific, nonfunctional routines or rituals
    c.) stereotyped and repetitive motor mannerisms (e.g., hand or finger flapping or twisting, or complex whole-body movements)
    d.) persistent preoccupation with parts or objects (rather than the whole object

B. Delays or abnormal functioning in *at least one* of the following areas with onset *prior* to age three: social interaction, language as used in social communication, or symbolic or imaginative play.

C. The disturbance is not better accounted for by Rett's disorder or childhood disintegrative disorder.

2. **Asperger's Disorder—299.80**
    A. Qualitative impairment in social interaction as manifested by *at least two* of the following:
        1. marked impairment in the use of multiple nonverbal behaviors such as eye-to-eye gaze, facial expression, body postures, and gestures to regulate social interaction
        2. failure to develop peer relationships appropriate to developmental level
        3. lack of spontaneous seeking to share enjoyment, interests, or achievements with others
        4. lack of social or emotional reciprocity

B. Restrictive, repetitive, and stereotyped patterns of behavior, interests, and activities, as manifested by *at least one* of the following:

    1. encompassing preoccupation with one or more stereotyped and restricted patterns of interest that is abnormal either in its intensity or focus

    2. apparently inflexible adherence to specific, nonfunctional routines or rituals

    3. stereotyped and repetitive motor mannerisms

    4. persistent preoccupation with parts of objects

C. The disturbance causes clinically significant impairment in social, occupational, or other important areas of functioning.

D. There is *no* clinically significant general delay in language (e.g., single words used by age two, communicative phrases used by age three).

E. There is *no* clinically significant delay in cognitive development or in the development of age appropriate self-help skills, adaptive behavior (other than in social interaction), and curiosity about the environment.

F. Criteria are *not* met for another pervasive developmental disorder or schizophrenia

3. **Rett Syndrome—299.80**

    A. *All* of the following:

        1. apparently normal prenatal and perinatal development

        2. apparently normal psychomotor development through the first five months after birth

        3. normal head circumference at birth

    B. Onset of *all* of the following after the period of normal development:

        1. deceleration of head growth between ages five and forty-eight months

2. loss of previously acquired purposeful hand skills between ages five and thirty months with the subsequent development of stereotyped hand movements (hand-wringing)
3. loss of social engagement early in the course (although some social interaction develops later
4. appearance of poorly coordinated gait or trunk movements
5. severely impaired expressive and receptive language development with severe psychomotor retardation

4. **Childhood Disintegrative Disorder—299.10**

   A. Apparently normal development for at least the first two years after birth as manifested by the presence of age-appropriate verbal and nonverbal communication, social relationships, play skills, and adaptive behavior.

   B. Clinically significant loss of previously acquired skills (before age ten) in *at least two* of the following areas:
      1. expressive or receptive language
      2. social skills or adaptive behavior
      3. bowel or bladder control
      4. play
      5. motor skills

   C. Abnormalities of functioning in *at least two* of the following areas:
      1. qualitative impairment in social interaction (e.g., impairment in nonverbal behaviors, failure to develop peer relationships, lack of social or emotional reciprocity)
      2. qualitative impairments in communication (e.g., delay or lack of spoken language, inability to initiate or sustain a conversation, stereotyped

and repetitive use of language, lack of varied make-believe play)

3. restrictive, repetitive, and stereotyped patterns of behavior, interests, and activities, including motor stereotypes and mannerisms

D. The disturbance is not better accounted for by another specific pervasive developmental disorder or by schizophrenia

5. Pervasive Developmental Disorder-Not Otherwise Specified—299.80

This category should be used when there is a severe and pervasive impairment in the development of reciprocal social interaction or verbal and nonverbal communication skills, or when stereotyped behavior, interests, and activities are present. However, the criteria are *not met* for a specific pervasive developmental disorder, schizophrenia, or avoidant personality disorder. For example, this category includes "atypical autism"—presentations that do *not* meet the criteria for autism disorder because of late age at onset, atypical symptomology, or subthreshold symptomology, or all of the above.

The *second* chart lists the diagnostic criteria for *autism spectrum disorder* as listed and described in the *DSM-V*:

Autism Spectrum Disorder—299.00

Currently or by history must meet criteria for A, B, C, and D.

A. Persistent deficits in social communication and social interaction across contexts, not accounted for by general developmental delays and manifested by *all three* of the following:

1. deficits in social-emotional reciprocity, which may range, for example, from abnormal social approach and failure of normal back and forth conversations to reduced sharing of interests, emotions, or affect to failure to initiate or respond in social situations

2. deficits in nonverbal communicative behaviors used for social interaction ranging from poorly integrated verbal and nonverbal communication to abnormalities in eye gaze and contact and body language or deficits in understanding and use of gestures to a total lack of facial expressions and nonverbal communication skills

3. deficits in developing and maintaining relationships ranging from difficulties adjusting behavior to suit various social contexts, difficulties in sharing, imaginative/make-believe play, or in making friends to absence of interest in peers.

B. Restrictive, repetitive patterns of behavior, interests, or activities as manifested by *at least two* of the following:

1. stereotyped or repetitive speech, motor movements, use of objects, or speech, such as simple motor stereotypes (e.g., lining up toys, spinning or flipping objects, echolalia, idiosyncratic phrases)

2. insistence on sameness, inflexible adherence to routines, ritualized patterns of verbal or nonverbal behavior, such as extreme distress at small changes, difficulties with transitions, rigid thinking patterns, greeting rituals, need to take same route or eat same foods every day, excessive resistance to change

3. highly restricted, fixated interests that are abnormal in intensity or focus, such as strong attachment to or preoccupation with usual objects, excessively circumscribed, or perseverative interests)

4. hyper or hypo-reactivity to sensory input or unusual interest in sensory aspects of the

MICHELLE A. SOUVIRON-KEHOE

environment, such as apparent indifference to pain/temperature, adverse response to specific sounds or textures, excessive smelling or touching of objects, visual fascination with lights or movement

C. Symptoms must be present in early childhood but may not become fully manifest until social demands exceed limited capacities.

D. Symptoms together limit and impair everyday functioning.

*Note that the *DSM-V* removes both childhood disintegrative disorder (CDD) and Rett syndrome as autism spectrum disorders.

The removal of these two disorders is justified as follows: CDD has important differences from other ASDs including the acuity and severity of regression that are associated with this disorder as well as comorbidity of specific physical symptoms that accompany this disorder such as bowel and bladder issues.

The removal of Rett syndrome is justified by the fact that typical ASD behaviors are not particularly prominent in individuals with Rett syndrome except for a brief period during early development. Also, ASDs are defined by *specific* sets of behaviors and characteristics and not etiologies (i.e., causes at the present time and, therefore, the inclusion Rett syndrome is considered to be atypical). Also, patients with Rett syndrome who also have autistic symptoms may still be described as having an ASD, but clinicians should be sure to indicate this with the *specifier* "with known genetic or medical condition" to indicate that these symptoms are specifically related to Rett syndrome.

The *DSM-IV* was in use from 1994, including its revision for text correction for PDD-NOS until 2013 when the current DSM-V went into effect. As per the *DSM-IV,* an individual would receive a diagnosis of any of the five *pervasive developmental disorders* listed in chart 1 if they met those criteria. Since May of 2013, an individual can receive a diagnosis of *autism spectrum disorder* rather than one of those five disorders previously mentioned. I have heard many parents as well as colleagues express a good deal of confusion regarding the differences between the two *DSMs* and what the specific diagnostic criteria mean to them and their children and students. Hopefully, this section of this guidebook will clear up any confusion and will explain precisely the changes that were made to the *DSM-IV* and that now appear in the *DSM-V.*

This chart compares and contrasts some of the differences in *DSM-IV* and *DSM-V.* (This is a condensed chart of comparisons. For full information, refer to previous complete charts.)

DSM-IV	**DSM-V**
A. *Impairment in social interactions*	**A.** *Persistent deficits in social communication and social interactions across multiple contexts*
1. Eye-to-eye gaze, facial expressions body postures and gestures	1. Deficits in social-emotional reciprocity
2. Failure to develop peer relationships	2. Deficits in communicative behaviors used in social interactions
3. Lack of spontaneous seeking to share interests and achievements	3. Deficits in developing, understanding, and maintaining relationships
4. Lack of social or emotional reciprocity	

MICHELLE A. SOUVIRON-KEHOE

B. *Qualitative impairment in communication*

1. Delay in or total lack of development of spoken language
2. If adequate speech is present, impairment in ability to initiate or sustain conversation
3. Stereotyped and repetitive use of language
4. Lack of varied, spontaneous make-believe play or social imitative play

C. *Restricted, repetitive, and stereotyped patterns of behavior, interests, and activities*

1. Encompassing preoccupation with one or more stereotyped patterns of interest that is abnormal in focus or intensity
2. Inflexible adherence to specific, nonfunctional routines or rituals
3. Stereotyped, repetitive motor mannerisms
4. Persistent preoccupation with parts of objects

B. *Restrictive, repetitive behaviors, interests*

1. Stereotyped, repetitive motor movements
2. Insistence on sameness, inflexible adherence to routines or ritualized patterns of verbal or nonverbal behavior
3. Highly restricted, fixated interests that are abnormal in focus and intensity
4. Hyper or hypo-reactivity to sensory input or sensory aspects of environment

While there seems to be something of an imbalance in the above listed characteristics, *all* the information represented by the *DSM-IV* does actually appear in the listed characteristics in the *DSM-V*. For example, the information in subcategory A.1. of *DSM-IV* appears in subcat A.2. of *DSM-V*. The information in A.2. of *DSM-IV* appears in subcat A.3. of *DSM-V*. A.3. of *DSM-IV* appears in A.1. of *DSM-V*.

The following chart lists the transmigration of all the information from the *DSM-IV* to the *DSM-V*:

DSM-IV	*DSM-V*
A.1.	A.2.
A.2.	A.3.
A.3.	A.1.
A.4.	A.1.
B.1.	A.2.
B.2.	A.1.
B.3.	B.1.
B.4.	A.3.
C.1.	B.3.
C.2.	B.2.
C.3.	B.1.
C.4.	B.3.

Note that the information in subcat B.4. of *DSM-V* is new and *did not* appear in the *DSM-IV*. This information is regarding *sensory* issues and concerns that many individuals with an autism spectrum disorder have; however, not all individual with sensory difficulties have an autism spectrum disorder. An overwhelming number of individuals on the spectrum experience a variety of sensory difficulties that make daily living extremely challenging, if not nearly impossible, so it is most beneficial that the *DSM-V* includes sensory as a diagnostic criteria.

MICHELLE A. SOUVIRON-KEHOE

The above chart seeks to explain the practical, meaningful differences and changes that have occurred between the previous *DSM* and the present *DSM*. For example, in the *DSM-IV*, the subcat A.3. describes a lack of spontaneous sharing of objects of interest. Most young children love to share items that they find interesting to them with others. However, many children on the spectrum do not readily do this. In the *DSM-V* subcat A.1., this information is described as a deficit in social-emotional reciprocity. This is basically stating the same thing only using different words. In fact, most of the changes made to the *DSM-V* are changes of wording and semantics rather than *different* information or criteria. Another example is in the *DSM-V* subcat A.3. Here we read that the individual presents as having difficulties in developing, understanding, and maintaining relationships; difficulties in adjusting behaviors to suit a variety of social contexts; and difficulties in imaginative/make-believe play or an absence of interest in peers. All this information is taken from *two* separate subcats in *DSM-IV*, A.2. and B.4. Again, the core information is the same albeit stated more succinctly and specifically. Several *DSM-V* subcats are the result of *combined* information taken from the *DSM-IV*. For example, subcat A.1. of *DSM-V* contains combined information from three different subcats in *DSM-IV*, namely A.3., A.4., and B.2. With the exception of only one subcat (B.2.) all of them are combinations of *DSM-IV* subcats, and one is an entirely new addition.

Other changes for the *DSM-V* regarding ASD are as follows:

1. The inclusion of *specifiers*—these give additional information regarding the following:
    - An association with a known medical or genetic condition or environmental factor that may have significant effect or bearing in relation to the individual's diagnosis. (e.g., Down syndrome, fragile X, prenatal substance exposure, or exposure to factory during pregnancy)
    - Verbal abilities

- Cognitive abilities
- Severity of symptoms in two or more domains

2. *Text descriptions* that include symptoms that may be unique to a variety of factors such as age, developmental stage, and verbal abilities

3. The inclusion of the *social communication disorder*

   A. Persistent difficulties in the social use of verbal and nonverbal communication as manifested by deficits in the following areas:

      1. Using communication for social purposes, such as greeting, sharing, and exchanging information in a way that is appropriate for the social context

      2. Changing communication to match the context or the need of the listener (e.g., speaking differently in a classroom than in a park, speaking differently to a child than to an adult, and avoiding the use of formal language)

      3. Following rules for conversation and storytelling, such as taking turns in conversation (volleying), restating when misunderstood, and knowing how to use verbal and nonverbal signals to regulate interactions

      4. Understanding what is not explicitly stated (e.g., inferences and nonliteral or vague, ambiguous meanings of language, such as idioms, jokes, metaphors, double entendres [two-way meaning], multiple meanings, and hyperboles), which depend on the context of the specific conversation for interpretation

   B. Deficits that result in functional limitations in effective communication, social participation, social relationships, academic achievement, or occupational performance.

MICHELLE A. SOUVIRON-KEHOE

C. Onset in the early developmental period (but deficits may not fully manifest until social communication demands exceed the individual's limited capacities.

D. Deficits are not better explained by low abilities in the domain of word structure and grammar or by intellectual disabilities, global developmental delay, ASD, or another mental or neurological disorder.

The rationale to include the new diagnostic area of the *social communication disorder* is due to the need for children who currently have a diagnosis of PDD-NOS on the basis of social communication deficits and individuals with significant social and language skills deficits. Additionally, it must be noted that this diagnosis should *not* be included in the ASD section because it defines and describes a group of individuals with related or similar, but *separate* symptoms.

Some *DSM-IV* cases lost their diagnosis with the new *DSM-V* criteria, but by and large, there was a significant increase in ASD cases. Also, when social communication disorder (SCD) cases were included, there was a nearly 15 percent increase in new diagnostic cases of ASD/SCD. Also, as per current case studies, a single dx of ASD will improve access to services for current diagnoses of Asperger's and PDD-NOS, who do *not* qualify for services in fourteen states.

Therefore, I must say that I am very pleased with the changes, definitions, explanations, rearrangements, and mergers in the *DSM-V.* There were many concerns previously about the application of the *DSM-IV* and the consistency of the diagnostic criteria for high-functioning autism versus Asperger's. There were concerns regarding the appropriateness of the use of certain diagnoses such as PDD-NOS as a mild neurodevelopmental disorder and Asperger's as presenting with odd behaviors. Also, there were concerns regarding the validity of the diagnosis of CDD as an ASD at all. Therefore, it was the goal of a neurodevelopmental disorders workgroup / advisory board that had been working to revise the *DSM* to apply more accurate, appropriate, consistent, and relevant diagnostic criteria for those individuals who may be on the autism spectrum. This advisory board worked tirelessly for over six years via biweekly teleconferences, semiannual in-person meetings, and addition web conferences. A total of more than 2,500 hours were devoted to this grand and daunting undertaking. Many expert consensus were supported by a vast array of current literature reviews, secondary data analyses, and clinical evaluations. This advisory board was vetted (i.e., appraised, verified) through public comments, presentations at scientific and advocacy meetings and reviewed by leading experts in the field of autism spectrum research and various advocacy group members.

The following list names the individuals who made up the *advisory board* and *workgroup members:*

Members:
Gillian Baird
Ed Cook
Francesca Happe
James Harris
Walter Kaufmann
Bryan King
Catherine Lord
Joseph Piven
Rosemary Tannock
Sally Rogers
Sarah Spence
Susan Swedo
Fred Volkmar
Amy Wetherby
Harry Wright

Advisors:
Jim Bodfish
Martha Denckla
Maureen Lefton-Grief
Nickola Nelson
Sally Ozonoff
Diane Paul
Eva Petkova
Daniel Pine
Alya Reeve
Mabel Rice
Joseph Sergeant
Bennet and Sally Shaywitz
Audrey Thurm
Keith Widaman
Warren Zigman

In recognition of the abovementioned individuals, I extend my gratitude to them for their boundless work and dedication toward the improvements and revisions of the diagnostic criteria regarding ASD made to the current *DSM-V.*

ICD-9 to ICD-10

ICD-9 and corresponding ICD-10 codes—the majority of ICD-9 and 10 codes that you'll need to are as follows:

314.0—attention-deficit disorder—**F82**

314.01—attention-deficit / hyperactivity disorder—**F82**

315.31—expressive language disorder—**F80.1**

315.32—mixed expressive-receptive disorder—**F80.2**

315.39—other developmental speech disorder / phonological disorder—**F80.89**

315.4—developmental coordination disorder—**F82**

315.5—mixed developmental disorder—**F88**

742.3—Congenital Hydrocephalus—**Q03.8**

742.2—Holoprosencephaly—**Q04.2**

758.0—Down syndrome (trisomy 21)—**Q91.1**

758.1—Patau syndrome (trisomy 13)—**Q91.7**

758.2—Edwards syndrome (trisomy 18)—**Q91.3**

758.6—Turner's syndrome—**Q91.4**

758.7—Klinefelter syndrome—**Q91.5**

758.9—Williams syndrome—**Q91.6**

759.81—Prader-Willi—**Q87.1**

299.00—autistic disorder—**F84**

299.10—childhood disintegrative disorder—**F84**

299.80—Asperger's syndrome—**F84.5**

299.80—perv. dev. dis.-not otherwise specified (PDD-NOS)—**F84.9**

313.9—disorder of infancy, childhood, or adolescence-no—**F93.3**

PAPI (Parents as Primary Interventionists)

PAPI IS AN acronym for parents as primary interventionists. In the last several years, there has been a movement toward involving parents and primary caregivers in their child's therapy as much and as frequently as possible. This school of thought makes perfect sense to many therapists and is something many therapists have been doing for some time. But now it has an official name and purpose under the auspices of early intervention.

It is well-known that children in general make better progress when parents are interested, invested, and involved in their academic and developmental progress. I have seen this phenomenon consistently over the past two decades as an EI special education teacher. I often remark about this to the parents during the initial visit. I believe that it is important that parents know that their involvement is essential. Many parents want to be involved but just need a little encouragement. After I began inviting parents to not only watch but to also participate in educational sessions, I noticed an increase in most of my students' overall progress. There are also a number of parents who want to be more involved in their children's therapy, but they are simply overwhelmed with other obligations: job, school, numerous appointments, other children, and the need for supplemental assistance such as counseling, social work services, or respite. The respite program offers monetary reimbursement toward childcare and babysitting services and is typically offered through the county's early intervention program. The OMRDD also has a respite program.

There are, of course, challenging cases, as is common with any situation or set of circumstances. For example, there are families that have difficultly devoting sufficient time and energy to their child's therapy and services. There are numerous factors that contribute to families needing extra assistance playing a larger role in their child's therapy. A fairly large percentage of mothers are either very young or overwhelmed with other children or both. Many mothers are either alone or have very little assistance or support. It's easy to imagine how I might feel if I were eighteen or nineteen, struggling to raise a two-year-old, work at a fast food restaurant, and go to GED classes with no help. I'd feel scared, vulnerable, and overwhelmed. I would also need and welcome help from an EI team member. Honestly, the majority of my students' families are most thankful for their team members' assistance and efforts; only a tiny handful seem to just have other priorities. These are the parents that sometimes need extra assistance helping their children to make as much progress developmentally as possible. EI team members regularly offer or suggest community services that can assist them financially, with childcare, parenting, counseling, education, employment, food, clothing, shelter, and recreation. Once families have these concerns taken care of, they'll be better able to assist in their child's therapy and development.

The PAPI system uses already existing family routines or modified routines as a framework for eliciting desired results/outcomes. Learning can and does take place while engaging in most any daily. Some families may have hectic, restrictive, or limited schedules due to frequent appointments. The PAPI model encourages "family training" sessions one time in every six-month IFSP period. Family training sessions offer families and team members an opportunity to discuss and hopefully resolve educational, behavioral, and other issues or concerns that may need addressing. Family training sessions are billable, unlike six-month and annual review meetings.

Many EI agencies want to see evidence or parent involvement and participation. On my daily progress note, I document when the parent/

MICHELLE A. SOUVIRON-KEHOE

caregiver asks a therapy-related question. I also document when I was able to provide the parent with.

Lastly, it may not be enough to invite, encourage, and involve parents in their child's therapy. It is important that therapists offer families as many possibilities for make up visits as they can so that the child has maximum opportunity for therapy. Some agencies may have their own policies regarding the implementation of makeup visits as well.

Infant/Toddler Observation Guide

	Social	Self-Help	Gross Motor	Fine Motor	Language
Birth	Quiets when fed and Comforted	Alerts to and is interested in sights and sounds	Wiggles and kicks; Thrusts arms and legs in play	Looks at objects or faces	Cries and makes small throaty sounds
1 mo.	Makes eye contact		Lifts head and chest	Visual tracking	Cries in special way when hungry
2 mos.	Recognizes mother	Reacts to sight of bottle or breast	Holds head steady when held sitting	Holds items placed in hands	Makes sounds (ah, eh, uh)
3 mos.	Recognizes other familiar adults	Increases activity when shown a toy	Makes crawling movements	Holds up hand and looks at it	Laughs out loud; squeals
4 mos.	Interested in own mirror image, smiles	Reaches for objects	Pivots around when lying on stomach	Puts toys/objects in mouth	Says "Ah-goo," "Ah-buh"

Age					
5 mos.	Reacts differently to strangers		Rolls over from stomach to back	Picks up items with one hand	Responds to voices; turns head to a voice
6 mos.	Reaches for familiar people	Looks for object after it 'disappears	Rolls over from back to stomach	Transfers objects from one hand to the other	Babbles; Responds to own name; turns and looks
7 mos.	Gets upset and cries if left alone	Feeds self cookie	Sits alone, steady	Holds items in each hand at same time- brings them together	Says da, ba, ga
8 mos.	Plays "peek-a-boo" while on stomach	Moves forward		Uses finger to poke, push, and roll small objects	Says "Dada," "Mama," "Baba"
9 mos.	Waves bye-bye	Resists having toy taken away	Crawls on hands and knees	Picks up small objects using thumb/finger grasp	Imitates sounds you make
10 mos.	Plays pat-a-cake	Picks up spoon by handle	Pulls self to standing position		
11 mos.	Cruises furniture or playpen	Puts small objects in cup or other container			Understands phrases such as "No-no" and "All done"

12 mos.	Initiates simple acts such as hugging a doll	Helps a little when getting dressed	Stands alone briefly then steadily	Turns pages of book two or more at a time	Says "Mama" and "Dada" for parents
13 mos.	Looks at or plays near other children	Lifts cup to mouth and drinks	Walks without help	Builds tower of two or more blocks	Shakes head for no; Hands objects to you upon request
14 mos.	Gives or blows kisses	Insists on feeding	Climbs up on to chairs, furniture	Marks with pencil or crayon	Asks for food or drink with sounds or words
15 mos.	Greets people with hi	Feeds self with spoon	Runs	Scribbles with pencil or crayon	Says two words other than mama or dada
18 mos.	Sometimes says no when interfered with	Can eat with a fork	Kicks a ball forward	Builds tower of four or more blocks	Strings sounds that resemble words
21 mos.			Has good balance and coordination		Uses five or more words to name things

MICHELLE A. SOUVIRON-KEHOE

24

Development of Language in Children

Birth–three months: responds to speech by gurgling or cooing and is attracted to parents' voices

Three–six months: talks to toy or mirror image of self

Seven–ten months: experiments with her voice, imitates sounds a caregiver makes, says and understands *dada*, *mama*, *bye-bye*, and *no*

Eleven–fifteen months: shows understanding of some words by pointing to people and objects, recognizes own name, understands simple instructions, imitates familiar words, waves bye-bye, uses the words *dada* and *mama* and other simple one-syllable words, and giggles and laughs frequently

Eighteen months: engages in "pattern to babbling" (sounds are strung together that resemble a rudimentary sentence), tries to participate in short songs, understands many common words, uses single words correctly, responds to or initiates simple games, and identifies several body parts by pointing

Two years: uses lots of single, two to three, and three-hundred-word vocabulary; says "What's this" frequently; uses negatives such as "No go" and "No want;" converses with toys, labels body parts; uses own name; follows one-step directions; uses some plurals; and asks for things like juice

Three years: knows one to two colors, knows night from day, asks why often, practices talking alone, knows address a bit, and knows three to four phrases and a thousand-word vocabulary

Four years: connects recent events, knows several colors and shapes, uses four to five phrases and 1,500-word vocabulary, uses past tense, follows two-step directions, asks many questions, and uses imagination expressions such as "I wish" and "I hope."

Five years: uses some pronouns; tries to imitate grammatical patterns of adults; defines objects by their function; eats with fork; knows many spatial relations (in, under); knows units of money; knows *same/different*, *big/little*, and *hard/soft*; has two-thousand-word vocabulary; uses five- to six-word phrases; counts to at least ten; uses future, present, and past tenses; and uses more complex sentences.

MICHELLE A. SOUVIRON-KEHOE

25

Typical Language Acquisition Skills

Child's Age	Expressive Language	Auditory Comprehension
Two–four months	Verbal play through cooing and laughing, vowel sounds such as *ooohh, eee, aahhh*	Turns head toward sounds and begins to tell one sound from another
Four–eight months	Begins to babble; some consonant sounds can be heard	Visually follows toy moving across floor, anticipates an activity (peek-a-boo), and visually attends to object with caregiver (joint attention)
Eight–twelve months	Produces variation of syllables (*gadabudagah*) and first-word approximations, engages in some nonverbal communication, jargon and other unintelligible speech	Associates words with a physical object (knows that the word *cup* actually the object cup) and responds to simple phrases such as "no touch"

One–two years	Has approx. ten to fifteen words at eighteen months and approx. forty to fifty at twenty-four months, uses mostly nouns and pronouns, jargon continues to be present	Displays increased attention to toys, changes behavior inresponse to comments made to her, understands simple commands and questions needing gestures at times, and points to simple pictures
Two–three years	Has approx. 150 words by twenty-four months, approx. three hundred to four hundred words by thirty-six months, frequently uses two- to three-word phrases, can ask simple questions, vowel sounds are stronger, jargon mostly gone	Comprehension rapidly increases, responds to more two-step commands with some prepositions— "Pick up the cup" and "Put it on the chair"
Three–four years	Has approx. six hundred to one thousand words and uses three- to four-word phrases; uses pronouns, adjectives, adverbs, prepositions, past tenses, and plural; answers what, where, and when type of questions	Understands up to 1,500 words and understands gender differences, plurals, pronouns, adjectives, and colors

MICHELLE A. SOUVIRON-KEHOE

Four–five years	Increases vocabulary to approx. 1,000 to 1,600 words; uses four-to six-word phrases; uses three-to four-syllable words, uses articles such as *the* and *a*; uses more adjectives, adverbs; and conjunctions, improves fluency	Understands 1,500 to 2,000 words; relates to *it, why, because,* and *when*; and follows more complex instructions
Five–six years	Has a vocabulary of approx. 1,500 to 2,100 words, uses complete five- to six-word phrases and sentences, has more fluent speech, uses many multisyllable words	Understands 2,500 to 2,800 words and understands more complicated words and phrases

26

Suggestions for Increasing Language Production Skills

- Narrate your and your child's actions. Talk about what you are doing in short two-word phrases (e.g., say, "Close door" as you close the door or "Lights on" as you turn on the light or "Down, down, down" as you go down the stairs.)
- Practice using familiar/useful single words (up, out, down, in, eat, more, and hot). Action words are very good first examples to use (run, jump, hop, and walk).
- During playtime, especially with activities that have multiple parts, hold some of the items back and give the child an opportunity to hear you modeling how to ask for the desired piece.
- When your child says words or tries to, model adding to what was just said (e.g., child says "Bye," so you say "Bye, kitty" and then "Bye, little kitty."
- Always provide choices. Show two items. Name each. "Here's a blue cup and a red ball." See which the child chooses and then model its name and how to ask for it. Say "Ball? Want ball?" Emphasize the first sound of the word *B-B-B-ball* or *C-C-C-cup*. The exaggerated sound is what will be repeated back first when the child is ready.
- Provide good speech models for your child.
- See if your child will repeat the initial sounds of very simple one-syllable words. Easier sounds include *b, m, p, t, d, h,* and *n*.

- Look at him/her and have him watch you and focus on your face as you say the word(s).
- Model slow and audible speech so your child can clearly hear what the words should sound like.
- Repeat what your child says, and say it back to her the way it should be said. She may or may not immediately repeat the word. That's okay. The more she hears the correct pronunciation of words, the better. Early on, accept whatever attempts your child makes, but keep repeating the correct pronunciation for her.

27

Important Milestones Acquired by Twelve Months

Social and Emotional Domains
- Shy and anxious with strangers
- Cries when parent leaves
- Enjoys imitating people during play
- Show specific preferences for certain people and toys
- Tests parental responses to actions during mealtimes
- Tests parental responses to behaviors
- May be fearful in some situations
- Prefers mother or regular caregiver over all others
- Repeats sounds or gestures for attention
- Hand/finger-feeds self
- Extends arm or leg during dressing

Cognitive Domain
- Explores objects in different ways—throwing, banging, shaking, and dropping
- Finds hidden objects easily
- Looks toward correct picture when named
- Begins to use objects correctly, appropriately
- Imitates gestures

Language Domain
- Pays more attention to speech
- Responds to simple verbal requests
- Responds to no

- Uses simple gestures, waves, and shakes head for no
- Babbles with inflection, intonation in voice
- Says "Mama" and "Dada"
- Uses exclamations such as "Oooh!"
- Tries to imitate words

Movement Domain
- Sits upright without assistance
- Crawls forward on stomach
- Assumes hands and knees position
- Creeps on hands and knees
- Can get from sitting to crawling to tummy position
- Pulls self up to stand
- Walks holding on to furniture (cruising)
- Stands momentarily without support
- May walk two or three steps without assistance

Hand/Finger Skills Domain
- Uses pincer grasp (thumb and finger)
- Bangs two objects together
- Puts objects into container (box or bag)
- Takes objects out of container
- Lets objects go voluntarily
- Pokes with index finger
- Tries to imitate scribbling

When to alert your child's pediatrician? It is when your child

- does not crawl (by twelve months);
- drags one side of body while crawling;
- cannot stand when given support;
- does not look for objects that are hidden even when he watches;
- says no single words *dada* and *mama* (by eight months);
- does not use gestures such as waving, nodding, or shaking head (by ten months);

- does not point to objects or pictures (by ten to twelve months); and
- experiences a drastic loss of skills that have already been acquired.

Note:

All babies develop at their own rate. It is nearly impossible to know exactly when your child will learn or even master a certain skill. The developmental milestones listed above represent only a broad idea of the changes in development that you can expect to see. Do not be alarmed though if your child's development presents somewhat differently.

Important Milestones Acquired by Twenty-Four Months

Social Domain
- Imitates behaviors of others—close adults and other children
- More aware of self as separate from others
- More excited about company of other children

Emotional Domain
- Demonstrates increasing independence
- Begins to show defiant behavior
- Separation anxiety begins to fade

Cognitive Domain
- Finds objects even when hidden under two or three covers
- Begins to sort by color and shape
- Begins to engage in pretend play

Language Domain
- Points to item upon request when named
- Recognizes names of familiar people, objects, and body parts
- Says several simple one- to two-syllable words (by fifteen to eighteen months)
- Uses simple two- to four-word phrases—*bye-bye* and *all done* (by eighteen to twenty-four months)
- Uses simple two- to five-word sentences—*I want more juice*
- Follows simple verbal instructions
- Repeats words overheard in conversation

Gross Motor Domain
- Walks without assistance
- Pulls a toy behind while walking
- Carries larger or more toys while walking
- Begins to run
- Stands on tiptoe to reach or see
- Kicks a ball
- Climbs onto and down from furniture by self
- Walks up and down the stairs with minimal assistance

Fine Motor Domain
- Scribbles on her own
- Turns over container to pour
- Builds tower of four or more blocks
- Might use one hand more often than the other

Alert your child's pediatrician when your child

- cannot walk by eighteen months;
- fails to develop a heel-toe pattern of walking after several months of walking or if walks on toes only;
- does not speak at least fifteen words by twenty to twenty-two months;
- does not use two-word phrases or sentences by twenty-four months;
- does not know the function of common household items—broom/sweep, fork/eat—by twenty to twenty-two months;
- does not imitate words or actions by twenty-two to twenty-four months;
- does not follow or seems confused by simple one step verbal direction by twenty-four months;
- cannot push a toy on wheels by twenty-one to twenty-three months; and
- experiences a marked loss of already acquired skills.

MICHELLE A. SOUVIRON-KEHOE

Note:

All children develop at a pace that is uniquely their own. It is, therefore, nearly impossible to precisely gage when they will acquire a specific skill or achieve a particular milestone. The above listed skills and milestones serve to provide you with an approximate sense of what to expect as your child grows. Do not be alarmed if your child's rate and course of development differs slightly.

Greenspan's Developmental Milestones by Age Groups

- Birth–three months: Exhibits growing self-regulation and an interest in the world
- Four–five months: Engages in relationships
- Six–nine months: Uses emotions in an interactive, purposeful manner
- Ten–fourteen months: Uses a series of interactive and emotional gestures to communicate
- Fifteen–eighteen months: Uses a series of interactive and emotional gestures to solve problems
- Nineteen–thirty months: Uses ideas to convey feelings, wishes, or intentions
- Thirty-one–forty-two months: Creates logical bridges between emotions and ideas

WHILE THIS IS largely a social-emotional developmental milestones chart, the above skills and abilities are linked to and associated with many speech and language skills and abilities.

ABA (Applied Behavior Analysis)

B OTH THE ABA (see common terms) and Stanley Greenspan's Floortime models are employed with children and older individuals with pervasive developmental disorders. ABA is one of the most common and evidence-based methods used to treat autism. It has been vigorously researched and tested and has been an effective learning tool and behavior modifiers for many individuals who are on the autism spectrum. Definitions of ABA are varied and are often questioned. Put simply, ABA is a procedure that investigates and adjusts behavior. It is specifically detailed according to the task at hand. It has been scrupulously tested and is known to be effective for many children and adults with autism. There are other definitions, but they tend to be honest fairly complicated or limited. For example, one definition states that ABA uses antecedent stimuli and consequences based on the findings of descriptive and functional analysis to produce socially practical change. ABA can be used to modify essentially any behavior regardless of its social importance. The first step in the ABA process is done by using the ABC model.

The ABC model is comprised of the following:

1. **A**ntecedent—a prompt to perform action
2. **B**ehavior—child's response whether it be compliance, noncompliance, or no response
3. **C**onsequence—reaction of therapist that can range from strong positive or strong negative

The ABA method uses *several techniques* such as the following:

- **Task analysis**—tasks are broken down into their basic parts or steps
- **Chaining**—desired skills are learned in small increments and linked together
- **Prompting**—prompts can be verbal or visual
- **Fading**—prompts are used more sparingly as time goes on
- **Shaping**—each undesired behavior is shaped each time it occurs by the caregiver through positive reinforcement to elicit desired behaviors
- **Differential reinforcement**—reinforcement is either positive (praise and tangible reward) or negative (at most an emphatic *no*); it is *differential* depending on the level of reinforcement that is used
- **Positive reinforcement**—can be widely varied from stickers and stamps to a pizza party or to a trip to the zoo
- **Generalization**—learned skills are taught in a variety of settings
- **Video modeling**—some students learn tasks by watching taped sequences of the desired behavior or task/skill.

Summary:

Virtually, any task, skill, or behavior can be taught either as a brand-new skill or can be retaught or shaped/modified to elicit skills or behaviors that are more functional, productive, or appropriate given the circumstances in which the skills or behaviors are occurring. In theory into a large extent or in practice as well, ABA therapy is extremely effective in teaching and modifying skills and behaviors. However, it does indeed have negative aspects. It is very expensive if it is not covered by insurance program for the grant. It is very time-consuming for the family as well as the child. Most children receive from twenty to forty hours per week. Most newly diagnosed children with autism receive between thirty and forty. This is a huge commitment, and it tends to consume the family's daily routine. However, with the time, resources, and competent ABA therapist and effort, a large percentage of families have experienced good to very good results with the ABA method of teaching and engaging children with autism.

31

DIR Model and Floortime

D IR STANDS FOR Developmental Individual differences
Relationship-based model. This therapeutic model was
developed by Dr. Stanley Greenspan in 1979 to challenge and
encourage children to move up a hierarchical ladder of emotional stages
or milestones that typically developing children to accomplish fairly
easily and without much intervention. DIR helps individuals on the
autism spectrum to achieve these milestones via one-to-one sustained
interaction between the individual and a caregiver (parent, teacher,
therapist, counselor, etc.).

The Floortime model was also developed by Dr. Greenspan in 1979.
It is a comprehensive developmental intervention that involves meeting
a child at his or her current developmental level. It encompasses the five
hierarchical emotional stages/milestones of the DIR model.

Floortime is child-directed, in that if the child wants to line up
blocks, he/she is allowed to, even encouraged to, and the therapist
engages fully in the same activity all while trying to "see" the world as
does the child. This, of course, takes some practice and a good deal of
patience to know the child fairly well. Therapist verbally describes the
activity and acknowledges that he/she too likes the blocks and likes
to line them up. Verbally acknowledging the child's interests on the
part of the therapist is a way of encouraging attention and intimacy.
The goal is that both caregiver and child are "tuned in" to each other
so as to cultivate a relationship between them. Another goal is two-
way communication, encouraging dialogue and promoting verbal
problem-solving.

Next, Floortime seeks to encourage the expression and use of feelings and ideas by facilitating play-drama, make-believe, and pretend-play skills. Lastly, the fourth goal is to promote logical thought and being able to cultivate a logical understanding of the child's world and to help the child connect his thoughts in ways that sense to him. Each emotional developmental milestone lays the foundation for the next. Therefore, the four educational goals of the Floortime model must be reached in sequential order as well.

To begin, the therapist must actually get rates down on the floor with the child and let him/her lead the session. The therapist simply follows the child's lead. If the child begins to, for example, stack blocks, stack with her and talk about what you're doing so that the child receives from you verbal acknowledgment regarding the activity. Point to objects, label them, be descriptive and repetitive, and elaborate them to reinforce the information the child absorbs. Try to provide information verbally as well as visually to further facilitate comprehension and promote language use.

This facilitates attention and engagement, which is the first goal of Floortime, and it corresponds to milestones 1 and 2. These two milestones are typically met by approximately eighteen months. So it may be difficult to start working on such a basic skill when the child is two or even three years old. Many typically developing twenty-four- to thirty-six-month-olds are learning communication skills, shapes, colors, and numbers.

It is essential, however, that the child has mastered these first two milestones before working on any goals that may follow afterward developmentally. Through the implementation of DIR/Floortime, children can learn to develop social, age-appropriate, emotional, interactive, and playful skills that will facilitate their ability to acquire future academic and social skills in later years.

Floortime Goals and DIR-Emotional Stages/Milestones

Floortime Goals	DIR-Emotional Stages/Milestones
1. Encouraging attention and intimacy	1. Regulation and interest
2. Facilitating two-way communication	2. Engagement and relating
3. Use/expression of feelings and ideas	3. Two-way intentional communication
4. Logical thought and reasoning	4. Continuous social problem
	5. Symbolic/dramatic play
	6. Bridging ideas

The first goal of Floortime corresponds to the first two emotional stages/milestones. The second goal corresponds to stages 2 and 3. The third goal corresponds to the fifth stage and the fourth goal corresponds to the sixth stage. Therefore, through symbolic and dramatic play (DIR stage 5), the child can develop his or her ability to use and express feelings, emotions, and ideas (Floortime goal 3). Eventually, the child will be able to engage in the beginnings of logical thought and reasoning (Floortime goal 4) by being able to answer simple task-related questions such as Where are the children on the school bus going? By *repetitively reinforcing* that the school bus takes children to school or home depending on time of day, the children will be able to eventually answer the question correctly, thereby encouraging the logical thought and reasoning skills that are necessary in the outside world.

Helpful Teaching
Techniques and Tips

I HAVE LEARNED and acquired a ton of clever, helpful little tips or techniques from many of my colleagues: speech paths, occupational therapists, physical therapists, and vision teachers. Also, I have developed a few tips of my own and would love to share them. Teachers and therapists who work with children are at their best professionally when they are willing to learn from their colleagues and are equally willing to share their talents with fellow teachers. Whenever another teacher or a child's family member comments on a particular technique, I ask them if it is mine specifically or someone else's. There are quite a few that I would love to take credit for, but I cannot. Here are just a few:

- Use a *child booster seat* while working on the floor with toddler-age children (eighteen to thirty months) to encourage greater focus and attending skills. When children are seated, they tend to be more focused and will attend to activities better and for longer periods. This is important for teaching basic building block skills such as shapes, colors, visual tracking skills, visual locating skills, visual matching skills, following visual models, and accepting manual assistance when necessary. These skills and others are essential for improving cognitive and language and communication skills.

- Use a *calm, slow, soothing voice* to calm a child down emotionally and to get them to slow down their pace. Many times, little children can become rather excited about a task or activity and may want to hurriedly rush through the task constantly, visually anticipating the next step or next activity but not really understanding the objective of the task at hand.

- Allow children to help *open and close containers, bags, boxes, etc.* This promotes a greater sense of interest in the task and a deeper level of learning and cognitive awareness of the skills that the task requires.

- Encourage children to *clean up* and put toys and materials away. This promotes a sense of emotional investment in the task and sense of responsibility, which will help them to carry these skills over in other areas of daily living.

- Save child's *favorite* activity or task until *last*. Trust me on this one. Bubbles are a favorite of most small children and are a great way to end a session and encourage hand/eye coordination and visual/motor accuracy.

- When children even attempt to complete a task verbally, *applaud and encourage* their efforts regardless of how small the effort is.

- Put as many verbal directions in *song* form, (i.e., sing to children what you want them to do). Kids love music and singing, so when you want them to complete a task, turn it into a little tune. It doesn't have to be fancy or even sound good. They respond more positively to singing because it makes the task more fun and enjoyable.

34

The Importance of Understanding Behaviors

N O MATTER WHAT behavior the child is engaging in, all behaviors are a form of communication. The child is trying to tell us how she feels. Without functional language and communication skills, children on the autism spectrum often engage in a good deal of challenging and problematic behaviors. When their behaviors begin to negatively impact other areas of growth and development, families must find useful and reliable ways to deal with these behaviors and their consequences.

Challenging behaviors can impede upon children's ability to learn, to establish meaningful relationships with others, and to engage in play and recreation. They can make a child's life and that of their families quite miserable if not addressed as early and effectively as possible. Many of the challenging behaviors typically seen with ASD are addressed with a type of ABA program once the child has received an ASD diagnosis. This doesn't usually happen until the child is around three years old; so until then, families need a way to face their children's behavioral issues.

Children who are on the autism spectrum typically have a few or many challenging and even problematic behaviors. These children do not engage in such behaviors to upset us or ruin our day. A variety of disordered sensory systems and the jumble of sensory information that affects them often overwhelm them resulting in behaviors that are resistant and noncompliant.

There are a few important considerations to keep in mind when trying to understand why the child is *acting out*:

1. **Sensory issues**—are the main reason many troublesome behaviors occur; therefore, the child's specific sensory challenges must be addressed in order to effectively deal with behaviors that will inevitably occur.

2. **Communication capabilities**—lack of communication skills lead to frustration and outburst. Without some form of communication system, children have only one way to tell others how they feel or what they need or want by presenting with noncompliant behaviors, emotional outbursts, meltdowns, or aggressive behaviors. Children need a form of communication so that *we* can help them to cope with and overcome their behavioral issues so they may learn.

3. **Unseen reasons for behavior**—child may not feel well or may be upset emotionally. This is fairly straightforward in that when anyone feels ill, their behavior often reflects that in some form. Many children who feel ill become quiet, passive, or withdrawn but some children who have sensory concerns or are on the autism spectrum may engage in more noncompliant or aggressive behaviors when either not feeling well or feeling sad or otherwise emotionally upset.

4. **Environmental factors**—are there sensory distractions or irritants present in the room? Make a thorough inspection of the child's immediate environment. If there are factors that present significant enough difficulty for the child, she will continue to present with behaviors that are not conducive to learning. Changes be need to be made in the immediate environment such as lighting, sounds, temperature, visual distractions, or physical layout of the room.

5. **Others affect behavior**—specifically the immediate caregiver or teacher who is present. This is to say that the child's parent, therapist, or teacher has a meaningful affect on the child's/student's behavior. This is because children are extremely adept at picking up on others' feelings. When we as parents or teachers are either upset or otherwise not pleased with their

behavior, they can indeed sense this, which in turn adds to their emotional and/or sensory turmoil. It will thereby increase the intensity of the tantrum and often increase the length of the outburst. Whenever possible, try to be in as positive a frame of mind as you can. Remember that our kiddos are not engaging in these difficult behaviors of their own volition. Rather, they are responding to inner turmoil—the only way they know how and without the benefit of functional language skills.

35

Important Considerations for Communication and Language Skills

I T IS IMPORTANT to remember that most children who are on the autism spectrum have difficulties with language and communication skills. Even children with Asperger's, who commonly have above-age level of vocabulary skills, lack the ability to understand the social and cultural aspects of language and communication. Therefore, as their parents, therapists, and teachers, we must search for other indicators that tell us the why, what, and how regarding our children and students. They *are* talking to us but in their own way. When a student is using mostly jargon (aka gibberish or chipmunk) to communicate with others, they are, in fact, actually trying to impart information to whomever can interpret their form of speech.

Those who are close with anyone on the autism spectrum must be aware of this and recognize a multitude of signs, clues, and signals as to what children want, how they feel, and what they are trying to tell us. And they are indeed trying to tell us all kinds of things. Also, it is important to remember that ASD kiddos are not just in their own little world as so many people might think. Once I begin to know a student, I recognize that so many of their behaviors and actions indicate how they feel and what they want. They are aware of others around them, but they often choose to engage in self-directed activities. We must bring them into "our world" because they do not normally possess the typical social impulses or emotional incentives to interact or connect with others as do those not on the spectrum.

36

The Importance of Addressing Social Awareness and Interaction Skills

EVERYONE IS A member of the world's human population, whether we like it or not and whether we are aware of it or not. An individual whose intellectual capacity is less than average may also have less than normal or typical social and situational awareness skills. Individuals with autism often also have difficulties with social situations. Their internal, innate social awareness system just does not function as instinctively as does ours. Their instinctual wiring is different, and most social information does not come naturally to them. Individuals with autism and Asperger's are virtually unable to acquire information about the social world and how to behave normally as do the rest of us. They only have as much knowledge and understanding about a social norm or skill as they experience in each individual social situation, and that is not enough to truly master social skills. This means that we parents and teachers must constantly facilitate and foster the awareness and development of healthy social skills in our children on the spectrum.

Theirs is a constant struggle to understand and process social information, which to them is largely foreign or even alien. It is truly easier for them to just "tune out" the rest of the world and retreat into theirs. This is understandable if you think about it. Imagine that each and every day, you have to try to figure out how to think, feel, and act in each and every social situation the day brings! It sounds like torture to me. I'd probably retreat too!

We parents, teachers, and therapists must try to provide our kids with every opportunity to engage in social situations across a variety of settings. Social skills vary from the library to the grocery store to a restaurant or a neighborhood party. Those are only a few examples of different social situations and settings. Encourage your child to at least observe social situations at first. Then gradually stimulate their interest in the situation by talking about it to them. Once the child feels comfortable, offer to join her in the situation. Then over time, these prompts and assistance can be diminished as needed so that the child feels he can be as in control and comfortable as possible in the social world. In short, we must find ways to safely and effectively teach them *how* to think, feel, and act normally (i.e., typical ways of social behavior). These concepts are foreign and strange to them, and the behaviors we are asking them to engage in are strange and uncomfortable to the point of them being unbearable.

There are no right or wrong ways to teach social interaction skills. For as many individuals with an ASD and social situations that exist, there are probably ten-fold the numbers of appropriate ways to teach the skills necessary to negotiate that situation even moderately well. Therefore, do not fret if your teaching methods gain looks of judgment or disapproval from on-lookers in a store, restaurant, or playground. Only a parent, teacher, or therapist (and not the general public) knows their child and their level of capability and tolerance and what they need in the way of instructional input.

Lastly, understand that it is often difficult for our kids on the spectrum to engage in social situations to any degree. Sometimes it's just uncomfortable but usually it's anywhere from painful to near torture for them. They must know that they're not alone—*we* know this, we understand, and we're there to help them. Most of my students on the spectrum respond very well to this approach. They want to be understood, to be reassured, and to know that they are okay. Often times, when students engage in a variety of self-stimulating and self-calming behaviors, it is because they are feeling uneasy or intimidated in a social situation. Engaging in *stims* eases their minds and basically calms them. Students also engage in stims just because they like to—plain and simple. The stims may have become an unchecked habit or a way to entertain them when bored. I tell my students that I understand that they need to engage in certain behaviors (stims), and I let them do so briefly and within reason. I describe what they are doing and even imitate the action. I must emphasis that after a short period of time, they must stop doing the action and engage in something more functional. Unfortunately the general public sees many stims as either inappropriate or disruptive. Therefore, it is our job and responsibility to help our children to modify or replace stims with more socially acceptable and developmentally functional behaviors. It may take a few incidents, but they will eventually be able to be redirected from repetitive, self-stimulating behaviors to more productive behaviors with less assistance, resistance, and drama. At that point, children can attend and learn and develop and grow!

37

The Importance of Addressing Daily Living Skills

ALL PARENTS WANT the same basic things for their children. We also want the best for our kids in the way of education and social skills and friendships. We would do anything to ensure their safety, success, and happiness. But we all know that we can only control so much ourselves; we must, therefore, do everything we can to teach them to achieve these goals themselves.

This is a challenging accomplishment even with typically developing children. When trying to teach children with developmental concerns, we must not only teach them the same skills but using specially adapted and individually tailored methods due to their specific needs and capabilities.

By daily living skills, we mean everything—from picking up their own messes and toys to helping to prepare meals and doing simple household chores and everything in between. In order to help our kiddos learn *and* master these and other similar skills, we must constantly repeat and reinforce daily living skills-related activities. We must transfer daily living skills acquisition to the classroom curriculum as well as in the community (e.g., restaurants and stores). When working with children at the EI level, daily living skills acquisition translates to helping them sit in a car seat, drink from a sippy cup, or hold an adult's hand to cross the street.

Daily living skills must be taught and instilled from a very early age and no matter their developmental level. Always take into consideration your child's ability level and start with small, repetitive steps until the particular skills is worked into a routine or set schedule and the skill is mastered.

Another equally important strategy for building children's sense of responsibility is to offer the child a variety of choices in order to make engaging in chores more appealing. For example, rather than saying "It's time to clean up your toys now," try "Should we pick up the blocks first or the dinosaurs?" Even very young children want to experience some measure of control in situations so as to gain a little independence and individuality. Having a simple choice of just two item/activities provides children with a small bit of these crucial developmental characteristics. Later, children can be offered three and then even more choices, depending on the situation and circumstances.

Try singing verbal directions. Really. Children love music, and when directives are sung or put to music, they generally comply much more readily or, at least, with fewer prompts.

Just come up with a silly little tune or rhyme such as, "Time to clean our toys and put them all away" to be sung to the tune of "Twinkle, Twinkle Little Star" or some other common nursery song. I've come up with several that I use every day and with every child. By the time people aren't singing directives to them anymore, they'll already be so used to these routine that they will follow through with few if any prompts. Any verbal directive can be sung to just about any tune. Just be creative, even quirky, and if it comes out sounding too silly or goofy, remember young children don't judge.

There are many ways we must accommodate the child by modifying the environment or adjusting the circumstances. Children, who are on the spectrum, often have developmental delays and concerns that limit their ability to process, learn, and master many daily living skills. For example, have the entire family brush their teeth at the same time to lessen the child's anxieties about tooth brushing, hair trimming, food preparation, meal times, etc.

Sometimes noise levels, lighting, and smells can also be modified to lessen children's anxieties or fear of trying new activities. Sometimes these factors cannot be altered, and we must try to sooth the child to ease their discomfort so that they may focus and learn new skills. Whenever possible, try to implement routines that make learning fun; modify or create environments that are welcoming and calming to promote our children in achieving success and becoming self-sufficient.

When children see that their parents/family members are involved in their well-being and daily living skills, they, too, are more likely to persist in developing these skills and are likely to carry them over into other areas and venues than their home.

Older toddlers and preschoolers are usually able to follow a simple picture chart listing each daily living skills/activities. Skills can be pictured and listed as a chore—for example, tooth brushing with a picture of the child brushing their own teeth. Putting toys away would be represented similarly.

Toddlers and preschoolers will significantly improve their ability to understand and follow through with a variety of simple, age-appropriate daily living skills, tasks, and activities with consistent parent/care involvement.

38

The Importance of Establishing Routines

ROUTINES PROVIDE STRUCTURE and a supportive framework for children to learn new skills. Children need and crave structures and routines. They learn a variety of essential skills and lessons from regular routines such as responsibility, teamwork, respect for authority, and myriad other skills that are the outcomes of specific routines.

The *first steps* in establishing routines are as follows:

- Identify and define the importance of specific activities.
- Learn and become familiar with the child's preferences, abilities, and the family's expectations and boundaries.
- Observe the child engaging in routines with another child.
- Identify appropriate outcomes for the routine(s).
- Identify specific strategies and sequences for the routines.
- Collect data, feedback, and monitor child's progress.

Routines have specific *components* or parts:

- Beginning/end
- Specific outcome
- Meaningful/useful
- Predictable
- Continuous/systematic
- Repetitious

Helping children and their families develop meaningful routines is crucial to the basic goal and mission of the early intervention program. All aspects of the program should strive to be as family centered and family oriented as possible. Early intervention clinicians are key to teaching families and other caregivers how to provide opportunities for children to broaden their skills while engaging in a variety of daily activities, thereby increasing their overall developmental skill base.

Note:

Not *all* activities or interactions will have every component of a routine, nor should they. Having a variety of well-established and expected routine activities is important, but spontaneous activities are equally as essential for a child to learn and develop.

39

The Importance of Having a Fabulous OSC (Ongoing Service Coordinator)

THE ONGOING SERVICE coordinator (OSC) is, in my opinion, the most crucial person on the child's therapeutic team. The OSC must act as the person who brings each team member together in a cohesive manner and should be "on the same page." Some children's cases are quite complicated and sensitive; therefore, they need an OSC who is experienced, thorough, diligent, dedicated, and efficient—put otherwise, a fabulous OSC. The child may be on the autism spectrum and need an OSC who will do a good deal of extra legwork. They will go above and beyond their job descriptions. They will have to make many phone calls to schools, agencies, parents, community organizations, doctors' offices, clinics, and more. They will have to accompany parents to doctor visits, evaluations and assessments, and school district committee meetings. They'll also have to do more paperwork. They must also devote more time and energy overall to cases of this nature. When my students have an OSC as I've described as being "fabulous," they experience more overall success. And while teachers, therapists, and parents are all also very important, if the OSC is less than *fabulous*, the success of the case will unfortunately be greatly compromised. I've had only a handful of truly fabulous OSCs, and when I get one, I let him or her know it because they are *that* valuable.

40

The Importance of Reading the Initial Evaluation Report

WHEN A THERAPIST receives a case, they are then sent or given the child's initial evaluation report along with other pertinent information such as initial intake data and the child's IFSP. The evaluation report presents a good first impression of the child's current strengths, abilities, needs, and more importantly, the child's current developmental levels. It documents the present concerns—why the child was referred. The family assessment is an optional part of the initial evaluation, which gives family members the opportunity to discuss any needs related to public assistance, health insurance, clothing, food, transportation, etc. in relation to the child's development. An observation of the evaluation is documented—who was there and how the child presented during the evaluation and if the child's behaviors were a typical representation of his/her current skills and abilities.

Next, a list of the assessment tools used is given. Many EI evaluations are used among other useful tools: the Preschool Language Scale (PLS), the Developmental Assessment of Young Children (DAYC birth to five years), the Hawaii Early Learning Profile (HELP birth to three years), the Westby Stages (Carol Westby assessment of cognitive and language abilities through play—nine months to five years), the Brigance Diagnostic Inventory of Early Development (birth to seven years), and the Early Learning Accomplishment Profile (E-LAP birth to three years). All these assessment tools are reliable and trusted for assessing young children's skills and abilities.

Next, the developmental assessment documents the child's physical development including medical history, audiological concerns, oral motor skills, and fine-and-gross motor skills. Next, adaptive and self-help skills are documented. Adaptive and self-help skills are those used to develop independence, including dressing, feeding, toileting, and household responsibility. These skills are based primarily on parent report. Cognitive development is documented next. This portion of the evaluation includes observing and assessing how the child learns, plays with toys, and solves problems.

Next, the child's language and communication skills (receptive, expressive, pragmatic, speech production, and voice skills) are documented. Receptive language refers to the child's understanding of spoken language and the ability to respond to verbally presented directions and information. Expressive language refers to the child's ability to communicate to others via spoken word or gestures. Pragmatic skills are those that an individual uses such as the speaker's intentions and all the elements in the environment surrounding the message, such as nonverbal communication. Social-emotional developmental is documented next. This includes the child's emotional responses, sense of self, attachment to and interactions, and relationships with others. Lastly, a report summary is given that will list the evaluators' clinical findings and their recommendations for therapy.

Sometimes, several weeks may have gone by since the evaluation, and when services actually begin and enough time may have passed that the child may have made some progress or even regressed. It is important, however, that the evaluation report is read and brought to the child's first visit. I will refer to the evaluation report during the initial visit. For example, if the child was experiencing difficulties—sleeping, eating, or transitioning from one activity to the next—I will ask the parent/caregiver if these concerns are still an issue. I will ask if the child's current skills and abilities are still what they were at the time of the initial evaluation, and if not, I will note how and why they differ. (Please refer to the initial visit checklist—appendix no.)

The initial evaluation report should include an *early intervention program hearing screening questionnaire*, which is a checklist of high risk indicators for hearing loss in children I have spoken to other therapists who may not have read the child's initial evaluation report and, therefore, are not as familiar with the child and their abilities upon beginning therapy. It is crucial to do so, and I am always amazed at either how similar to or different from the day of the initial evaluation the child is when I meet him for the first time.

MICHELLE A. SOUVIRON-KEHOE

41

The Initial Visit

A TEACHER OR therapist's initial visit is very important as it is the family and child's first encounter with and impression of you. I have found that the process goes much more easily and effectively if I approach it as an interview of sorts. I bring the child's paperwork (basic child and family information and the child's IFSP) with me to go over it with the family. I make sure that all the pertinent information is correct, and I make sure that the family understands all the information included in the paperwork.

Then I go over any consent forms there may be that need to be signed, and I explain what each form means. After this, I go over the initial visit checklist, which I have included here in section 48. The topics and questions that have devised work best for the families and students with whom I work. Look at the list and see if those questions and topics work for you and your purposes. The list can be altered or added to as you see fit.

I do not take a bag of toys on the initial visit anymore, expecting the child to come to me because I have toys. I am a stranger to them, and they do not know me. At their age, they cannot understand the difference between a good person with toys (i.e., teacher/therapist) and someone with nefarious intentions. Therefore, I want the child to see me talking with his mom, dad, grandparents, or whoever the primary caregiver is. I want them to become familiar with me, including my voice and face, before I ask them to sit with me for a session.

So many young children are all too willing to go with an adult who might entice them with a smile, friendly voice, and fun toys. This is a bit alarming, and it is the reason I stopped taking toys on the first visit.

I explain my reservations and reasoning behind this decision with the families and the vast majority agree and wish other therapists would do the same. I, of course, can only answer for myself. But since I've adopted this practice, subsequent visits tend to go much more smoothly. Also, parents appreciate this and feel more comfortable with and appreciated by me as their child's teacher.

Lastly, I finish the initial visit by asking the family if they have any concerns or questions for me. Many times, parents want to know just exactly what it is that I'll be doing with their child. So I explain to them what I will be working on with their child as per the child's IFSP goals. This is an important piece, which helps the family to feel as though they, too, matter in their child's therapy process. I want the families to know that they have a voice and the ability to express any concerns or issues they might feel uncomfortable about asking or discussing with a professional. It is my goal that families know that I am there to not only help their child but also to help them as well. Early intervention is designed to include and be centered around the child and the family unit as a whole. Therefore, it is important that families understand this right from the beginning of the therapy process.

MICHELLE A. SOUVIRON-KEHOE

42

Communicating Concerns with Team Members and Child's Family

A VARIETY OF communication methods are used to maintain communication. Many therapists use a notebook that they may write a little progress update for parents. The notebook can be kept in a place where each team member and parent can have access to it. Phone calls on an occasional basis to other team members, service coordinators, and parents can be especially helpful in making sure everyone is kept abreast of the child's progress and development on a regular basis.

Many special educators working closely with children on a daily basis will be able to recognize many characteristics of autism soon after meeting the child. Many very young children (eighteen months to thirty months) who will most likely be diagnosed with an ASD at a later date exhibit some similar traits as those listed in appendix 2. Many act as if they are in their own little world. Many exhibit limited and/ or vague eye contact. They either avoid making eye contact, or they appear to look right through you. Many of these toddlers engage in a variety of self-stimulating behaviors or stimming, such as vocal, visual, tactile, vestibular, and auditory. Each of these stimming behaviors will be described in greater detail in the sensory section.

Once the educator is fairly certain that the child exhibits at least two characteristics in the three major ASD characteristic subgroups, the next step is to call the ongoing service coordinator (OSC) to discuss what the next step should be. It is never advisable to approach the child's parents with your suspicions. As special educators, we cannot officially diagnose a child with a *DSM-IV* recognized developmental condition. Only medical doctors can engage in evaluation and assessment so as to diagnose a child with an ASD. As sure as we may be that the child is autistic, we are not specifically trained to evaluate, assess, and diagnose a medical condition. Therefore, after the service coordinator is notified, it is advisable that the entire professional team meet and discuss what to do next. While the parents are also viewed as team members, they are not professionally trained to deal with what the diagnosis means until explained by a medical doctor. It is our job to formulate a concise and understandable plan with which to approach the family. This will be heartbreaking news for the family. It is our job professionally to prepare them for the initial evaluation and assessment process, which could most likely lead to a diagnosis of autism.

Therefore, we never act as if we can diagnose the child. However, as you complete the first few sessions with the child, watch his movements, his eye gaze, how long he stays seated, and if he plays productively and appropriately with toys. Certain odd or different physical movements such as toe walking, hand flapping, and rocketing may indicate the presence of an ASD. Also, children who frequently make vague, distant, and limited eye contact with toys and caregivers are often diagnosed with an ASD. Many children with considerable sensory difficulties, but not an ASD necessarily, have trouble staying seated and visually focused for age-appropriate lengths of time as opposed to children with autism. Engaging in productive play skills are sometimes difficult for children with sensory integration difficulties but are especially difficult for children with autism. Children with an ASD typically focus exclusively on small parts or aspects of a toy rather than the whole toy itself. It is believed that these children engage in such behaviors because it may be visually calming for them and engaging in productive functional play skills, especially with the teacher may be too demanding and stressful. Engaging in such behaviors is referred to as self-stimulating behaviors or "stimming." This indicates a behavior or mannerism that is nonfunctional in nature and repeatedly employed largely to calm

MICHELLE A. SOUVIRON-KEHOE

and relax a child. Many times, these behaviors seem to make the child "zone out." I do not believe so. I think that some of these behaviors may be self or other injurious or socially inappropriate or dangerous. These behaviors are manifested in a number of ways: visually, auditory, tactically, vocally, proprioceptively, or vestibularly. The following are examples of such behaviors:

- **Visual stimming**—watching things spin or move vertically or horizontally
- **Auditory stimming**—fixating on sounds or voices
- **Tactile stimming**—touching things constantly or routinely
- **Vocal stimming**—repeating words, sounds, and parts of words
- **Proprioceptive stimming**—tightening or loosening muscles by various movements
- **Vestibular stimming**—may include positioning self to achieve bodily balance/equilibrium

If the child exhibits any of these behaviors, notify the OSC to meet with the other team members and decide how to best approach the child's family. Many parents may already have a suspicion of the child having a delay or concern. Nonetheless, this is a difficult news to process and accept. Therefore, it is highly advisable that the parents are given the utmost respect and consideration in this situation. Parents must understand that it is important that a developmental pediatrician or child psychologist to rule out or be diagnosed with autism evaluate their child. The assessment process begins with a lengthy waiting period to get on a list. The assessment itself usually takes two afternoons— sometimes less, sometimes more. One or more standardize evaluation measurements may be used. Among the most common assessment tools for diagnosing ASD are the M-CHAT and the A-DOS. Please refer to the list of acronyms for descriptions. These two assessment tools are only two of many other tools. They are two of the most relied upon and trustworthy assessment tools in young children for autistic spectrum disorders.

After the assessment process, the child will receive a diagnosis of autism or not. I have not yet had a student goes through the assessment process without receiving a diagnosis of autism. The sooner the child receives the diagnosis and then more intensive the therapy, the better, for no time can be wasted. The earliest of diagnoses has a better chance of yielding more satisfying result for the child and his family. Once the child has the diagnosis of autism, she will be able to receive many services that will greatly facilitate her progress and development. Many communities also have outreach programs and counseling services for parents and other family members of children with autism.

Summary:

This section contains basic information regarding the importance of maintaining open communication with parents and other team members. Children experience greater levels of progress and success when all team members are working together and parents are kept abreast of all changes and developments with their child's progress.

MICHELLE A. SOUVIRON-KEHOE

43

Mandated Reporting

N EW YORK STATE, as does each state, recognizes that certain professionals are specially equipped to perform the important role of mandated reporter of child abuse or maltreatment. Those professionals include but are *not* limited to the following:

- Physician
- Registered physician's assistant
- Registered nurse, LPN and PN
- Social worker
- Emergency medical technician
- Psychologist
- School official
- Teacher
- School coach
- School bus driver
- Police officer or other law enforcement official
- District attorney or assistant DA
- Mental health professional
- Substance abuse counselor
- Day-care worker
- School age childcare worker
- Foster care worker

A more complete list of legally mandated reporters can be found at the following website: New York State Office of Children and Family Services—www.Ocfs.State.Ny.us

Needless to say, as a mandated reporter, you will need to be vigilant and mindful of the fact that *whenever* you feel a child is at risk of child abuse, neglect, or maltreatment, you are *legally required* to report your reasons for concern. I have had to do this three times in the past twenty years. It is not easy. It tears at your heart, knowing that it may result in a child (or children) being removed from his or her home and placed in foster care. While this end may be in the child's best interest, it is *always* traumatic and emotionally devastating for a child to be removed from his parent(s). Each early intervention contracting agency and school district gives in services or workshops to inform its therapists and teachers of their responsibilities regarding mandated reporting.

44

Codes of Dress and Conduct

A S AN EARLY intervention therapist or teacher, you'll be working with babies and toddlers. Most EI therapists work with their students on the floor so comfortable, sensible, appropriate clothing is important—no high heels, dresses, skirts, etc. Modesty is essential as well. In warm weather, for example, one wants to be as cool as possible but short shorts, flip-flops, and halter tops are just not appropriate for an EI visit with a child. Wearing excessive jewelry is also not advisable. It is distracting to children, and they may pull at it or break it.

As for conduct, knowing what to do or say in certain, shall I say "tricky" situations, is largely a matter of common sense and good old fashioned "on the job/learn as you go" training. For example, I have encountered situations that were domestically uncomfortable to witness. This *can* happen because you're *in* people's homes at least twice monthly, if not once or twice weekly. You become familiar with the family, even close to them due to the fact that you're working so closely with their child. But it is very important that you maintain a professional distance with the family since your role there *is* of a professional nature and not a social one. You are still a teacher/therapist, but one that conducts lessons/therapy in-home rather than in a professional setting (e.g., school, hospital, etc.) While you may genuinely like and care for the family, it is not advisable to extend oneself beyond the professional boundary.

45

Cancellations and Missed Visits

AN OCCASIONAL CANCELLATION is to be expected. Even a forgotten visit can happen when parents' lives are so busy and hectic, but when these incidents become habitual, team members need to find out what the reason is. My rule of thumb is, if I have to cancel for whatever reason, I feel that I am obligated to make up for that visit as soon as possible. If the family misses a visit, it is my professional duty to ask the family if they would *like* a makeup visit, which will be done as soon as possible. However, if the family is a no show, meaning "no one is home at the time of the scheduled visit and there is no courtesy call," I will try to discuss the importance of keeping scheduled appointments the next time I speak to a parent/caregiver, mostly so that the child receives her therapy regularly and consistently. This is so that she can have her therapeutic needs met while making developmental progress.

These are situations in which many therapists tend to feel wary of scheduling further appointments, not wanting to waste time and gas when they may show up to an empty house. I've been in this situation countless times actually, and it is frustrating for many reasons, especially because I know that these situations often lead to a child falling through the cracks and not receiving their much-needed therapy. Most agencies have policies regarding *habitual absenteeism*. Some agencies have a "three strikes and you're out" policy for incidents of excessive no shows. Therapeutic services at the EI level are not mandated, so a parent can end services at any time and for any reason. Therefore, after a certain number of no-show visits or habitually canceled sessions, a letter is typically sent to the family/parent(s), and if there is no response to the letter, the case will be closed. Cases can, as well, be reopened in the future, if the parent so chooses.

46

New Teacher/Therapist's Requests

WHEN A FAMILY wants a new teacher or therapist for whatever reason, they are encouraged to contact their (ongoing) service coordinator to begin this process. I had been itinerant teaching for only a year or so when one of my agencies called me to say that I need not return to the home of a particular student. I was devastated knowing that this family wanted another teacher. *What had I done wrong?* I thought. Probably nothing, but sometimes no matter how nice, sweet, qualified, or well-intentioned you may be, a disconnect may exist or sometimes certain kiddos just don't "mesh" with certain teachers/adults. Well, twenty years later, this has happened a few more times, and no doubt, it will happen again. My point being that families can request new teachers/therapists for whatever reason they want. Sometimes it is a matter of the teacher or therapist not being a good fit for the child and the child's individual needs. Sometimes there is a clash of schedules.

Sometimes families are looking for someone to provide their child with a specific type of therapy/instruction. I do not take it personally when this happens because often times, the family's reasons are as simple and understandable as some of the reasons previously mentioned. One time, I had a family who just wanted someone to entertain their other two children while providing therapy for the intended student. Well, not only is this next to impossible to do, but it takes time and attention away from the intended student and her allotted therapy time. It is, therefore, not a professional nor ethical way to conduct a session. Another time, the family wanted all the therapists to be from the same agency, so I was let go. Or quite simply, you may just not be the right teacher/therapist for that particular set of circumstances, and that's okay. You may have to search your soul a bit to find out why. I do not think that *every* teacher will be a perfect fit for every student. We all have our own unique strengths, abilities, and preferences. The child may need a different teaching style or method in order to achieve their developmental goals. So when a family requests another teacher/therapist, try to put the situation into perspective and either learn and grow from it or simply look forward to your next student!

Declining a Case

T EACHERS AND THERAPISTS can also decline a case. This can happen for a wide variety of reasons. A therapist may not feel safe or comfortable in a certain area or situation. A family might move away to an area that the teacher may not service. Or perhaps the teacher needs to cut back on his caseload. Most early intervention contracting agencies have their teachers and therapists submit list of service area preference and availability. This way, therapists and teachers only provide services in the areas they've already chosen. But this is not to say that early into a case, a situation may not occur that could prompt a teacher or therapist to feel the need to decline the case. I do have trouble declining cases because it is never the child that I want or need to decline, it is a situation or set of circumstances that warrant the need to drop a case. This decision always weighs heavily on me, but I try to focus on being able to devote that much more time and attention on my currents students. That being said, it is wise not to overload yourself so that you can provide your current caseload with all your talents as possible so that your students receives the quality early intervention services they deserve.

Transition and Aging Out of the EIP (Early Intervention Program)

I N THE EARLY intervention program, children are eligible for services, providing that they continue to qualify until the day before their third birthday. When a child is making good progress and the therapist/teacher feels that the child no longer needs the same level or frequency of services, a part 2 is submitted and services are either decreased or discontinued. However, when the child continues to need services, they must go through the transition process. Around the child's second birthday, the very involved and somewhat complicated transition process is to begin. There is a good deal of paperwork that must be filled out and submitted to the appropriate people in the transition process. The child's service coordinator is the team member who is responsible for beginning the transition process. It is important that they guide the family by explaining each step and its purpose. I also help to explain the process to families when students are nearing their second birthdays.

Several steps in the process need to be completed properly and in sequential order so that children may receive a committee meeting with their school district's committee on preschool special education (CPSE committee). Ideally, the child will receive transition testing at around twenty-eight to thirty-two months. The sooner, the better because the larger the school district, the longer the wait for a meeting date. At the committee meeting, all in attendance will discuss the child's progress in the EI program, their current needs, and what type and level of services they will receive once in the preschool special education (CPSE) program. The child's parents are able to express their wishes for their child's developmental and educational needs. If the parents choose, their child may stay in the EI program until the cutoff date. For children born from January 1 to August 31, their cutoff date is August 31 (e.g., a child born on January 16 can continue receiving EI services until August 31). Too many times, however, I've seen children not receive a committee meeting by the day before their third birthdays because something went wrong in the transition process, and it is so unfortunate. Children who have a beginning of the year birthday especially suffer when this happens, and instead of being able to continue with EI services or receive a center-based preschool program, they're made to sit at home until September. Therefore, it is of the utmost importance that the transition process be started at least by the child's second birthday. The other cutoff date is December 31. Children who turn three from September 1 to December 3 can receive EI services until December 31 if their parents choose to continue with EI services. In January, they will be placed in a center-based preschool program if they qualified at their committee meeting.

49

Templates

Important Parent Notifications

An initial notification letter:

Dear Parent(s):   Date:_____

    My name is_____. As _____'s EI special education teacher, I am looking forward to working with you and your child. It is important for _____'s progress and development that we work together to make sure that the educational sessions take place in a timely manner. If I cannot complete a session, I will give at least a twenty-four-hour notice to cancel and reschedule the session. Likewise, if you need to cancel, please do so within twenty-four hours so that I can fill that time slot with another child and be able to reschedule with your child as well. Makeup visits can be completed within one month of the original missed visit. I will make every effort to complete as many makeup visits as you would like me to do. When your child receives consistent, scheduled visits, he/she will have greater opportunities to make developmental improvements.

Thank you for your attention to these matters.

Sincerely,

_____

*This letter may be given to the parent/caregiver at the initial visit

Sick-Child Cancellations

*Most agencies / schools / day care facilities send or give parents a letter regarding sick-child cancellations. If the child has a fever of 99.5 or higher, rash-colored discharge, etc., the parents should cancel the session so that the child has an opportunity to get well. Below is one example of a letter of this nature that can be modified as needed.

Dear Parents: Date:_____

In order to ensure the health and safety of your child, it is requested that you cancel services for your child if they exhibit or are experiencing any of the following symptoms:

a.) a temperature of 101 or any fever accompanied by a cough, earache, or draining ear or sore throat

b.) a rash of any kind until diagnosed, treated, or declared harmless by a physician

c.) diarrhea and/or vomiting the previous evening or before scheduled therapy session

d.) red, runny, or crusty eyes

Sincerely,

X_____

Initial Visit Checklist

1. When does your child get up in the morning?
2. Does your child have breakfast right away?
3. What does he/she eat for breakfast, lunch, snack, and dinner?
4. Does your child have any known food allergies? What?
5. What kinds of toys/activities does your child like?

6. How does your child play with toys? Is play functional/appropriate?
7. Is your child familiar with and cooperative for the following routines?

  • meals (seek/offer details)
  • bathing / hair washing
  • diaper changes
  • toothbrushing
  • bedtime routine

8. How does your child get along with family members: siblings, grandparents, and other children?
9. Does your child have opportunities to play with peers?
10. Does your child have temper tantrums? How often, and what are they like?
11. Does your child ever display any self-injurious behaviors? Explain.
12. Does your child have any problems chewing or swallowing food?
13. Has your child had any colds or ear infections?

*Feel free to add whatever questions you may have for the child's family.

MICHELLE A. SOUVIRON-KEHOE

50

List of Early Intervention Level Assessment Tools

- Ages and Stages Questionnaire (ASQ-3)
  by Jane Squires, PhD and Diane Bricker, PhD

- Assessment, Evaluation, and Programming System for Infants and Children (AEPS)
  by Diane Bricker, PhD

- Bilingual Language Proficiency Questionnaire
  by L. J. Mattes and G. Santiago

- Bracken Basic Concept Scale-R
  by Bruce A. Bracken

- Brief Infant Toddler Social Emotional Assessment (BITSEA)
  by M. J. Briggs-Gowan, PhD and Alice Carter, PhD

- Child Development Inventory
  by Harold Ireton, PhD

- Communication and Symbolic Behavior Scales (CSBS)
  by A. M. Wetherby and B. M. Prizant

- Development Indicators for the Assessment of Learning
  by C. Mardell-Czudnowski and D. S. Goldenberg

- Devereaux Early Childhood Assessment Program (DECA)
  by P. A. LeBuffe and J. A. Naglieri

- Early Learning Assessment Profile (ELAP)
  by M. E. Glover, J. L. Preminger, and A. R. Sanford

- Early Screening Inventory Revised
  by S. J. Meisels, D. B. Marsden, M. S. Wiske, and L. W. Henderson

- Gilliam Autism Rating Scale-3 (GARS-3)
  by James E. Gilliam

- Greenspan Social-Emotional Growth Chart
  by Stanley Greenspan

- Hawaii Early Learning Profile (HELP)
  by S. P. Warshaw

- Infant–Toddler and Family Instrument (IFTI)
  by N. H. Apfel and S. Provence

- Landmarks of Normal Psychosocial Development
  by Amy Lin Tan

- Modified Checklist for Autism in Toddlers-R (M-CHAT-R)
  by Diana Robins, Deborah Fein, and Marianne Barton

- Preschool Language Scale (PLS)
  by I. L. Zimmerman, V. G. Steiner, and R. E. Pond

- Speech and Language Screening
  by Amy Lin Tan-Kai Ming Head Start

- Vineland Social-Emotional Early Childhood Scales (SEEC)
  by S. S. Sparrow, D. A. Balla, and C. V. Cicchetti

MICHELLE A. SOUVIRON-KEHOE

51

Resources

Autism- and sensory-processing-disorder-related websites:

www.autisminternetmodules.org
www.texasautism.com
www.ocali.org
www.asha.org
www.speech-language-therapy.com
www.webmd.com
www.villagespeech.com
www.childdevelopment.com
www.ohsu.edu
www.gallaudet.edu
www.theautismsite.greatergood.com
www.centerforautism.com
www.autismspeaks.org
www.autism-society.org
www.activebeat.co/autism
www.autismnow.org
www.myautismteam.com
www.phdinspecialeducation.com/autism-asperger's
www.spdfoundation.net (sensory processing disorder foundation website)

Down syndrome–related sites:

www.ndss.org (National Down Syndrome Society website)
www.downsyndrome.com

www.nads.org (National Association for Down Syndrome website)
www.down-syndrome.org
www.familiesexploringdownsyndrome.org

Speech/language, autism and sensory-related apps (these sites list iPad and iPhone applications):

www.parenting.com/gallery/autism-apps
www.autismapps.wikispaces.com
www.autismlanguagelearning.net
www.autismtoday.com/top-10 autism apps
www.ausm.org/autism-apps
www.speechassociates.ca/Therapy
www.nojitter.com/autism-apps
www.pinterest.com/autism-sensory-apps
www.researchautism.net/autismapps
www.baycoastbehavioral.com/autism-apps
www.autismfamilyonline.com
www.childrensucceed.com

52

Recommended Reading

Autism and related spectrum disorders:

Colby Trott, Maryann, *Sense Abilities: Understanding Sensory Integration*

Gagnon, Elisa and Miles, Brenda, *This Is Asperger's Syndrome*

Grandin, T., and Scariano, Margaret, *Emergence: Labeled Autistic*

Grandin, Temple, *Thinking in Pictures: My Life with Autism*

Grandin, Temple, *The Unwritten Rules of Social Relationships*

Greenspan, Stanley, and Wieder, Serena, *The Child with Special Needs: Encouraging Intellectual and Emotional Growth*

Greenspan, Stanley, Thorndike Greenspan, Nancy, *The Learning Tree: Overcoming Autism from the Ground Up*

Hannaford, Carla, *Smart Moves, Why Learning Isn't All in Your Head*

Pitman, Stephen, *Beyond the Autism Plateau—a Parent's Story and Practical Help with Autism*

Le Blanc, Raymond, *Autism and Asperger's Syndrome in Layman's Terms. Your Guide to Understanding Autism, Asperger's Syndrome, PPD-NOS, and Other Autism Spectrum Disorders (ASDs)*

Le Blanc, Raymond, *Autism—What Do You Need to Know? A Parent's Guide to Autism Causes, Diagnosis, and Treatments DSM-5 Ready*

Sensory Integration International Inc., *A Parent's Guide to Understanding Sensory Integration*

Tammet, Daniel, *Born on a Blue Day: Inside the Extraordinary Mind of an Autistic Savant*

LaZebnik, Claire, *Growing Up on the Spectrum: A Guide to Life, Love, and Learning for Teens and Young Adults with Autism and Asperger's*

Collins, Paul, *Not Even Wrong: Adventures in Autism*

McCarthy, Jenny, *Louder Than Words: A Mother's Journey in Healing Autism*

Kranowitz, Carol, *The Out-of-Sync Child: Recognizing and Coping with Sensory Processing Disorder*

Greenspan, Stanley, *Respecting Autism: The Rebecca School DIR Casebook for Parents and Professionals*

Grinker, Roy, *Unstrange Minds: Remapping the World of Autism*

Paterson, Cecily, *Love, Tears & Autism*

Moor, Julia, *Playing, Laughing, and Learning with Children on the Autism Spectrum*

Keenan, Mickey, Kerr, Ken P., Dillenburger, Karola, *Parents' Education as Autism Therapists*

Robinson, John E, *Look Me in the Eye*

Higashida, Naoki, *The Reason I Jump*

Notbohm, Ellen and Zysk, Veronica, *1001 Great Ideas for Teaching and Raising Children with Autism or Asperger's*

Conclusion: Final Words of Wisdom and Thanks

I SIMPLY CANNOT imagine doing anything else but teaching at the early intervention level. Yes, my job is very stressful at times, but it is very rewarding and happily much more so the former than the latter. I liken it to the bell curve, as I do with many situations and occurrences. For example, most of my days teaching and interacting with students and parents are good—some are a real drag and others are fabulous. So the vast majority of cases are clustered around the center with some of each extreme at either end. Thankfully, the days that are trying are far fewer than the wonderfully rewarding encounters that I experience on the ever changing and challenging itinerant teaching path that I've chosen. Just seeing a child at the door or window jump for joy because someone is coming to their home to play with them is simply magical. And it is those days that I must keep in mind when the not-so-magical days occur.

My students and their families are my joy and inspiration. They also teach me that as they change and grow, so must I. There is a constant need to stay informed and up-to-date on the latest research and info regarding all things autism and sensory. This way, I can give my students and their families the most recent and accurate information as possible. But mostly, my students and their families are the inspiration for writing this guidebook. I not only want this book to help new teachers and therapists to the field but to also guide parents of pre- and newly diagnosed young children on the autism spectrum. Hopefully this book will provide families with an easy-to-read, comprehensive guide to help them cope during a difficult experience and to promote progress and learning in children. All this assistance then leads to children receiving the most they can out of the early intervention program and that leads to overall progress, growth, and development.

I especially wish to thank my students' parents and close caregivers. Close caregivers can include older siblings, grandparents, aunts/uncles, etc. They are faced with overwhelming and heartbreaking new realities for their children and are still able to manage daily life amid therapies, doctor appointments, evaluations and studies, demanding schedules, little or no sleep, other children, jobs, housework, etc. I am truly in awe of so many of my students' parents, and I tell them so. I feel it is important that parents know that others understand and appreciate what they go through in order to *manage life* with a child on the autism spectrum. They accomplish stunning feats of endurance, strength, courage, perseverance, flexibility, creativity, understanding, compassion, determination, adaptability, resourcefulness, dedication, responsibility, proactivity, self-reliance, and *patience,* all on a daily basis! They receive only a fraction of the appreciation and recognition they deserve, and they deserve medals.

Lastly, I wish to thank my students. They, too, are fighting a never-ending battle to live and grow in a world that is baffling, confusing, and uncomfortable for them on a daily basis. They have taught me to be more thoughtful, inquisitive, creative, understanding, determined, and *patient.* None of these traits equal those of their parents however, but I've acquired much more than I had when I began teaching—that's for sure! Any teacher of young children with special needs must possess at least a modicum of the above qualities or should not be in this field. These children require every person who works with them to have higher than average levels of these above-mentioned characteristics almost as a *prerequisite.* As the teacher grows and develops as an educator, he or she learns to hone these traits, as the circumstances require. I have learned from my students more about autism and "what makes them tick" by just watching them, playing with them, talking to them, listening to them, and laughing with them than all the workshops, conferences, and seminars I have attended. My students have taught me that they feel the same, love the same, and want the same as anyone else. They just interpret and process feelings and information differently than anyone else. They've also taught me that they need *us* to be patient with them—for with patience, all the other traits will develop and grow along with the child.

53

References

Premack, D. G. and G. Woodruff. 1978. "Does the Chimpanzee Have a Theory of Mind?" *Behavioral and Brain Sciences,* 1, 515–526.

Gopnik, A. and J. W. Astington. 1988. "Children's Understanding of Representational Change and Its Relation to the Understanding of False Belief and the Appearance-Reality Distinction." *Child Development,* 59, 26–37.

Baron-Cohen, S., A. M. Leslie, and U. Frith. 1985. "Does the Autistic Child Have a Theory of Mind?" *Cognition,* 21, 37–46.

Shamay-Tsoory, S. and J. Aharon-Peretz. 2007. "Dissociable Prefrontal Networks for Cognitive and Affective Theory of Mind: A Lesion Study." *Neuropsychologia,* 45, 3054–3067.

Lucariello, J., M. Le Donne, T. Durand, and L. Yamell. 2006. "Social and Interpersonal Theory of Mind." *Theory of Mind in Language and Development Contexts.* pp. 149–171. New York: Springer.

Notbohm, E. and V. Zysk. 2010. *1001 Great Ideas for Teaching and Raising Children with Autism or Asperger's,* pp. 2, 4, 6, 59, 65, 79, 109, 148–149, 220. Arlington, TX: Future Horizons.

Hart, C. 1993. *A Parent's Guide to Autism,* pp. 5–9.

Grandin, T. 1995. *Thinking in Pictures,* pp. 4, 9, 11, 14, 17–19.

Jameson, T. A. and C. E. Thompson. 2010. *The Everything Parent's Guide to Children with Autism, 2nd ed.,* pp. 2–13, 14–29.

Myles, B. S., K. T. Cook, N. E. Miller, L. Rinner, and L. A. Robbins. 2000. *Asperger's Syndrome and Sensory Issues: Practical Solutions for Making Sense of the World.* pp. 1–4, 6–11.

Grandin, T., 2011. *The Way I See It: A Personal Look at Autism and Asperger's.* pp. 5, 7–11.

INDEX

A

ABA (applied behavior analysis), 9, 99, 107

ABC model, 99

ADD (attention-deficit disorder), 9

ADHD (attention-deficit / hyperactivity disorder), 9–10, 20

A-DOS (autism diagnostic observation schedule), 9, 127

AEPS (assessment evaluation and programming system for infants and children), 11, 141

American Psychiatric Association, 15

ASD (Autism Spectrum Disorder), i, iii, 4, 9–10, 16, 19, 22–23, 30, 32–33, 40, 42, 45, 62, 67, 69–70, 72–73, 75, 77, 107, 112, 125–26, 145

Asperger's syndrome, 10–11, 20, 22–23, 45, 58, 62, 64, 75, 78, 110–11, 145–47, 151–52

ASQ (ages and stages questionnaires), 10

auditory association, 11

auditory discrimination, 11

autism, 9–11, 13, 16, 19, 22, 31, 45, 49–50, 58, 62–63, 67, 69–70, 72, 75–76, 99–101, 107–8, 111, 125–28, 142–49, 151–52

autosomes, 60

awareness, 32, 44, 53–54, 111

B

BBCS—R (Bracken basic concept scale—revised), 12

Behavioral Neuroscience, 49

behaviorism, 9

bell curve, 11, 148

bilateral coordination, 12, 48

bilingual language proficiency questionnaire, 12, 141

BITSEA (brief infant toddler social emotional assessment), 12, 141

Briggs-Gowan, Margaret, 12

C

Carter, Alice S., 12

CDD (childhood disintegrative disorder), 12–13, 22–23, 69, 75

chromosomes, 60–61

CNS (central nervous system), 13

CPSE (Committee on Preschool Special Education), 13, 136

CSBS (communication and symbolic behavior scale), 13, 141

CSE (Committee on Special Education), 13

D

DAS (differential ability scales), 13

DD (developmental delay), 14

DECA (Devereux early childhood assessment program), 14, 141

deletion, 61

DIAL-3 (developmental indicators for the assessment of learning), 14

DIR model (developmental, individual differences, relationship-based model), 14, 102

Down syndrome, 60–61, 73, 78

translocation, 61
trisomy, 60–61, 78

V

vestibular system, 44

vestibulum, 44
Vineland Social-Emotional Early Childhood Scales, 28, 142
visual discrimination, 28, 48
visual motor integration, 28, 48
visual tracking, 29, 82

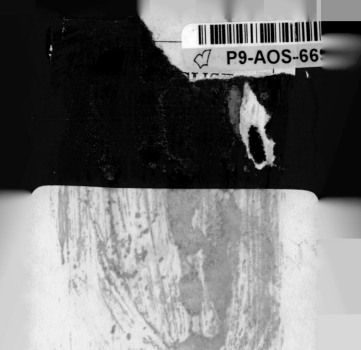

P9-AOS-66

UNIVERSITY COLLEGE LIBRA

Economics and the policy
maker.

FUND FOR ADULT EDUCATION
LIBRARY

UN 0 2 1995
SEP 15 1995   MAY 1 2 1995

ECONOMICS AND THE POLICY MAKER

ECONOMICS
and the
POLICY MAKER

Brookings Lectures, 1958-1959

SIDNEY S. ALEXANDER   ROBERT V. ROOSA

GERHARD COLM   SUMNER H. SLICHTER

NEIL H. JACOBY   MARK S. MASSEL

LOUIS SHERE   EVERETT E. HAGEN

FUND FOR ADULT EDUCATION
LIBRARY

THE BROOKINGS INSTITUTION
Washington, D. C.

© 1959 BY

THE BROOKINGS INSTITUTION

Published November 1959

Library of Congress Catalog Card Number 59-15669

Printed in the United States of America
The George Banta Company, Inc.
Menasha, Wisconsin

THE BROOKINGS INSTITUTION is an independent organization engaged in research and education in the social sciences. Its principal purposes are to aid in the development of sound public policies and to provide advanced training for students in the social sciences.

The Institution was founded December 8, 1927, as a consolidation of three antecedent organizations: the Institute for Government Research, 1916; the Institute of Economics, 1922; and the Robert Brookings Graduate School of Economics and Government, 1924.

The general administration of the Institution is the responsibility of a self-perpetuating Board of Trustees. In addition to this general responsibility the By-Laws provide that, "It is the function of the Trustees to make possible the conduct of scientific research and publication, under the most favorable conditions, and to safeguard the independence of the research staff in the pursuit of their studies and in the publication of the results of such studies. It is not a part of their function to determine, control, or influence the conduct of particular investigations or the conclusions reached." The immediate direction of the policies, program, and staff of the Institution is vested in the President, who is assisted by an advisory council, chosen from the professional staff of the Institution.

In publishing a study the Institution presents it as a competent treatment of a subject worthy of public consideration. The interpretations and conclusions in such publications are those of the author or authors and do not necessarily reflect the views of other members of the Brookings staff or of the administrative officers of the Institution.

BOARD OF TRUSTEES

WILLIAM R. BIGGS, *Chairman*
ROBERT BROOKINGS SMITH, *Vice-Chairman*
DANIEL W. BELL, *Chairman, Executive Committee*

Arthur Stanton Adams
Dillon Anderson
Elliott V. Bell
Robert D. Calkins
Leonard Carmichael
Arthur H. Compton
Colgate W. Darden, Jr.
Marion B. Folsom
William C. Foster
Huntington Gilchrist
John E. Lockwood

George C. McGhee
Morehead Patterson
Gilbert F. White
Laurence F. Whittemore
Donald B. Woodward

Honorary Trustees

Robert Perkins Bass
Mrs. Robert S. Brookings
John Lee Pratt

HAROLD G. MOULTON, *President Emeritus*
ROBERT D. CALKINS, *President*
ROBERT W. HARTLEY, *Vice-President and Director of International Studies*
GEORGE A. GRAHAM, *Director of Governmental Studies*
RALPH J. WATKINS, *Director of Economic Studies*

Foreword

THE FOURTH SERIES of Brookings Lectures for professional specialists and public officials was held during the winter of 1958-59. The series was designed to present a review of the uses of economics by policy makers in the conduct of public and private affairs. Economists who have engaged in the application of economics were invited to discuss the eight subjects here presented before an audience of practicing economists and officials in the Washington area. The lectures are published as given with minor modifications.

Previous Brookings Lectures were published under the following titles: *Economics and Public Policy* (1954) by Arthur Smithies, Joseph J. Spengler, Frank H. Knight, John Jewkes, Jacob Viner, and Lionel Robbins; *Research Frontiers in Politics and Government* (1955) by Stephen K. Bailey, Herbert A. Simon, Robert A. Dahl, Richard C. Snyder, Alfred de Grazia, Malcolm Moos, Paul T. David, and David B. Truman; *Changing Environment of International Relations* (1956) by Grayson Kirk, Harrison S. Brown, Denis W. Brogan, Edward S. Mason, Harold H. Fisher, and Willard L. Thorp.

In the present series, the task of applying economic analysis to the problems of business and government is considered from several points of view.

Sidney Alexander discusses the contribution that economics can make to the conduct of a business enterprise. As a theorist who has had broad experience as a consultant in business, he points out that although the application of the tools of economic analysis is "neither simple nor direct," it may nonetheless be substantial. Macroeconomics can be an aid in short-run forecasting of the business cycle and microeconomics in long-run planning and profit-maximizing; descriptive economics, which gives practical content to the analysis, can be useful in relating the firm to its environment and in long-run planning. Within this traditional framework, he provides an unconventional, lively, and incisive synthesis of how the economist works in substituting explicit analysis for intuitive appraisal, and in forming judgments about considerations that are left out of theoretical formulations.

Underlying Gerhard Colm's discussion of stabilization policy is his interest in the development of tools useful to the policy maker. Traditional economic analysis, he points out from his experience in government, has often been unable to provide the kind of guidance needed by public officials, and so —unable to wait until economics as a science has been perfected—officials and their economic advisers have often been forced to use makeshift tools. Indeed, many of the concepts and tools of stabilization policy have originated on the "firing line" of economics rather than in the academic development of the science. This is not to disparage the academic theorists since much of the inspiration for the new concepts came from academic thinkers. Rather it serves to point up the real need to re-establish closer communication between academic economics and economics in action.

In *The Problem of Creeping Inflation*, Neil H. Jacoby, a former member of the Council of Economic Advisers, urges economists to devote more time to the great issues of public policy. He asserts that "The value of economics as a field of intellectual activity must, in the long run, rest upon the extent to which it really helps man advance toward a better life." In illustration of his thesis, he uses "familiar concepts of economic analysis" to deal with the problem of reconciling full employment and a stable price level in a growing, free-market economy. Creeping inflation, he contends, is the result of general systematic faults in economic structure and policy and not the result of misbehavior by certain groups. Monetary and fiscal measures are not sufficiently flexible to offset cyclical changes in private demand and to hold aggregate demand around full employment, he argues, and there is insufficient flexibility in prices and movements of resources because of inadequate competition and government interference with competitive markets. He proposes reforms in five fields of economic policy: antimonopoly, agriculture, international trade, stockpiling, and federal taxation.

Louis Shere argues that tax policy suffers unduly from two major defects: the failure to apply the little economics we know and confusion about the areas of tax policy that fall outside the economist's competence. He illustrates his position by considering several issues: the distribution of the tax burden, level of taxation, limits to taxable capacity, tax incentives, inflation, budgetary policy, and the structure of the tax system. In his opinion, the economist's main weakness as an adviser is timing, since he is better at appraising long-run implications than their short-run effects. Hopefully, the analytical tools of the economist will be better in the future than they are now. But we can make great strides through the consistent and systematic exploration of the potentialities of currently available tools. He recommends a review of the American tax system in its entirety.

Monetary and Credit Policy, the lecture by Robert V. Roosa, is a view of the policy-making problem "from the doorstep of the central bank." What Mr. Roosa still considers to be the essence of effective central banking—the responsive adaptation to changing phenomena—is examined in the context of the objectives of central banking policy: the ultimate objectives relating to output, employment, income and prices, and the intermediate objectives relating to general financial conditions that promote the fulfillment of ultimate objectives. He places particular emphasis on the role of uncertainty and the need for flexibility of interest rates.

In the sixth lecture, a keen observer and outspoken commentator on our "laboristic" economy explores the consequences of collective bargaining and the policy of encouraging monopoly in the sale of labor in an economy ostensibly dedicated to the principle of competition. "Unions," says Sumner H. Slichter,[1] "are by far the most powerful monopolies to be found anywhere in the economy." But they are also "income-creating organizations": they obtain wage increases that may have an effect on the economy similar to the effect of an autonomous increase in government spending. His analysis of why he believes this view to be true is the central part of his lecture. He concludes with an examination of what his analysis implies regarding economic growth and stability and public control of union activities.

Mark S. Massel—lawyer, accountant, and economist—brings the weight of this varied experience to bear on the troubling problems of competition and monopoly. The tools of economic analysis, he points out, will not be utilized adequately until lawyers and economists learn how to co-ordinate their disciplines effectively. Since lawyers dominate the administration of antitrust policies and generally prefer to try their cases on familiar legal grounds, economists face the task of making their tools operationally useful in adversary proceedings. In the broader realm of policy formation affecting competition, the economist's role is different, and the distinction between the economist's task in the administration of antitrust laws and in influencing decisions about public policy is a major theme of Mr. Massel's essay. Economists unfamiliar with legal practice will find the review of trial procedure particularly useful for illuminating both the limits and the opportunities for economic analysis in the antitrust field.

Economic theorists have shaped increasingly keen analytical tools to deal with the problems of prices, competition, international economic relations, distribution of income and

---

[1] While this book was in press, word was received of Professor Slichter's death on September 27, 1959.

the level of employment, but, in the opinion of Everett E. Hagen, they have had little or less to contribute to the question of how growth begins. At the heart of economic growth is creativity, he says, and we must look outside economics for an explanation of the appearance of technological creativity. Economic theory concerning the beginnings of growth has been inadequate or wrong. But once economic development has begun, economic analysis has a great deal to contribute. Here, unfortunately, the advice of the economist about decisions regarding the allocation of resources for economic development is largely disregarded, at least in the low-income countries to which it is addressed.

The Institution is indebted to Ralph J. Watkins, Director of Economic Studies, who planned and directed this lecture series. The Institution is grateful to the Ford Foundation for financial support which has made these lectures possible.

ROBERT D. CALKINS
President

October 1959

Contents

1

Economics and Business Planning
SIDNEY S. ALEXANDER[1]

WHAT CAN ECONOMICS CONTRIBUTE to the conduct of a business enterprise? To this question there is a simple and obvious answer: Economics is the study of the fundamentals governing business, and it stands in the same relationship to the practice of business as knowledge of physical laws and facts to the practice of engineering.

But this proposition, like so many others that are simple and obvious, is just not true. There is no economic handbook, comparable to an engineering handbook, such that a skilled practitioner can consult the appropriate table and find the answer to his practical problem. It may be true, in some sense, that economics is to business as physics is to engineering, but the relationship must be more obscure and possibly more profound than the direct application of scientific study to the solution of the practical problem. As an analogy, I might ask you to consider how useful Einstein's theory of relativity would have been in helping you to get your automobile engine started when it had failed—purely an exercise in applied physics.

The tools and the modes of thought of economics are clearly not the tools of business practice. They can, however, be useful in the practice of business, and it is my purpose

[1] School of Industrial Management, Massachusetts Institute of Technology.

to indicate how. But the application is neither simple nor direct.

An economist friend of mine, exploring job opportunities in the motion picture business, was told by a movie tycoon: "If I had an economist on my staff I wouldn't know what to do with him." It is my impression that the heads of some of our greatest corporations who have hired economists have not known what to do with them either. Nor did the economists have a clear idea of what they were to do. Yet, I think a notable contribution is being made by economists to the businesses which they serve, and the full potentialities have not yet been realized. In this, as in so many other human affairs, what can be done is worked out by facing up to the problems as they emerge rather than by the construction of an orderly and complete blueprint in advance.

Economics can be divided into three broad subjects: *macroeconomics,* national income and all that; *microeconomics,* supply and demand and all that; and *descriptive economics,* all that. The great name in macroeconomics is Keynes, in microeconomics, Marshall, in descriptive economics, the National Bureau of Economic Research.

The coat of arms of macroeconomics is the rising curve of expenditure as a function of income intersecting the forty-five degree line of the equality of expenditure and income. The motto: Saving Equals Investment. The coat of arms of microeconomics is the ancient and honorable supply and demand curves crossed in a field. The motto: Supply Equals Demand. Descriptive economics can best be broken down into two branches, statistical and institutional, and the statistical, in turn, into two types: statistical methods, or applied calculus, and statistical practice, or applied arithmetic. Their respective coats of arms are white and black balls in an urn and a chart of the Bureau of Labor Statistics index of the cost of living. The other branch of descriptive economics, the institutional, has a coat of arms in the style of an old civic mural, with panels showing scenes from industry, agriculture, commerce, and government.

Each of these broad fields of economics has its own contribution to make to business. Macroeconomics is useful principally in the short-run forecasting of aggregate business activity, microeconomics in long-run planning and in profit-maximizing. Descriptive economics, which lends practical content to what would otherwise be barren theory, is useful both in relating the firm to its environment and in long-run planning.

Short-term Forecasting

The most obvious contribution that economics can make to the conduct of a business is in short-term forecasting of the business cycle. The study of the business cycle is clearly recognized as the special province of economists, and it was in their role of analysts of the current and prospective state of business that economists were first hired in private business. The large metropolitan banks were among the first to recognize the contribution that economists can make to the analysis of business prospects—for somebody else. Some 30 years ago the characteristic job of a bank economist was the publication of a monthly letter on business conditions to be made available to the bank's customers. Internal consumption was not prohibited but there is no evidence that it was widely indulged in. Economists, by and large, were not directly involved in the business conduct of the banks at that time. The large downtown New York banks often had huge pillars in front of their buildings, but the pillars did not really support the roof. They also had economists inside, but the economists did not help guide portfolio policies. The pillars remain, or in more recent structures, their prestige value is served by large expanses of glass, but the economist's role has changed. Undoubtedly, this change is a consequence of the development of a more specialized professional approach to the analysis of aggregate business activity, largely a combination of Keynesian theory with the empirical work on the national accounts pioneered by the National Bureau of Economic Research and further developed by the Department of Commerce.

In government as well, the first important use of economists, I believe, was in the public information function. The statistical work of the Bureau of Labor Statistics and the Department of Commerce was instituted largely as a service to the economic community rather than as a guide to governmental policy. For, at least in the formative period of this work, the federal government hardly had a policy with respect to the subject matter of these statistical inquiries. I suspect you have to look to the Tariff Commission, or perhaps to the Interstate Commerce Commission, to find an economist before 1929 furnishing information or counsel in the policy-making process. With the New Deal, however, and especially since the Employment Act of 1946, the participation of economists in governmental policy formation has certainly increased. Their participation in business planning is, to a considerable extent, an extension of this sort of activity.

At any rate, the first thing that is usually expected of an economist in business is the short-run forecasting of business conditions, the application of macroeconomics to current problems.

A distinction is clearly required here between the contribution that economics can make to the conduct of a firm's business and the contribution that the resident economist can make. Much of the short-term forecasting useful to the business firm is supplied externally rather than internally. A company's own economist can seldom improve substantially on the forecasting analyses available in the business press or from specialized forecasting services. At least, he cannot greatly improve on the best of them. Part of his function must be to select from among the available analyses those which he deems best, but his principal task is to convert this external information into a form useful for his company and to inject it into the internal flow of information so that it can be brought to bear upon the firm's own problems.

While this injection sometimes takes the form of a disembodied general appraisal of business conditions circulated within the top management, it is frequently also embodied in the budgeting procedure. For most large corporations the periodic short-term budgets start off from the assumptions of business conditions forecast by the economist. The individual divisions, on those assumptions, then prepare their own forecasts of total sales of their products for the entire industry, and the company's share of the industry's sales. The economist then reviews the divisions' forecasts for their consistency with his own forecasts for the economy and for the industry.

In this review function, the economist depends not only on his skill in macroeconomic analysis, but also on his training and experience in descriptive economics, particularly in empirical statistics. That is, the economist serves not only as the forecaster of general economic conditions, but as the window upon the world for the company. In the latter capacity, he depends upon specialized skill in the interpretation of industry statistics as well as specialized analysis of the consequences of emerging developments. The tool of analysis corresponding to this function has no concise name, but proceeds from the tradition of empirical research in economics. An economist is by no means the only one who could extract information and predictions useful to the firm from statistics and general economic developments external to the direct experience of the corporation. But he is certainly more nearly fitted than one not trained in economics, and the responsibility will usually fall to an economist if the corporation employs one.

What are the economic tools of analysis for forecasting general business conditions? The most pretentious tool is the elaborate econometric model. But neither in business nor in government has this tool been utilized extensively in a practical way. These models do indeed have great promise, but the promise still lies in the future. Less comprehensive or less systematically organized techniques are those in principal use at present.

A second tool is that of the economic indicators, time series useful in predicting levels of economic activity. Some of these indicators are like Ambrose Bierce's definition of a barometer —an ingenious instrument that tells you the sort of weather you are having. But some of them do have forecasting value. The work of Geoffrey Moore at the National Bureau of Economic Research, based upon the earlier work of Arthur F. Burns and Wesley C. Mitchell, suggests that certain economic time series, called the leading series, characteristically reach their cyclical turning points well ahead of the turning points of the general business cycle. My own investigation of these leading series as forecasters suggests that while they do in fact lead turning points of the business cycle with a lead averaging about six months, the length of lead is highly variable.

Even worse, these leading series frequently yield false leads. They often show turning points when the business cycle does not. Just how frequently they yield false leads depends upon the extent to which they are smoothed. The more they are smoothed the fewer false leads they indicate, but smoothing also cuts down the length of their lead. Their predictive power can roughly be summarized, so far as my studies are concerned, by the observation that the leading series can, with a given degree of reliability, signal business cycle turning points some four months ahead, on the average, of the Federal Reserve index of industrial production's signal of equal reliability. This four-month average lead is, of course, subject to a good deal of variation.

Essentially, these series lead because they are sensitive to the rate of change of business activity. When an upswing slows down, they turn down. A slowdown of an upswing frequently does precede a business cycle downturn. In such cases the leading series yield true leads. But it frequently happens that an upswing renews its vigor after a short lull. In such cases the leading series yield false leads. While the frequency of false leads and the high variability in the length of true leads limits the forecasting value of the leading series, that value is still considerable.

By far the most common method of forecasting in business, as in government, is the lost horse method. The name is based on the old prescription for finding a lost horse. You go where the horse was last seen and ask, "Where would I go next if I were a horse?" This technique is, in particular, applied within the framework of the Keynesian analysis. According to that analysis, the gross national product is determined by the aggregate level of expenditure, part of which is itself geared closely to the level of the gross national product, while the remainder has a more nearly autonomous variation. The lost horse technique then is applied to the autonomous elements such as investment in plant and equipment, government expenditure, exports, and the autonomous component of consumption expenditure.

While this method is operated within the theoretical framework of the Keynesian analysis, its application at critical points is an art rather than a science. It requires the identification of the areas where autonomous variation in expenditures can be expected, and the quantitative estimation of these autonomous variations. Of course, government expenditure is one of the most important of the autonomous components and the amateur can be separated from the professional practitioner of the lost horse method according to whether the forecaster relies on the budget estimates or makes his own independently. For, in spite of the fact that the budgetary expenditures and receipts are officially estimated by the government, the errors in forecasts of the governmental sector are among the most important errors in actual practice in forecasting levels of aggregate economic activity. The strengths and the weaknesses of this general approach to forecasting are well discussed by Gerhard Colm elsewhere in this volume. It should be clear from his discussion that the process is far from perfect and is still beset with difficulties.

While the lost horse method is undoubtedly the one in most general use by economists both in government and in business, second place among economists and first place among businessmen is certainly occupied by the persistence method, the so-called naive model. Even in meteorology, I am told, one of the best predictions of tomorrow's weather is that it will be the same as today's, outside of New England. Possibly meteorology has passed beyond this point, but there is some question whether economics has. The chief economist of one of our largest corporations tells me that when his short-term forecast actually has to be committed to paper a very high respect is paid to the likelihood that economic conditions will continue to move in the direction in which they have most recently been moving.

Two sorts of persistence models should be distinguished. The first is persistence of level, the second, persistence of change. The first says that next year's business will be about the same as this year's, the second, that next year's rate of change will be about the same as this year's. The persistence of change assumption is the more popular, at least among economists.

Let us not be too scornful of the persistence assumption. In at least one thorough test of econometric models of forecasting, the persistence models were used as a basis for comparison, and they certainly were not outclassed. But the great flaw in the persistence method is that it cannot predict a turning point. It is like Napoleon's drummer boy who knew very well how to beat a charge but had never learned how to beat a retreat. Yet in short-term forecasting, the prediction of turning points is the very heart of the problem.

While complaints are often made of the unpredictability of economic affairs, it can be argued that there is actually a great deal of predictability. Thus a persistence type estimate of the Federal Reserve Index three months hence as equal to this month's index plus two thirds of the change over the past three months will explain about 94 per cent of the variance of the FRB Index in the postwar period. But that hardly qualifies as a prediction. What we are really interested in is reducing the remaining errors. What is simply predictable is taken for granted, only what is as yet unpredictable is regarded as worthy of prediction. That is why the persistence models may be taken as the base line from which the value of other forecasting techniques can be measured.

Also similar to a technique used in meteorology is the specific analogy method. If you can find days in the past when the weather maps strongly resemble today's map you can expect tomorrow's weather to be about the same as followed those previous examples. Similarly, the economic prospects for the immediate future may be forecast on the basis of what happened the last time things shaped up as they are now shaping up. This technique, in economics, is subject to the limitation that the number of recorded business cycle configurations is infinitely smaller than the number of recorded weather maps. Consequently, the specific analogy method is used principally at times of great structural change such as the onset of war or its termination. At such times it may be helpful to inquire what happened the last time that a similar event occurred.

Another forecasting technique, more frequently used by noneconomists than economists, is the periodicity method. In its extreme form this implies a uniformly timed succession of ups and downs of the business cycle. Its forecasts are based on time alone, or on the time since the last turning point.

While this notion of rigid periodicity is generally scorned by economists as in the witch doctor stage, nevertheless, in the postwar period when a downswing approaches twelve months, or an upswing approaches three years in duration, it is reasonable to look closely for signs of a turning point.

The coexistence of dubious methods of short-term forecasting with the more respectable ones does reflect the limited claims that can be made for the best of the methods in present use, the lost horse technique. The tools of short-term economic forecasting may not be very sharp, but they are useful nonetheless. They are most useful in the hands of an artist; they cannot be applied mechanically, which means that they tell only part of the story. The remainder depends on the judgment and insight of the economist, bred by familiarity with the workings of the economy, but not yet reducible to a scientific technique. The economist can bring to this process a theoretical structure for conditional forecasts, the governing conditions being the actual variations of the autonomous expenditures.

While conditional forecasts are useful for government and for monetary authorities who have power to alter some of the basic conditions, they are not of interest to business men who require unconditional forecasts. In order to convert a conditional forecast to an unconditional one, the governing conditions must be estimated. This is where the art of finding the lost horse comes in. The forecaster must use his best judgment, based on his familiarity with the current data and his intuitive "feel" for the workings of the economy, in estimating the governing conditions.

Long-term Planning

While the most obvious task of the economist in the large corporation is short-run forecasting, his most valuable contribution, it seems to me, is in long-run planning. To some extent, this is a consequence of the greater amenability of long-run developments to economic forecasting techniques. While it is often quite hard to estimate whether the fourth quarter of next year will have a gross national product higher or lower than the fourth quarter of this year, it can quite reliably be estimated that the gross national product ten years from now will be some 35 per cent higher than it was this year. More precisely, it can be estimated that the long-term trend value that economic historians will come to assign to 1969 will be some 35 per cent greater than the long-term trend value they will come to assign to 1959.

The persistence method of forecasting, which works only indifferently well in the short run and misses all the turning points altogether, works very well in the long run, at least for aggregate output. Of course, the persistence method cannot be so appropriately applied to the components of the gross national product as to the aggregate. Individual industries wax and wane, and the firms within them are traditionally likened to the trees of the forest. But the other techniques applicable to the estimates of long-run developments will usually be found to be simpler than those applicable to the short-run. Asymptotic solutions are frequently possible even when general solutions are beyond our power. In more homely language, you can often say where you are going to end up without knowing exactly how you are going to get there or when.

I hope that a personal reminiscence of the greatest economist of our time may be cited in support of this point. Keynes once set the future of the rate of interest as the topic for tutorial discussion. I wasn't sure whether he meant the short-run or the long-run future, but as the London bond market was acting up just at that time, I tried to analyze the factors likely to govern the near-term course of bond prices. Keynes picked up my paper and sailed it across the room to the waste basket. "Alexander," he said, "any decent economist should be able to say what will happen to the rate of interest over the next ten years, but no one knows what's going to happen to the bond market tomorrow."

Even though long-run developments are both more important and more easily appraised than short-run, the short-run problems get the lion's share of attention in business, as in government. The businessman, deeply immersed in the day-to-day affairs of the business, never has the time and very rarely has the temperament for study of the long run. His experience in meeting urgent problems of the moment tends to emphasize, in his thinking, the short-run factors at the expense of obscuring the underlying long-run factors. The flow of information to him is from everyday experience of circumstances as they are. Long-run problems require projection into circumstances as they will become or can be made to become. Consequently there is a real opportunity for a valuable contribution by the economist in bringing long-run considerations to bear on a firm's decisions.

Even a summary discussion of how to analyze long-run problems would require, in itself, several lectures the length of this one. But the rough outline of the approach is essentially to construct a model of the developing situation and to project that model into the future. Now this is the sort of thing economists are accustomed to doing. And they can be expected to have some skill in doing it.

The economist's principal contribution is the realization that such a model can be constructed. I am not referring to an elaborate mathematical model, but merely to a conceptual model, whether simple or elaborate. A simple one is involved in the traditional Marshallian analysis of supply and demand. There are long-run supply curves based on costs, ultimately on technological relationships, and long-run demand curves based on tastes and incomes. In the long run, prices and quantities produced will tend to approach their equilibrium level at the point of intersection of supply and demand. This is a simple example of the character of long-run analysis drawn straight out of microanalysis.

It would be a false statement of the role that economic thinking can play to say that if you have a long-run problem you should get an economist to work on it. Much more important, if you have an economist working on your problems he is more likely to look to their long-run aspects—if he is a good economist. Even for an economist, however, once he is injected into a business situation, the temptation is strong to get into the urgent problems of the day and to neglect the long-run aspects.

The major contribution that an economic mode of thought in particular, or a scientific mode of thought in general, can make to the analysis of business problems, and those of government too, is the reduction of the problems to rational study, the transfer of as much as possible out of the field of the intuitively and implicitly appraised to that of the rationally and explicitly appraised.

The best consultants I know are uniform in their agreement that they contribute to their clients little more than applied common sense. But why can applied common sense be a contribution? Essentially because in attacking the problem the first task is to recognize the problem explicitly, and this is not habitually done by an active type. No discredit is implied here; the contemplative type is probably not very good at making and executing decisions. We should not be surprised that in this activity as in others, productivity can be increased by the division of labor, provided, as always, the extent of the market will support the division of labor. One man can profitably specialize in running a business and meeting its day-to-day problems and another in studying those factors that are likely to affect the business in the long run. Different skills and temperaments are suited to each of these activities.

Many of the critical decisions of long-run planning are

once in a decade decisions, some are once in a lifetime. It can hardly be expected that anyone could handle such problems on the basis of his own personal experience. There should be no wonder that this sort of analysis is a field for specialization. Those skills most important for the businessman—skills in negotiation, in execution, and in administration—are not usually associated with the sort of introspective analysis appropriate for the projection into an "as if" world of the future. But the economist is a specialist in the analysis of the "as if." As one Brookings author has stated, "Economic analysis is a substitute for the sixth sense of businessmen." The sixth sense probably does better in sensing the short-run situation, but not as well in sensing the long-run. Even when the businessman himself would be highly skilled at making such a study, the doctrine of comparative advantage suggests that it may be more advantageous to turn the study over to a specialist in analysis while the businessman concentrates on problems of administration and execution.

The characteristic long-run problem of the business enterprise is what business should it be in and on what scale. This is the principal content of business planning, and it centers on capital budgeting.

Long-range planning, or LRP, as it is frequently referred to, is now a big word in business. The devotees of LRP speak of its advantages much as the old line socialists spoke of society under socialism—when everything will be better. "Fuzzy management disappears when LRP is applied." "Crisis management becomes less pronounced." "Short-term dips assume less significance." "New markets are entered as soon as possible." "Money and men come easier." "Long-range planning . . . is a mark of industrial leadership by which good management is made more effective and good companies retain or attain recognition in their industry." These statements, taken out of their context of a discussion of long-range planning in a management journal, possibly give an oversimplified picture of the enthusiasm for long-range planning on the part of its advocates, but they do not exaggerate the intensity of that enthusiasm.

Clearly, planning can confer such benefits only if it is good planning. Most of the literature on planning in business is aimed at the form rather than the substance of planning. Implicit in this is the idea that even a poor plan is better than none at all, since the planning process is unlikely to result in a worse outcome than unplanned behavior. And there's probably some truth in this. Because the very act of planning does require explicit consideration of the relevant factors, it is less likely that an important consideration will be ignored. But most of the literature stops short of the substantive problem of how, in fact, the future is to be projected as the basic assumption for the long-range plans. That is the great opportunity for the economist.

How does one actually go about making projections of future developments which can serve as the basis for long-run planning? Once again, the lost horse method is the dominant technique, but in a different and less well-defined framework. Microanalysis does not furnish as neat a combination of theory with descriptive statistical categories as is available in macroeconomics in the relationship of the Keynesian theory with the national accounts. In the short-term analysis, one need merely run down the categories of the national accounts to make sure one has included the relevant categories. In long-term projection of sub-aggregates the elements of the analysis cannot be so clearly identified in advance. Like the famous recipe for rabbit stew, which begins "catch a rabbit," a long-run projection must begin with the identification of the relevant variables. The second step is the estimation of the direction and extent of their variation.

The principal claim of the economist to expertise in long-run projection of business situations must be based on his feeling for the relevant variables. Lawyers are sometimes said to be experts in relevance, but that claim can probably be made by all scientific workers as well. Only recently has it been recognized in the natural sciences that the so-called scientific method describes the process of demonstration rather than discovery. Discovery depends on insight and belief—in the tradition of Columbus, not of Euclid. Even in pure mathematics, one generation makes the great discoveries and the next cleans up the proofs. So, too, in the much humbler field of applied business analysis, there is great room for insight and intuition informed by experience and by perception of the relevant facts.

Macroeconomics helps only in the first step, the estimation of the level of aggregate economic activity over the period for which the plans are being made. The next steps are to determine the movement of the output of the particular industry relative to aggregate business activity, and beyond that the change in the share of the firm within the industry, and how that will depend on what the firm does. Here a combination of microeconomics and descriptive economics comes to the fore.

I recently asked an economic consultant, studying whether his client should abandon operations in a particular geographical area or should build a whole new organization there, why the client could not perform the analysis for himself. The reply was that he wouldn't know where to begin. This very simply sums up the position of the economist as a specialist in knowing where to begin, and hopefully, where to go from there, in the analysis of a projected situation.

What is required is skill in appraising an analytical problem, in identifying the relevant variables, and in using empirical techniques to estimate them and theoretical analysis to integrate the estimates into a picture of possible future developments under assumed conditions. This, of course, is a rough description of the requirements for successful empirical research in any discipline. The skills are not restricted to economists, and, indeed, others than economists, natural scientists in particular, now offer consultation services in the analysis of long-run problems for business firms. It is quite interesting to see how much economics they are rediscovering in the process.

An economist may be permitted to believe, however, that a person trained in economics, and more particularly, experienced in economic research, can appraise these problems from a somewhat richer background, relative to the needs of the problem, than can one trained in other disciplines. Thus, to give a somewhat oversimplified example, natural scientists in operations research have been known to set up the problem as maximizing output per unit of input in the same spirit as they would approach the design of an electric power plant, rather than maximizing the difference between the value of output and the cost of input along the lines of maximizing the profitability of an economic process. It is an elementary proposition of economics that in the maximization process you should push the process beyond the point of maximum return per unit of input to the point of equality of marginal return to marginal cost.

A more fundamental claim that can be made by the economist for special competence in the long-run analysis of business problems is that of familiarity with the general context of these problems and insight into the nature of the relationships. Plato was fond of arguing that the horse trainer is the one most likely to be well informed of the nature of horses, and the musician of the nature of music. This familiarity with the nature of the process is principally the contribution of descriptive economics, both institutional and statistical.

In preparation for this talk, I asked several economic consultants, some of whom I consider the best in the business, what tools of economic analysis were most useful in their activities. I must confess that I never got to first base. Each of them took for granted the sort of analysis that could be made and stressed almost exclusively the role of the outsider versus the insider. The process of decision making in the large corporation, they maintained, usually involves a strong identification of emotional feeling with the lines of policy that come to be favored in that organization. Consequently, there is not likely to come from within the company the sort of critical analysis that the outsider can supply.

As to what the concrete content of that critical analysis is likely to be, all that I could find out was that it usually has a large component of the distinction between the short run and the long run. The external pressures on the officers of a large corporation frequently run in terms of the annual profit statement, so that there is a real possibility that long-run objectives may be sacrificed to short-run. It is not claimed that this sacrifice is done on a conscious basis, but merely that the daily decisions which must be taken immediately—the "fires that must be put out"—do concern matters of short-run adjustment. There is no comparable imperative to make the long-run decision or to introduce the long-run consideration into the short-run decision. There is a human tendency to push off into the background those questions which do not require immediate decision. "Let tomorrow take care of itself" is certainly not a consciously adopted policy of any great corporation, but it is frequently adopted by default not only by large businesses but by government and by you and me.

The great contribution that the outsider can play, and to a certain extent the economist within the corporation can be regarded as an outsider for this purpose, is to bring into explicit consideration the pattern of long-run factors that should be kept in mind both as the background for short-run decisions and the substance of long-run decisions. This is the nugget of truth in the claims, sometimes extravagant, for the benefits of long-range planning. Long-range planning does bring into open discussion the problems of the long run that might otherwise go by default. It imposes upon the corporation the task of consciously facing up to the problems of the long run, of bringing the background into the picture instead of pushing it out of sight.

I know of at least one major proposed line of approach, extensively and favorably considered by a giant company, that was shattered by a three sentence description of the way it looked to an outsider. That three sentences could do the job convinces me that the management of the company was really aware of the unpleasant truth all the time, but could suppress that knowledge in a congenial and hopeful atmosphere. But when faced by the facts as seen by an outsider, the company officers immediately recognized the truth that had previously been successfully suppressed. This experience is not confined to business, however. In academic work as well, many a soaring plan is shot down by a well-placed criticism. Wherever there is an opportunity, in business or in academic circles, to achieve truth through discussion, criticism has a major contribution to offer, and criticism that comes from an outsider can have the great advantages of broader perspective and freedom from emotional involvement.

But certainly, criticism from any old outsider will not do. If an outsider is to make a constructive contribution, critical or otherwise, to the conduct of a firm's long-run planning, he must be skilled in the art of analysis of long-run business problems. While this skill is by no means confined to economists, training and experience in economic analysis and research is certainly one of the best bases from which to approach a problem of business from outside the business itself. The economist cannot hope to have the same familiarity with the internal facts of the business as those who have spent a lifetime in it. He must substitute for knowledge of the particular facts a knowledge of the general configuration of business relationships, so that he can readily learn the relevant facts and fit them into an analytic framework designed to appraise the long-run consequences of any given decision.

The contribution of the outsider is not only that of criticism based on a broader perspective. There is also the opportunity, indeed the necessity, of asking the questions that should be asked but aren't. Sometimes they are unasked for lack of time or skill on the part of those intimately engaged in the business, but sometimes the inquiry is suppressed for fear of what will be found out, just as some people can't find time to visit the doctor or dentist. Once these questions are raised, however, they do require explicit consideration of what was previously taken for granted, the starting point on the road to improvement.

This process may be illustrated by the simple example of the adoption of punch card methods of accounting. In order to convert an accounting system to a punch card installation, the whole system has to be re-examined and the question asked about each element, "What is its purpose?" As a result, activities which have been carried on for a long time without specific justification other than custom are brought before the bar of utility. The new system is likely to be superior to the old, not only because of the advantages of machine over hand methods of computation, but also because of the rationalization of the process, which is an incident of the new installation. Of the two elements, the second is usually the more valuable.

The same principle frequently applies to more complicated situations. For example, the application to business problems of recent developments in mathematical programing requires, as the first step, a thoroughgoing analysis of the problems in order to fit the new techniques to them. This analysis will frequently be found to suggest improvements at least equal in value to the benefits of the new techniques themselves.

In sum, the economist can make a valuable contribution to the solution of long-run business problems because his mode of thought, based on microeconomics and descriptive economics, is particularly attuned to the analysis of the long run, and because his role of outsider affords a broader perspective and leads to explicit examination of practices that would otherwise be taken for granted. Any scientifically trained person would share many of these characteristics, but the economist has the further advantage of familiarity with the class of problems encountered in business and with the data and the techniques of empirical research appropriate to this class of problems.

Marginal Analysis for Business Decisions

One outstanding feature of microeconomics is valuable not only in long-run analysis but in many operating problems as well. That is the concept of incremental variation, or marginal analysis. The practices of accountants are so permeated with cost allocation directed at average costs that there is, in any large corporation, a full time job for an economist in undoing the work of the accountant. In order to analyze the probable effects of a business decision on the corporation's profits it is necessary to estimate the incremental revenues and the incremental costs associated with that decision. Because of the many interactions among different activities at any point of time, or among different time periods for any given activity, there is likely to be a substantial difference between the costs of the activity as reflected in the books of account, and the incremental costs relevant to the decision.

This situation is well illustrated by the experience of the consultant who wearied of arguing that a machine which could not meet average cost but could more than meet incremental cost should be put back into production. He actually bought the idle machine at a fair price, in view of its present efficiency. "Now," he said, "I'll sell it back to you at the same fair price. And now it will pay you to operate it."

Resistance to thinking in incremental terms runs deeper

than the practices of accountants. It depends fundamentally, I believe, on the fact that the whole business cannot make a profit unless average costs are met. The argument that a machine should be kept in operation, or a line of business maintained or expanded, as long as the proposed activity makes a contribution in excess of its incremental cost is likely to elicit the response that nobody ever made a profit without meeting average cost—not just incremental cost.

Whatever the reason, incremental analysis is sufficiently different from the common customs of business that it can frequently point the way to increased profits. Thus, it could be demonstrated to commercial banks that, in the consumer finance field, more bad loans should be made. Credit standards should be softened to the point where the incremental risk just balances the incremental profitability of these loans, as compared with alternative lending opportunities. Similarly, insurance companies could be told that a high interest rate on policy loans, however high minded the intent of discouraging the impairment of the protection to the beneficiaries, was likely to shift these loans to other lenders. Advertisers who base their budgets on percentage of sales could be reminded that the appropriate criterion is whether the incremental dollar of advertising brings in more or less than an additional dollar of net revenue. A large corporation which takes pride in the fact that its interdivisional transactions involve prices that are the same as would be charged outsiders can be shown that its interdivisional sales are unprofitably restricted by this policy. The Air Force can be advised that to maintain a given number of airplanes in flying condition there is a tradeoff possible between the number of planes purchased and the amount spent on their servicing. Each of these cases depends, not on high powered analysis, but on opening the doors of thought to the simplest propositions in the textbook.

A similar observation may be made about the application

of the statistical mode of thought to quality control. An outstanding quality control expert told me that, trained as an engineer, he used to regard all the screws produced by a given setting of a screw machine as substantially identical. A whole new approach was opened up once he realized that their dimensions were subject to a probability distribution.

There is an important difference in the two cases, however. In the case of quality control, once the new mode of thought is adopted, the methods of its application are fairly direct, the numerical measurements straightforward. But the incremental analysis of economics can usually serve only as a general guide, rather than a specific. For example, what advertiser, outside of the mail-order field, knows the marginal productivity of his advertising? There is usually a very large step to be taken between the adoption of the incremental principle and its successful application. But even as a general guide it is of great value.

Other Examples of the Contribution of Economic Concepts

There are other aspects of the mode of thought of economists, some of which are almost trivial intellectually, that can nevertheless make valuable contributions. I may cite an experience of the President's Materials Policy Commission to illustrate how a small difference in approach can lead to a tremendous difference in a conclusion. The staff of the commission projected aluminum consumption in 1975 at four and one half times the high level of 1950. Industry sources expressed themselves as pleased by this ebullient projection but wondered whether it would not be more reasonable to expect over the next 25 years something closer to a doubling, in view of the record breaking growth that had already taken place. Both parties were projecting growth over the next 25 years at the same rate as the past 25 years, but the industry people had in mind an arithmetic rate of growth and the economists a geometric rate of growth.

Another simple example may be drawn from interpretation of weekly statistics on business activities subject to strong seasonal influences. It is often customary, in such cases, to make an allowance for seasonal effects by comparing the current week's figure with that of the corresponding week in the preceding year. Figures on department store sales and railroad car loadings are frequently published in this manner. This type of seasonal adjustment suffers from the serious defect that it introduces a lag of about six months in the portrayal of the cyclical movements of the processes involved. That is, only about six months after department store sales or car loadings have passed their peaks can we expect this week's figures to run below those of the corresponding week of the previous year. There are several statistical methods, not at all complicated, that can fairly effectively adjust for seasonal fluctuations without introducing a lag comparable to that introduced by the comparison with the previous year. It is amazing how much more valuable the data become when they are adjusted for seasonal variation by these more effective methods.

You may be surprised that I have left almost unmentioned the new techniques in mathematical programing, game theory, and other aspects of that broad field known as operations research. Mathematical programing clearly has a contribution to make to problems of scheduling over time or space: problems of transportation, warehousing, inventory control, production scheduling and product mix. I have already mentioned the valuable by-product of these techniques in requiring a rational examination of the processes to which they are applied. Beyond that, few business problems fit these techniques, as presently developed, so well as to justify their reclassification as problems of engineering rather than of business management. Most of the problems to which these techniques can be applied are usually more complicated than can be handled within the well-defined limits of the techniques. A Procrustean approach is usually required to cut the problems down to the capabilities of the analysis, so that solutions will frequently be offered, not to the problem in hand, but to a somewhat similar problem, from which we may learn something. Furthermore, the limiting conditions which must be set in defining the problem, such as the cost to be assigned to running out of stock in inventory control, usually have to be set on the basis of management's judgment rather than by a scientific technique. It is certainly possible to determine some of these limiting conditions by empirical research, thus pushing back a little further the line between managerial judgment and routine applications of well-defined techniques.

It remains to be seen, however, how broad a class of problems can be transferred out of the field of general management into what is now ambitiously called management science. The present indications are that there will be, for a long time to come, enough room for the exercise of personal judgment for business management to retain its challenging character, and to benefit from the broad modes of thought of the economist.

Having made strong claims for what economics can do for business, I feel it appropriate, in closing, to ask whether it is, in fact, likely to do what it can do. For the successful application of economics to business a great deal of judgment is required. Economics can help to form the judgments, but the judgments, to be sound, must also take into account the context of facts from which economic theory habitually abstracts. The frequent complaint that economic analysis is too theoretical to be useful in practice is usually based on the belief that abstraction has been made from some of the fundamental facts. Economics can be valuable in business only to the extent that it comes to grips with the facts of the situation, making allowance in particular for those considerations that are left out of the theoretical formulations. There is a type of business consultant who tries to apply "the book" to the particular problem in hand. Usually the book does not fit. There are others who come with an open mind, guided by theoretical principles but adapting them to the facts as they find them. These are the ones who may be aided to superior insights by their training and experience in economics.

The most important problems of business are problems of adjustment to uncertainties. In this context the economist in business does well to adopt as his motto the old proverb, "In the land of the blind, the one-eyed man is king."

2

Economic Stabilization Policy

GERHARD COLM[1]

WE ARE DEALING in this series with economics as an aid in decision making—decisions by government, by business managers, trade union leaders and other agents in the economic process. My topic has to do with one particular field of government decision making, namely, economic stabilization policy. Stabilization policy I interpret broadly as the promotion of balanced economic growth and the encouragement of a fair degree of stability, both in employment and prices. In other words, I include in stabilization policies the objectives stated or implied in the Employment Act of 1946.

The emphasis on decision making may appear unrealistic to those who know that most human actions and inactions do not result from deliberate decisions but from drifting, emulating, yielding to pressure, or simply from chance. Actions or inactions brought about in this fashion fortunately need not always be bad. Nevertheless, our claim to some rationality impels us to assume that a deliberate decision gives us a chance of generally better results. In any case, individual, corporate, or government actions can be appraised only by reviewing them on an "as if" basis, using a rational decision as criterion of their soundness.

[1] Chief Economist, National Planning Association.

Whenever we ponder a decision, we grope for answers to these three questions: Where do we want to go? Are we moving in the right direction now? If not, what changes are necessary? These questions apply to all decisions—where to go for a drink, how to conduct our business, how to obtain an increase in wages, how to promote economic growth and stability, or any other worthy objective.

The philosophy of the Employment Act is based on recognition of this three-stage procedure in the determination of stabilization policy. The Employment Act specifically requests the President to state in the Economic Report:

1. The economic goal (*i.e.,* "levels of employment, production, and purchasing power needed to carry out the policy declared" in the preamble of the act);

2. Current and foreseeable trends in the levels of employment, production, and purchasing power under existing policies;

3. A review of the effects of existing policies and recommendations of policies needed to accomplish the objectives of the act.

Here I may remind you of the legislative history of the Employment Act. In the original version of the Full Employment Bill of 1945, the three-stage estimates were required in dollar terms for the ensuing year. The present act is not specific about requiring dollar estimates and leaves also open the time period for which the statement should be made. It is my understanding that the language was changed because it was not always best suited for the purpose. I believe the wording of the present legislation suggests that quantitative estimates should be given where feasible, but the legislators refrained from putting the President in a legislative strait jacket. I interpret this part of the Employment Act as saying to the President: "Go as far as it is feasible in the quantification of economic goals, trends, and programs, but use general or alternative terms when a definite quantitative expression is not yet feasible."

It seems to me that this should be the procedure for developing and examining a national stabilization policy, even if it were not prescribed by a basic statute.

I will now discuss what is required of economics if it is to contribute at each of these stages towards the formulation of an economic stabilization policy.

The Setting of Goals

The use of goals or targets in the formulation of policy is essential because without a goal the policy maker has nothing to guide him; he would be tempted to use the past rather than the future for his aim. At present (fall 1958), Gross National Product is running at a rate above $440 billion, which is near the prerecession level of 1957. Does that mean we have reached a satisfactory level of production? We can answer that question only by a forward look. In order to reach a satisfactory level of production and employment a year from now, an increase in GNP by at least $35 billion in present prices or at least 8 per cent in over-all production is needed.

Before such estimates can be regarded as targets for economic stabilization policy, the question must be asked whether there are other considerations of national policy that require a modification of the objective. There is a specific reference in the Employment Act to "maximum purchasing power," which implies consideration of the value of the dollar, that is, of the inflation problem. I believe that the difficult problems of price stabilization can be tackled better when the economy is growing at a reasonable pace than when the economy is in slack condition and low rates of operations cause a rise in unit costs.

Also noneconomic considerations—the other "needs, obligations and essential considerations of national policy," in the language of the Employment Act—must be reconciled with the full employment objective. For example, considerations of national security measures and foreign policy may be important in this respect. I believe adequate provisions for national security and foreign aid are more feasible in a growing than in a stagnant economy. Furthermore, nothing would do greater harm to the United States position in the world than a failure to solve our domestic problems. As a general rule, it appears that a fair approximation of maximum production and employment promotes rather than impairs these noneconomic policy objectives. Therefore, I do not believe that there are important "obligations and other essential considerations of national policy" which would compel the government to modify the pursuit of economic growth and stability incorporated in the objectives of the Employment Act.

There can hardly be any question about our ability to estimate such maximum employment and production targets for a period of a few years ahead. Stating "needed" levels of employment and production in the aggregate is a relatively simple technical task. At least within a short time, only gradual changes will take place in the crucial factors, such as preferences for hours of work, the development of labor participation rates, with respect to advances in management, technology, and other factors affecting productivity. It is true, there have been substantial fluctuations in some of these factors resulting from underemployment or overemployment of men and factories. However, these are cyclical fluctuations, not fluctuations in the full employment levels of activity.

Thus aggregate estimates of "needed" levels of employment and production do not present particularly difficult problems either from a technical or a political aspect (even though recent economic reports of the President have failed to provide quantitative estimates of these needed levels). More difficult problems arise when longer-term projections with a meaningful breakdown of the aggregates are prepared.

Such a breakdown of the aggregates is essential for a detailed analysis of stabilization policies.

It is, for example, of utmost importance for economic stabilization policy to have an appraisal of that relationship between investments in plant and equipment and total GNP which is sustainable, that is, the relationship which leads neither to an inadequate growth rate nor to excess capacity. We know that in 1957 aggregate consumer and government demand were inadequate in relation to existing capacity. That was proven by the emergence of idle capacity. In order to formulate an opinion on such questions, projections are needed which reflect a desirable rate of growth and a corresponding increase in productive capacity.

For purposes of general economic and fiscal policy formulation, it is sufficient to present the GNP aggregate target with a few component parts, such as consumption, investment in plant and equipment, and so on. However, for purposes of a broader stabilization policy a much finer industry by industry breakdown would be desirable.

The national stabilization policy can succeed only if it is not merely a government effort but also an effort in which business enterprise, labor, and other groups participate. Economic projections can serve as a link between government policies and business investment policies. If businessmen know the aim of government policy and have confidence in the government's determination and ability to approximate the objective, they will in their own self-interest use these objectives as general guides in their management decisions. For that purpose it would be most desirable if the general GNP aggregates would be broken down by industry groups. These projections of industry groups could then be used by business managers as guides in formulating their own investment programs. Let me emphasize that we are speaking here of guides and not of blueprints. There is a radical difference between economic projections as an aid for government and business policy and five-year plans which are enforced by government dictate.

GNP projections have been broken down by industries with the help of input-output or interindustry tables. Unfortunately, the tables which were prepared for 1947 are now out-of-date. A more current interindustry table would be of great value in a broad effort at promoting balanced economic expansion.

Setting goals and preparing economic projections is a task quite alien to the thinking of an economist trained in the tradition of classical economics. He doubts the wisdom of any such undertaking. For him, the performance of the economy is the result of the automatic forces of the market. Good economic policy would only serve to remove man-made obstacles that hinder the working of this preordained *ordre naturel*. According to classical philosophy, the economist should learn to understand how an unimpeded market economy behaves—as the astronomer tries to understand the movements of stars and planets. "Understanding" and not "action" is the key word. The economist reared in the classical tradition regards it as almost sacrilegious if he is asked to aid in formulating goals for the economy.

The economics of stabilization policy is based on a different philosophy. It, too, recognizes the essential role of self-responsible decisions by the consumer, by business, and by labor. In a complex society it is important to use the market mechanism for reconciling individual decision making with organized achievement. Yet, the market mechanism is not an end in itself but a means. If the market mechanism does not give the desired results, the government has the responsibility of using its various programs and resources for supplementing the activities organized in the market economy. This requires a full understanding of the way the market economy works or fails to work in reaching the goals.

Setting of goals is not just an expression of what the

economist thinks is desirable. Let me make quite clear that it is not incumbent upon the economist to prescribe economic goals for the community. Present national objectives and existing consumer preferences are for him the point of departure. Most of the projected increase in future production is pre-empted by the requirements of labor and business without which the increase in production would not be feasible. There remains, however, a discretionary margin which can be used either for higher consumption, expanded government programs, or more rapid modernization and expansion of plant and equipment or larger capital export or any combination of these. The economist can only spell out in figures the alternative choices. Each alternative, however, must be economically feasible and internally consistent. By presenting such alternatives, the economist can help in the process of clarifying policy objectives.

Great advances have been made during the last 15 years in developing the art of economic projections in this country and many foreign countries. A great deal of work has been done in constructing internally consistent alternative projections, based on different plausible assumptions with respect to government, business, worker, and consumer attitudes and behavior, and different possible internal developments. Economic analysis was of help in the clarification of such concepts as sustainable economic growth. However, in constructing operational quantifiable models, the economists had largely to create their own tools of analysis.

Hypothetical Forecasts

The second stage in the process of developing an economic stabilization policy requires an estimate of the course of economic activity—of production, employment, and purchasing power—assuming no change in economic policies.

With respect to our ability to make accurate economic forecasts, I am a skeptic. However, fortunately for purposes of formulating economic stabilization policies, hypothetical forecasts are used which are somewhat less hazardous than absolute forecasts. Absolute economic forecasts involve, at least in logic, if not in computation, three steps.[2]

First, we survey *present* intentions with respect to *future* actions of government, business, and consumers. Government budgets and procurement plans, business intentions to invest in plant and equipment, and consumer propensities to buy are examples of such intentions about which some knowledge can be obtained. These are building blocks for a first tentative forecast. This first step in the forecast is based, for the beginning, on the assumption that neither government, nor business, nor consumers change their plans.

The second step considers that all economic agents do change their plans in response to the unfolding economic outlook. If because of recessionary forces some prices or interest rates should drop, some buying and investment might be stimulated. There are, however, also factors that tend to aggravate recessionary tendencies. If a slackening of economic activities is expected or appears to make itself felt, then business may become uneasy, hold back on expansion plans, and cut back on inventories. Workers who begin to be uncertain about their job security may hesitate to make commitments and postpone purchases. These are feedback effects that are likely to aggravate a primary cyclical development. The examination of the relative strength of the factors involved should enable one to judge whether the aggravating responses are likely to outweigh the mitigating reactions or the other way around.

Third, we have a response by the government—the built-in stabilizers which result in rising transfer payments and re-

---

[2] I recognize that in a mathematical procedure these three steps could be rolled into one.

duced tax payments as the result of a recession. In addition, there are deliberate policies, particularly by the monetary and fiscal authorities. If they try to counteract a recessionary development by compensatory measures, we may speak of a counter-feedback effect.

The feedback and counter-feedback effects create a difficulty for the forecaster because they cannot be estimated solely on the basis of past experience and the responses may change from one recession to the next. In the recession of 1957-58, for example, business cut inventories severely when a slight downturn became visible, making the downturn thereby more severe than could be expected on the basis of previous intentions. In the fall of 1958 some businesses found themselves with short inventories, which explains the speedy recovery that ensued.

For our hypothetical forecasts we need not worry about guessing what the government is likely to do because, unlike the absolute forecasts, hypothetical forecasts *assume* no change in government policies. The only complicating factor is that business and consumers react in part in anticipation of expected government policies—a kind of feedback effect of the counter-feedback effect. All this very much complicates actual business forecasting. But it impairs to a lesser extent the ability to estimate the direction and intensity of movement which results from primary changes in existing plans and intentions.

Again, I feel as in the case of goal-setting that much of the work done by theoretical and statistical business cycle analysis, valuable as it is, should be supplemented by research into the factors that I have called the feedback effects. It would be of particular interest, for example, to study to what extent experiences of business, workers, and consumers in one recession condition their responses in the next recession. It is in this field that realistic studies of consumer behavior could be of great value.

With present knowledge, it should be possible to make statements about the direction in which economic activities are likely to move—assuming no change in government policies. This will certainly be true when improvements in the intention surveys have been adopted which are under active consideration.[3]

In the present situation (fall 1958), for example, there is fairly general agreement among economists that the outlook is for rising activity in the coming year. Surveys indicate that the contraction of investments in plant and equipment has come to a halt and that a small rise from recent levels may be expected. Budget data indicate that government programs for defense and nondefense (for example, road construction and schools) will rise above the 1958 level. Some rise in consumer spending is indicated. On the negative side is the possibility that the present mildly restrictive credit policy, if further tightened, will lead to a curtailment in the level of residential construction. In total, a rise in gross national product appears likely. It is, with available data, much more difficult to say if the rise will continue at the present pace. In recent months, the shift in inventory policies from sharp liquidation either to very mild reduction or to some accumulation of inventories has given a strong push to production, and a further rise is most probable. The push from the shift in inventory policy will, however, have exhausted its steam in the near future. On the basis of present indications, there may be some doubt as to whether the rate of expansion in consumption, investment, and government will be adequate to reach a satisfactory level of production, will absorb the addition to the labor force, and will reduce the still high level of unemployment within a year or so.

The possibility can, however, not be excluded that a con-

---

[3] See the Federal Statistics Users' Conference study of the fields in which additional intention surveys could be obtained without large additional costs, released under the title, *The Economic Road Ahead* (1958).

tinued modest rise in activity may have such a feedback effect on business investment (including inventories) and consumer purchases that the initial modest impulse may become a rapid rise in demand. The financing of a large government deficit if supported by the Federal Reserve may, in this view, supply the monetary means for financing such an expansion. Those who focus attention on this possibility fear that demand may tend to press against capacities with inflationary price rise as a result. This is a possibility but in my opinion not a probability. Yet the fact that there is the possibility of such divergence of views demonstrates the difficulty of economic forecasting.

Absolute prediction is highly uncertain. Therefore, in the present situation, it would be best to develop alternative estimates for a faster or slower rate of growth and analyze the factors on which realization of the one or the other alternative depends. Also, the consequences of each of these alternative estimates should be analyzed, in terms of remaining unused capacity, lost production potential, and unemployment in case of a slow rise in activity, or inflationary pressure as the opposite case. This is the kind of information needed by the political decision maker who has perforce to make his decision in the face of uncertainties.

The Appraisal of Policy Measures

The third stage in the process of formation of economic stabilization measures consists in appraising the effects of existing government programs and of possible changes in policies.

During the last 25 years, much work has been done on the appraisal of economic policy measures. There is a broad area of agreement that is supported both by economic analysis and practical experience. Only few economists would doubt that economic recovery can be stimulated by an easing of credit, by an increase in well-selected government programs, or by a reduction in taxes. Still there are differences of opinion with respect to the best timing and size, and the best combination of such measures as the events of 1958 have demonstrated. More fundamental disagreement exists, however, with respect to policy measures designed to combat a price rise.

I will discuss some of the reasons why there are such basic differences in the appraisal of policy measures among experts and laymen alike.

I believe one reason for difference of opinion results from the fact that an opinion about the effect of policy measures has often been formed in the past and applied to quite different circumstances of today. For example, there are economists who maintain that a price rise, every price rise, is indicative of excess monetary demand and calls for restrictive fiscal and credit policies. Another group of economists contends that costs and prices may rise for other reasons; they have risen in the most recent past actually at times when there was no excess demand. If in such circumstances restrictive credit and fiscal policies are applied they may not halt the price rise but almost certainly will hinder a desirable rate of economic growth and possibly cause a recession.

Specifically, it has been suggested that a tight money policy which raises the rate of interest will not bring costs down but rather may add to the costs of production. Only if the policy of credit restraint should succeed in creating a recession would it exert a downward pressure on some cost factors and some prices. Other prices would not be forced down even by a recession, particularly in industries with a relatively inelastic demand and in industries in which unit costs rise when the rate of operation is reduced.

Similar controversy exists with respect to taxes. One group of economists takes it for granted that rising tax rates absorb purchasing power and reduce demand for either consumers' or producers' goods, thereby leading to price declines. Others insist that, at least beyond a certain point, an increase in taxes adds to the upward pressure on prices. This argument applies, with some variation in degree, to all taxes—most directly to excise and sales taxes which affect the cost-of-living index and thereby wages; to corporate taxes which affect the financial requirements of business for expansion and thereby their pricing policy; and to individual income taxes which affect the pressure for compensating increases in wages, salaries, and other income. The drastic use of tax policy for combating a price rise requires supplementary policies designed to prevent such shifting of the burden.

Also, the economic effects of either a budget surplus or deficit are by no means clear. Actual experience with relative price stability in periods of large budget deficits (for example, the calendar years 1956 and 1957) refutes the simple statement that budget deficits necessarily mean price rises, and vice versa.

Those economists who doubt that price stability can be maintained solely by fiscal and monetary policies have the responsibility of proposing alternative policy measures. Time does not permit a discussion of the many proposals that have been made.

Another reason for conflicting views about policy measures results from different emphasis on short-range and long-range effects of various measures. In periods of demand inflation, an increase in government programs will add to current inflation but at the same time other programs, such as those in research or training, may strengthen production capacity and thereby help in combating long-run inflationary trends.

A different evaluation results from focusing not only on the short-range spending effect but also on the longer-range program effect of a government undertaking. The increase in industrial production which is not accompanied by a corresponding increase in industrial employment presents an example. The persisting high unemployment is in part a cyclical, in part a structural phenomenon. It may be that anticyclical policies may not be suitable to deal with the whole of the present unemployment problem. It may be that full absorption of the unemployed requires not only measures promoting a rise in economic activities but also measures for retraining and resettling some of the unemployed and special measures for aid of especially depressed areas. The view an economist takes of various policy measures depends in part on his attention to short-range, cyclical or long-range, structural problems.

Another example of conflicting views: one economist may recommend public works, another tax reduction as an antirecession device. The reason for the difference may result from their attention or lack of attention to the preparatory measures that have been taken to implement such policies promptly. Or, one economist may take political feasibility into consideration while another one regards that as outside his competence.

Finally, let us assume a situation of uncertainty in which a recession is threatening, but the severity of the recession is doubtful. In such a situation one economist may recommend a government program because he feels that it is better to act too early than to run the risk involved in acting too late; while another recommends waiting because he wants to avoid the risk of unnecessary action. There are also economists who fear that a recommendation of antirecession measures in the earliest stage of a recession may create pessimism and supply additional fuel to the recessionary forces. I personally believe the opposite is more likely. For example, the announcement of an antirecession program late in 1957, in my opinion, could have prevented some of the inventory liquidation, mitigated the recession, and resulted in lesser budget deficits than are now expected for the fiscal year 1959. Here we have differences in the evaluation of risks and business psychology which lead to different possible economic strategies.

Thus, an appraisal of policy measures is at best a complex task. Those who drafted the Full Employment Bill of 1945 thought that the estimates of full employment production and the estimates of current trends would automatically give us a figure, representing either an inflationary excess demand or a demand deficiency. This figure would then indicate to the policy maker the dollar amount of addition to, or absorption from, total demand which would have to be brought about by changes in government measures. We know today that the task is more complicated than was envisaged at that time. Yet basically, the objective and the general approach were right. The decision maker needs a quantifiable goal; he needs an evaluation of current trends; he needs an appraisal of the existing policies and of policy measures which deserve consideration in support of an economic development that will bring us nearer to the goal. This appraisal of alternative policy measures should not be in generalities but in specifics— quantified wherever feasible. On the basis of such advice, it should be possible to devise a stabilization policy which may not always be right but which is designed with full consideration of the unavoidable conditions of uncertainty and incomplete knowledge. It would follow the principles of "minimum risk," recognizing the possibility of erroneous economic analysis.

This is a difficult task. However, the fact that the task is difficult is no justification for theoretical economists to escape into the "pure" realm of mere inapplicable mathematical symbols or for action economists to escape into the realm of mere "factual" statistical descriptions. Economics in action can be neither merely pure nor merely factual. Economists have to concern themselves with these tasks because the men who have to make decisions cannot wait until economics as a science has been perfected. There is nobody better equipped to give that advice. We have got to work with what we have and improve it at the same time.

Conclusion

All intellectual endeavors are stimulated by two kinds of developments. There is, first, in each intellectual field an immanent movement. The solution of one question often opens up new vistas, with new problems. Or a new finding sheds doubts on previous findings. The research workers are thus driven by the inner logic of the subject matter from one step to the next. This I propose to call—without any value judgment—the "academic" development of science.

There are, second, the challenges that come from the outside. Constantly, decisions involving economic affairs have to be made by business, by labor organizations, by government, by consumers, and so on. These decision makers are usually influenced in their thinking, consciously or unconsciously, by the economic theories of a previous period. Ever so often, situations arise in which it becomes obvious that economics, which in one way or another must be used as a guide by the decision makers, is inadequate for the task. Then the decision makers or their advisers have to construct their own tools, often in a make shift manner. In such situations, "economics in action" is ahead of the "academic" economics. It seems to me that this was largely the case with the economics of economic stabilization policies, during recent decades.

Unfortunately, we cannot always assume that the policy makers or policy advisers will meet the challenge by devising the right tools. They may be so deeply steeped in traditional economics that their imagination is blocked, and they do not see the need for developing or adopting new tools of analysis. Or, in the other extreme, they may miss the critical faculty and use tools which are so crude that they do more harm than good.

Nevertheless, an appraisal of the work done by the Joint Economic Committee in Congress, by the Council of Economic Advisers in the Executive Office of the President, and by private organizations of business, labor, and research demonstrates that substantial progress in the development of appropriate tools of analysis has been made.

Economics has become a "how-to-do-it profession." We have discovered "that 'it' is awfully hard to do," as Tom Schelling has so aptly put it.[4]

Economic projections, hypothetical forecasts, appraisals of various policy devices, "built-in" stabilizers, compensatory policies—all these concepts and tools of stabilization policy did not originate in the course of what we called the immanent "academic" development of science. They originated on the "firing line" of economics.

This does not mean that all these tools were developed without the benefit of the academic profession. As a matter of fact, much of the stabilization policies of the 'thirties originated directly from academic thinking which was deeply shaken up by the experience of the depression. Keynesian thinking had a great influence on this development. His was the case in which the immanent scientific development and the responses to the outside challenge were inextricably blended.

However, in recent years, with the refinement of economic theory on the one side and the development of stabilization tools on the other side, the gulf has widened again. Repeated efforts have been made, here and in other countries, to reestablish a closer communication. Such efforts were made by the Council of Economic Advisers in frequent consultation with academic economists and on a larger scale by the Joint Economic Committee, and most recently also by other congressional committees concerned with fiscal and economic matters. Also such organizations as the Committee for Economic Development and the National Planning Association, and other research organizations, have helped to bridge the gap between economics in action and academic economics. Textbooks,

[4] *Review of Economics and Statistics,* Vol. 40 (August 1958), p. 222.

lectures, academic periodicals, and particularly the symposia of congressional committees show that academic economics has begun to respond again to the challenge of "economics in action."

However, let me close with the observation that this process of amalgamation has not yet gone far enough. There is still a considerable gap between pure theory and a theory that lends itself to application in the formulation of stabilization policies. No scientific progress is possible without the thinking that can best be done in the contemplative atmosphere of the ivory tower. But the work in the ivory tower can be fruitful only if it is in two-way communication with the decision makers or with those who aid the decision makers. In this respect, what Veblen wrote exactly sixty years ago in his article, "In Dispraise of Economics," is still true: "There is the economic life process still in great measure awaiting theoretical formulation." If I understand the purpose of this series of lectures, it is to promote that mutual communication. I will be happy if these comments have contributed a bit to it.

3

The Problem of Creeping Inflation

NEIL H. JACOBY [1]

MY THESES ARE SIMPLE but fundamental. I hold that the economist performs his highest and best function when applying his craft to the great issues of public policy in his times, and that American economists should devote more time to this activity. We stand in greater need today of lucid and courageous application of familiar concepts of economic analysis than we do of new tools of thought. These propositions are illustrated by our failure so far to deal effectively with the problem of reconciling full employment with a stable price level in a growing, free-market economy. I shall try to diagnose this problem and to show how traditional economic theory suggests the elements of a solution.

Economics Is A Policy Science

It is hardly necessary to remind economists that their science had its origins and growth in efforts to analyze contemporary issues of public policy, and to communicate the results to literate people through political tracts as well as

[1] Dean, Graduate School of Business Administration, University of California, Los Angeles.

systematic treatises. The theoretical structure of a competitive free-market price system was worked out, in the main, by men trying to find answers to insistent political questions. The great pioneers in British classical economics faced the hard political issues of their times. Smith, Mill, Ricardo, Marshall, Pigou, and Keynes all served as Royal commissioners, bankers, or public servants. All wrote for popular consumption as well as for fellow scholars. The marriage of academic speculation to policy formation was peculiarly fruitful in the evolution of British classical economics. Through application, concepts were tested and either sharpened or abandoned. First-hand contact with public policy issues gave economists fresh information and perspectives which they used to formulate new theories.

The value of economics as a field of intellectual activity must in the long run rest upon the extent to which it really helps man advance toward a better life. The theorists who are long remembered are those whose concepts have had operational value. Adam Smith is remembered for the free trade policies based upon his devastating attack on mercantilism. Keynes is honored for the fiscal policy consequences of his theory that the level of employment required conscious intervention by government.

Being specialists in the allocation of resources, economists might be expected to deploy their intellectual talents in the most productive way. Yet a scanning of the economic journals in recent years suggests that we are not thinking and writing as much as we should about the primary economic problems of our country. There are many skillful refinements of theory. Problems of stabilization are extensively discussed. One notes penetrating contributions to monetary theory, wage theory, fiscal policy, monopoly and competition. Great advances have been made in operations analysis and business decision making. There is a burgeoning literature on the development of primitive economies. But applications of economic reasoning to basic issues of public policy seems to be reserved nowadays for the farewell addresses of out-going presidents of the American Economic Association!

One must go back many years to find penetrating analyses of the scope of Schumpeter's *Capitalism, Socialism and Democracy* (1942) or Simon's *Economic Policy for a Free Society* (1947)—to cite two examples. The most prominent recent effort to deal with contemporary economic policy comprehensively is that of Professor Galbraith, whose *The Affluent Society* (1958) is the only work of its type to become a best-seller in recent years. Despite its useful insights and the author's brilliant rhetoric, this work advances the erroneous thesis that productivity and output deserve less emphasis in the United States economy today. By failing to identify many important economic policy issues of our society, and by making certain recommendations that would impair the vitality of the American economy, Galbraith's book threatens to mislead many laymen.[2] We economists need to resist the powerful

[2] Galbraith asserts that the primary economic problems of our society include: (1) how to create sufficient consumer demand to keep the economy fully employed; (2) how to finance sufficient consumer demand without increasing consumer debt to a point where it threatens to produce economic instability; and (3) how to achieve a "social balance" between public and private expenditures so as to put an end to "public poverty" and "private opulence."

It is untrue that the United States need no longer emphasize increased productivity and output. Its economy requires vast amounts of capital for education, transportation, resource development, housing and community facilities, and huge increases in the output of consumer goods in order to meet the demands of an exploding population. Ninety-five billions of dollars is required, according to a recent McGraw-Hill survey, merely to modernize our obsolete industrial equipment. Foreign investment must be increased by many billions a year, if the United States is to play its economic role in the world. Yet Galbraith urges less emphasis on production!

Consumer credit is certainly not as important an issue of economic policy as agricultural adjustment, labor union regulation, international trade and investment, or stimulating technological progress. Because consumer credit does tend to amplify business cycles, a good case exists for regulation of its terms by government. However, in view of the fact that outstanding consumer instalment credit forms only about one and one-half months of consumer expenditure, and forms a much smaller fraction

tendency to become narrow specialists, cultivate a capacity to relate vignettes to the whole picture, and develop the literary talent to command a wide audience for our writings.

Price Stability and Growth

Unquestionably, a primary problem of economic policy of our time is how to maintain reasonable stability of the price level in a free economy that is growing vigorously. We may assume that the American people wish to have full production and employment and economic freedom along with a dollar of dependable buying power. In the end they will accept neither stunted economic growth nor a network of governmental controls of prices and wages as the price of a stable dollar.

Despite a few dissenters, there is a growing consensus that creeping inflation—a persistent rise of between 2 and 5 per cent a year in the price level—is in the long run a drag upon national progress, and that it is both feasible and desirable to prevent its occurrence. Direct controls to repress inflation, and escalator clauses to accommodate to it, are now generally seen as evasions of the problem. The reasoning that underlies these conclusions has been set forth fully elsewhere and

---

of consumer assets than it did a decade ago, it cannot be viewed as a major destabilizing factor.

Galbraith asserts that a large relative increase in public expenditures would be beneficial. Governmental purchases of the GNP have not only held their position but have risen since 1947 as a percentage of the total. While our happiness might be greater if the governmental percentage were larger, the figures do not indicate that Americans have kept their governments in penury. The choice between public and private expenditures may be tipped in favor of the latter by advertising and sales promotion. It is also tipped the other way by political "log-rolling" and the absence of a direct personal link between the benefit and cost of public services. Bringing about an expansion of governmental expenditures must surely be considered one of our less difficult problems of public policy!

need not be repeated here.[3] Despite general agreement that a stable price level fosters economic growth and should, along with full employment and free markets, be an accepted goal of public policy, surprisingly little has been written on ways and means of achieving this end. There is much dissension over the causes of inflation.[4]

The popular view is that creeping inflation arises from excessive federal spending,[5] and from wage increases that outrun gains in productivity and force up prices. Hence the remedies most often suggested are a reduction in federal expenditure and "restraint" by union and management officers in making wage agreements. But this diagnosis and remedy are plainly deficient. Although systematic control of federal expenditures is important, they cannot be *the* salient cause of inflation because they form only about 15 per cent of aggregate demand. If the pull of excessive aggregate demand causes inflation, we should be more likely to find the culprits among those who spend the other 85 per cent! Moreover, there have been extended periods of rising price levels when federal expenditures were falling (for example, 1945-48), and stable price levels when federal outlays were rising (for example, 1951-53). Granted that the upward push of wages on prices has played an important role in inflation, experience

[3] The consensus against creeping inflation is well expressed by G. L. Bach, *Inflation—A Study in Economic Ethics and Politics* (1958) and by A. F. Burns, "Monetary Policy and the Threat of Inflation, *United States Monetary Policy,* The American Assembly (1959). My own views on the economic effects of creeping inflation appear in *Harvard Business Review,* Vol. 35 (May-June 1957) and Vol. 36 (January-February 1958) and in *Problems of U.S. Economic Development,* Vol. I (1958), p. 153. S. H. Slichter and A. H. Hansen, on the contrary, accept creeping inflation as a desirable or at least inevitable concomitant of economic policies to maintain full employment. Cf. Hansen, *The American Economy* (1957) and Slichter, "On the Side of Inflation," *Harvard Business Review,* Vol. 35 (September-October 1957).

[4] This conclusion is suggested by a reading of papers submitted to the Joint Economic Committee of Congress. See *The Relationship of Prices to Economic Stability and Growth* (March 31, 1958).

[5] Even when the Federal budget is balanced on a consolidated cash basis.

has shown that admonitions to use "restraint" are not very effective in producing noninflationary wage agreements. Restraint must grow out of the bargaining parties' conception of their own interests rather than out of their regard for the general interests of society.

The popular analysis of creeping inflation is not only unsatisfactory, but it leads to futile efforts to assign the blame to particular groups of people, such as "aggressive" union leaders, "monopolistic" business executives, congressional "spenders," and so on. As a result, public discussion of the problem becomes emotional and remedial action is stultified. The problem really arises, as I shall attempt to demonstrate, from general systemic faults in economic structure and policy, and not from the misbehavior of certain people.

Let us view creeping inflation in a long perspective, develop a theory to account for it, and then deduce from this theory a feasible program of public policies to prevent it in the future. Time allows us to paint only with broad strokes of the brush; the work of many economists and policy makers will be required to fill in necessary details.

A Theory of Creeping Inflation

In formulating a theory of creeping inflation, we do well to recall some simple arithmetic. Inflation is defined as a significant rise in the Consumers Price Index, an average of the prices of 300 commodities and services sold in a sample of retail establishments in 46 cities. Now if we are to avoid inflation in the short run, when some *individual* prices rise, it is clearly necessary that other individual prices shall decline. And if we are to avoid inflation in the long run, if the *average* of prices lifts during the expansionary phases of business cycles, it is necessary that the average level of prices shall decline at other times. Simple arithmetic demonstrates the need for more two-way flexibility in individual prices and in the average of prices if we are to avoid creeping inflation. It indicates that avoidance of inflation requires attention to what may be called the "structural flexibility" of our economy as well as to the maintenance of aggregate demand at an appropriate level through time.

The creeping inflation which has marred the performance of the United States economy in recent years has resulted from two major defects: *first,* insufficiently flexible monetary and fiscal measures to offset cyclical changes in private demand and to hold aggregate demand around full employment levels;[6] *secondly,* insufficient flexibility in prices and in movements of resources, caused by inadequate competition and by the interference of government with competitive markets. The remedy for creeping inflation requires both more sensitive and powerful monetary and fiscal actions to regulate aggregate demand, and governmental measures to make the United States economy structurally flexible with respect to individual prices and movements of resources.

Recent efforts to stop creeping inflation have been disappointing because they have involved reliance only upon restrictive monetary and fiscal policies, without concurrent actions to increase structural flexibility. Highly restrictive monetary and fiscal measures, which cut governmental expenditures to the bone, raise taxes, and make credit expensive and hard to get, can probably stop inflation. They reduce aggregate demand so severely as to create unemployment, hold down prices and moderate wage agreements to a point where the wage-cost push on prices is diminished. But in an economy where resource movements have become too slow, competition is not pervasive, and enough individual prices do not decline quickly enough in the face of lowered demand, a highly restrictive monetary-fiscal policy will produce persistent unemployment. It will require a sacrifice of normal economic progress which the American people will not accept indefinitely.

[6] Defined to mean that at least 96 per cent of the labor force is productively employed, as an annual average.

The restoration of structural flexibility is basically a matter of creating the framework for workable competition in many markets from which it is now absent. Competition in *open markets* is *the* fundamental principle of a free versus a centrally-directed economy. If competition is pervasive and resources are mobile, enough prices will decline quickly enough when aggregate demand is shrinking and enough resources will move into more remunerative industries, so that sensitive monetary-fiscal restraints will serve to prevent inflation without creating excessively large and persistent "pockets" of unemployment and economic stagnation. Conversely, an expansionary monetary-fiscal policy will more rapidly induce movements of resources into the most urgent uses, enabling total output to grow for a longer time without producing "bottlenecks" and inordinate price increases. If the people of the United States squarely face the need to increase the structural flexibility of the economy as well as to improve monetary and fiscal controls, we will succeed in realizing our full potential of growth without bringing on a debilitating depreciation of the dollar. Even moderate gains in structural flexibility will suffice to keep the price level reasonably stable, so long as productivity rises steadily.

Let us now outline the elements of a program of public policy which will help solve the problem of creeping inflation. Because structural flexibility has received relatively little attention in discussions of inflation, it merits fuller attention than improvements in monetary-fiscal policy. Although they do not exhaust the subject, I shall focus attention on necessary reforms in five fields of economic policy: antimonopoly, agriculture, international trade, stockpiling, and federal taxation.[7]

[7] Removal of structural rigidities in the economy suggests many additional lines of policy action. For example, private pension and retirement programs tend to impede occupational and geographical changes of employment, by not vesting the employer's contribution in the employee. This problem requires public attention.

Antimonopoly Policies

Actions to make competition more vigorous and pervasive in the United States are an important part of a program for price-level stability. Stern enforcement of the antitrust laws, their extension to all kinds of private economic activity, and other measures to invigorate competition will help to make individual prices and wage rates more responsive to changes in demand, will augment productivity, will moderate the wage-price spiral, and thereby reduce inflationary pressures.

While competition should be enforced in all segments of the economy, labor union activities are of greatest present concern. The main legal instruments for enforcing competition, the Sherman and Clayton Acts, were designed to apply primarily to business firms and to commodity markets; labor unions and most professional and cooperative organizations are exempt from most of their provisions. Meanwhile, some unions have acquired great power over labor markets, which they exercise in a number of ways to push up prices or to prevent prices from falling. While inflationary wage agreements have received most attention, union restrictions upon entry of workers into trades, and union working rules to reduce productivity ("featherbedding") are also important inflationary factors. Being exempt from the antitrust laws, unions may do many things to "restrain trade" which businessmen cannot do. Indeed Professor Chamberlin avers that "indirectly, unions may already have more influence in raising costs and thus prices than do businessmen."[8] Because labor income comprises 62 per cent of national income, it is evident that the impact of wages on the consumer's price level is powerful. Public regulation of labor unions is therefore necessary to assure that their activities will be compatible with the public

[8] E. H. Chamberlin, *Labor Unions and Public Policy,* American Enterprise Association (1958), p. 18.

interest in a stable price level, efficient production, and workable competition.

Labor markets differ in many ways from commodity markets, and a fresh body of law needs to be developed to deal with their special problems. These problems include gross inequality of bargaining power between big unions and small employers, organizational and jurisdictional strikes, undue restrictions upon union membership, picketing, secondary boycotts, union support of price-fixing agreements, and internal union affairs. Some union activities should be made illegal; others are imperfectly understood and the relevant law would have to be developed on a case-by-case basis. In any event, it is difficult to understand how objection can be made to the principle that antimonopoly legislation should apply to *all* kinds of private economic activities whether carried on by businesses, unions, professional associations, cooperatives, or any other individual or group. A comprehensive rather than a fragmentary approach to the maintenance of a competitive order is needed.

Agricultural Policy

Food and apparel have 38 per cent of the weighting in the Consumers Price Index.[9] Because prices of most such items are directly or indirectly affected by current agricultural policies, it is clear that our efforts to support prices of basic farm commodities at "parity" are a potent source of inflationary pressure. Our agricultural policies have operated to maintain or raise the prices of food and fiber in the face of striking technological advances that have reduced costs of production and would have brought lower prices in the absence of gov-

[9] U. S. Department of Labor, *Average Retail Prices: Collection and Calculation Techniques and Problems,* Bulletin No. 1182 (June 1955), p. 62.

ernmental intervention. At the same time, our policies have
built up huge surpluses, whose disposal abroad impairs
friendly relations with other countries. Farm prices would
have declined in free markets, helping to keep the cost of
living stable and removing some of the wage-push exerted
on costs *via* escalation clauses in wage agreements. About 4
million workers are employed under contracts requiring quarterly or annual adjustment of wages to movements of the
Consumers Price Index, and this Index is a consideration in
virtually every wage determination.[10]

A new policy for agricultural adjustment is urgently needed
for many reasons. Output per man-hour has been rising more
rapidly in agriculture than in the rest of the United States
economy for at least twenty years. Because technological progress has made the large commercial farm relatively efficient
and the small farm inefficient, 44 per cent of our farms now
produce 91 per cent of the value of marketed farm produce.[11]
It is impossible to provide the remaining 56 per cent of the
farmers with a satisfactory income by means of farm price
supports, because they do not produce enough for sale. Present policies subsidize the affluent farmer while giving little
help to the needy one. The game has continued to the point
that the cost of supporting farm prices will be more than $5
billions in the current fiscal year, federal payments will com-
prise about 40 per cent of net farm income, and the federal-
held surplus will total about $9 billions by mid-1959.

A rational agricultural program—as the Committee for
Economic Development and other objective students of the
farm problem now agree—calls for gradual removal within
definite time limits of farm price supports, acreage allotments

[10] H. E. Riley, "The Price Indexes of the Bureau of Labor Statistics" in
The Relationship of Prices to Economic Stability and Growth, op. cit.,
p. 113.
[11] Committee for Economic Development, *Toward A Realistic Farm
Program* (1957).

and marketing controls. Such a program should embrace relocation and retraining grants to assist the submarginal farmer to enter more promising employment and to assure him a minimum income. It must embrace a program to dispose of existing surpluses. A programed return to free-market agricultural prices would remove a source of tension in our international relationships and diminish inflationary pressures. Even if a rational farm program cost the taxpayers as much as the present policy—which is most unlikely—the gains would be great.

International Trade

An essential element of an anti-inflationary policy is reduction of tariffs, import quotas, and other impediments to international trade. These help keep up domestic prices and shelter inefficiency and monopoly. A truly liberal international trade policy is the best safeguard of high productivity and a stable domestic price level in a world in which the leading trading nations seek monetary stability. The United States makes its economy strong by exposing its producers to fair (that is, unsubsidized) competition from abroad. If we expect to market our products in foreign countries, and ask them to expose their producers to our competition, we must be willing to receive their products.

The recent record of the United States in international trade policy has not been bad. We can applaud the renewal of the Reciprocal Trade Agreements Act. Yet there have been lapses from the path of virtue, in our tariff increases on watch movements and bicycles and our quotas on imports of Middle East and Canadian oil and Japanese textiles and apparel. There are now powerful reasons for more energetic action to remove trade restrictions. There is the ideological consideration that the United States, as primary exponent of competitive capitalism, cannot preach competition at home and reject it from abroad. There is the national security consideration that the Free World is strengthened when its member nations are closely bound together in a network of trading and investing relationships. There is the economic growth consideration that the United States needs increasing amounts of foreign raw materials to feed its growing industrial machine and must find ever larger markets throughout the world in which to dispose of its products. These factors constitute a convincing case for a more liberal international trade policy, quite apart from the real contribution it would make to the stability of the dollar.

Stockpiling

Revision of federal programs of stockpiling defense materials would also contribute to the fight against inflation. Federal stockpiles of "strategic and critical materials" (in which copper, lead, zinc, and platinum are important items) were valued at $6.4 billions at June 30, 1958, and the government also owned $3.3 billions of machine tools.[12] Most of these commodities were purchased when the concept prevailed that World War III would resemble World War II. In the light of present nuclear war potentialities, these huge stockpiles make little sense. There is a danger that "national security" may become a cloak for governmental price-supporting operations for many commodities, as has already been the case for lead and zinc. If so, additional elements of inflexibility in the price indexes would be created.

The United States has wisely refrained from participation

---

[12] *Annual Report of Office of Civil and Defense Mobilization,* Submitted to the Joint Committee on Defense Production (1958).

in Western hemisphere price stabilization schemes on the ground that they violate our basic economic tenets, and fail in the end. Clearly, we should not operate domestic schemes of our own under any guise, especially when they contribute to inflation and impede economic readjustment.

Tax Reform

Reform of the federal tax system is an important part of any effort to increase the efficiency and structural flexibility of the United States economy, and to make it less inflation-prone. In tax reform, the main emphasis should be upon measures that will offer both incentives and means of financing research and development and the modernization of our industrial machinery, and thus help to keep down costs and prices.

The immense cost-reducing potentialities of industrial modernization have been shown by a recent McGraw-Hill survey of American manufacturing industries. It was found that the cost of replacing all obsolete facilities with equipment of the most modern and efficient type would be $95 billions—a sum equal to *all* of the expenditure on plant and equipment by American business, for additional capacity as well as modernization, during the three boom years 1955, 1956, and 1957.[13]

If we add to this modernization backlog the future capital requirements for *replacement,* in the light of an accelerating pace of technological change, plus the capital required for *additions* to our industrial plant to serve the needs of a population that may double within the next 50 years, United States capital requirements are astronomical. Yet they must be met

[13] "How and Why Industry Modernizes," *Business Week* (Sept. 27, 1958), p. 21.

if we are to retain our economic leadership in the face of rapid Sino-Soviet growth in production and influence. Nor should we forget that other Free World nations have become formidable competitors in world markets. Some of them have *relatively* more post-World War II equipment than the United States possesses.

Americans would be wise to ask themselves how rapidly they wish their economy to grow, and then consider what kind of tax system will be consistent with this rate of growth. While the present federal tax system possesses valuable "built-in" countercyclical powers, as a result of its very heavy reliance upon progressive income taxes, it lays so heavy a burden on both the incentives and the ability to finance risky investment as to reduce the rate of capital formation, innovation, and economic growth.

The main lines of necessary federal tax reform are reasonably clear:

First, reduction of the top bracket personal income tax rates to realistic levels. The 91 per cent rate is really a phantom rate, paid by few and producing little revenue, while deterring productive effort and distorting investment.

Second, inauguration of a workable system of averaging personal incomes over periods of, say, five years. This would remove the penalty now imposed upon persons with unstable annual incomes (usually derived from entrepreneurial activities) in comparison with those having stable incomes (usually from salaried employment).

Third, reduction of the rate on corporate income, now 52 per cent. The present rate makes the federal government, in effect, the majority stockholder of every business corporation of substantial size. It favors wage inflation and inefficiency by charging the bulk of labor and other costs to the government. It diminishes both the incentive to make and the means of financing new investments.

Fourth, modernization of depreciation laws to give business managers wider latitude to write off fixed assets and thus foster earlier replacement of obsolete facilities. Headway was made in this direction in the tax revisions of 1954 and 1958, but the basic United States rules continue to be illiberal in comparison with those of other industrialized countries.

These federal tax reforms would stimulate economic growth, help to reduce costs, and contribute to price-level stability. Our state and local tax systems should be reformed with the same purposes in view.

Countercyclical Monetary and Fiscal Policies

My discussion of measures to increase the structural flexibility of the United States economy has left me time to make only brief observations about increasing the effectiveness of monetary and fiscal measures.

The recent record of countercyclical monetary action is, I believe, fairly good;[14] that of fiscal action is less favorable. Stabilization policies could be improved in the future by more complete knowledge of the time lags involved, by augmenting their potency and availability for use, and by better administrative coordination.

The economic stabilization process involves three kinds of time lags: a lag between the emergence of a stabilization problem and its identification by policy makers; a lag between problem identification and policy action; and a lag between governmental action and its corrective effect on the economy. The first two lags could be reduced by more accurate and

[14] This was the consensus of participants in an American Assembly meeting October 16-19, 1958. See *United States Monetary Policy,* pp. 116, 222. For a contrary view see Ascher Achinstein, *Federal Reserve Policy and Economic Stability, 1951-57,* A Study Prepared for the Committee on Banking and Currency (1958).

promptly available economic statistics and by better economic analysis. The third kind of lag probably cannot be reduced in length, being inherent in the institutional structure of the economy, yet the timing of countercyclical actions could be improved if we knew its magnitude. Here is an urgent subject of research.

Increasing the potency and availability of countercyclical policy measures also requires reform of certain monetary and fiscal arrangements. It is likely, for example, that revisions of the legal reserve system for commercial banks and placement of nonbank financial institutions under some general monetary controls would be salutary. Such matters are now being examined by the Commission on Money and Credit. In the execution of fiscal policy a greater flexibility of tax rates is desirable. A delegation of congressional power to the President to change personal tax liabilities within specified limits is one possibility. A system of automatic adjustments in personal income tax rates geared to changes in price or employment levels is another concept worth study.

Finally, we need to attain a better coordination of stabilization policies and actions within the Federal Executive, so that the monetary, taxation, expenditure, lending and loan insuring operations of government reinforce each other. One means to this end would be the establishment of a National Economic Council under the chairmanship of the President, analogous to the National Security Council in the area of defense.

Economics and Politics

Creeping inflation can be stopped in a free and vigorously growing economy only by reforms in many fields of public policy. The political obstacles to these reforms are indeed formidable. Inflation raises the most difficult political problems because it pits the general interest in a dollar of stable buying power against many organized and articulate special interests. They include the farm lobby with a desire for continued high and rigid supports of farm prices; oil and mining interests with built-in profits from inflation, import quotas, and stock-piling programs; union officials with a desire for unbridled economic power; and business groups seeking protected markets to shelter their inefficiencies. All of these groups must be educated to understand that their own welfare turns in the long run upon an efficient American economy competing in open markets and capable of flexible adaptation to change.

Ability to solve the problem of creeping inflation will be a supreme test of the economic wisdom of Americans and of the vitality of our political institutions. Will good economics prove to be good politics? American efforts to stabilize the dollar are being observed throughout the world, especially by people in nations yet wavering in their choice of economic development under freedom or under totalitarian control. We must not fail to pass the test. The United States must form a visible example to the world of an advanced industrial nation operated on the principles of economic freedom and financial probity. Here lies a great challenge to the economists and policy makers of our time.

4

Taxation Policy

LOUIS SHERE[1]

FEW ISSUES OF TAXATION policy fail to be resolved for lack of adequate analytical tools in comparison with those that divide us because we tilt in ignorance of the facts. Indeed, for the economist, the chief obstacle to formulation of effective tax policy, both now and in the foreseeable future, will be found in the shortage of factual information rather than in the breakdown of economic analysis. In the absence of data, refined techniques of analysis lie unused or yield mischievous results. In the presence of data, even relatively simple and crude techniques of analysis can yield significant results.

But the optimum factual information and analytic tools would still leave an enormous gap in the requirements for deciding tax policy, because these requirements go beyond economics. The economic aspects of tax policy problems are complex enough, but this complexity is aggravated by political considerations. In general, it is the voting mechanism that plays the dominant role in the formulation of tax policy, as in all public policy. The findings resulting from economic analysis of relevant data constitute important information

[1] Professor of Economics and Director of Tax Research, Indiana University.

63

that should be widely disseminated among the people, if they are to exercise effectively their sovereign democratic rights at the polls.

Even within the realm of economics tax policy cannot be determined effectively in isolation. By now this is well understood. All public policies that affect the economy—budgetary, debt management, monetary, expenditure, regulatory—as well as price, wage, and other policies being pursued in the private sector, play a greater or lesser role in the determination of tax policy. Effective tax policy blends several economic objectives, some of which are conflicting. The level of public expenditures, the distribution of wealth and income, the current standard of living, the rate of growth, stability, cost of compliance and administration, incentives to work, save and invest, regulation and control of consumption and industry, and the impact on the structure of the federal system of government are among the considerations that must be weighed in the formulation of tax policy. It is not desirable to stress any one to the exclusion of the others. The optimum mix certainly will disappoint all the ardent proponents of each objective. There is no agreement on how best to attain any one goal and still less on what constitutes the optimum mix. These are the fundamental reasons why tax policy is highly complex and controversial and destined to remain so.

The economist can play an important role in the formulation of tax policy, but he should distinguish clearly what falls within his special competence. In the ultimate choice of objectives, he has the status of a layman. He is an expert only in analyzing the economic consequences of alternative policies. The results of such analyses may provide critically important data for the guidance of the policy maker and more generally the public. In this way, the economist can play a key role in influencing policy decisions.

His knowledge of the structure of the economy and its economic processes, in the aggregate or segments, is far from complete. His major weakness as a policy adviser is timing. He can appraise long-run implications of alternative tax policies better than the short-run effects, yet as a practical matter it is frequently important to be able to evaluate such short-run effects. It is almost always extremely difficult to foresee how and when short-run deviations from desirable long-run trends are to be brought into harmony with them. The economist is as baffled as others by this perplexing problem, but he is better able to calculate the social costs of favoring the short view or the long in tax policy decisions. It is because the existing tools of economic analysis have their limitations and existing knowledge is limited that it is important to encourage experimental economic research and to adopt a sympathetic attitude towards several different approaches to economic investigation. In this way there is promise that the analytic tools of the future will be stronger than those presently available.

I believe, however, that what needs to be emphasized now is that a more consistent and systematic exploration of the potentialities of currently available tools of economic analysis could yield rich returns. We can make enormous strides with the little we know, if we have the intelligence and the fortitude to use it. This is a case where a little knowledge is not so dangerous that it is unwise to apply it practically.

My thesis is that tax policy suffers unduly from two major defects: (1) the failure to apply the little economics we know and (2) confusion about the areas of tax policy that fall outside the economist's competence. I shall illustrate this position by brief discussion of a few tax policy issues—the distribution of the tax burden, the level of taxation, the limits to taxable capacity, tax incentives, inflation, budgetary policy, and the structure of the tax system.

Distribution of the Tax Burden

Everyone agrees that the tax system should distribute the tax burden equitably (fairly or justly) among the taxpayers. In a democracy, after a transitional period, it would seem reasonable to expect that this result had been attained. Yet from all taxpayer groups one hears the persistent outcry that the tax system discriminates unfairly. In part, this reflects a wholesome clash of economic interests, tending to assure the proper consideration of all segments of the population in tax policy formulation. In part, it reflects the great uncertainty that prevails regarding the incidence and economic effects of taxation. So long as this uncertainty prevails, the public is without an adequate frame of reference as regards the distribution of the tax burden, yet it is asked to pass on a rapid succession of tax measures, each of which is inadequately analyzed in relation to the existing over-all distribution of the tax burden.

To some extent, this gap in information has been closed. We are indebted to a few courageous economists who, working primarily with price theory and with a liberal mixture of assumptions where facts failed them, have provided for a few specific years a distribution of the federal, state, and local tax burden by net income classes. The results of these efforts are not in controversy because of any defects in the tools of economic analysis used, but because of a lack of agreement on the factual foundation and the nature of the assumptions used in the absence of data. We are indebted also to others who have extended the analysis of the incidence and economic effects of taxation by the application of macroeconomic theory. The results are much more sophisticated but more difficult to understand and less specific than those yielded by the partial analysis which stops with the application of microeconomic theory. Recently more attention has been focused on empirical evidence relating to the incidence of taxation. The corporation net income tax, in particular, has been the subject of several such studies. Analysts have also turned to empirical work in testing the incidence of sales, excise, and other taxes. Each analyst refers to different data and employs different analytic techniques in reaching his conclusions.

There is little agreement at this stage on problems of tax incidence and consequently on how the burden of the present tax system is distributed by net income classes. We have a long way to go before the technical analysis of this problem is complete. If the information is to make some impact on those who initiate tax proposals in the government, on the legislative bodies that pass on the proposals, and most importantly on the public, the ultimate arbiters of tax policy, the results of economic analyses relating to the distribution of the tax burden must be presented in a form that can be readily understood.

Suppose, optimistically, that the uncertainties with respect to the incidence and economic effects of taxation will soon be dispelled. Suppose also that newly found powers of exposition and dissemination of information make it crystal clear to all concerned precisely how the tax burden is distributed by income groups. The public would still not have enough background information for a proper evaluation of current tax proposals. It needs to know the nature of the existing distribution of wealth and income before it can decide whether any incremental change conforms with or departs from the desired goal. We have scarcely any information on the distribution of wealth and far from satisfactory information on the distribution of income. There are scarcely any data on the distribution of income with atypical variations, such as appear in cross-sectional annual data, eliminated. Yet, this concept has long been recognized as fundamentally important in appraising the noneconomic considerations relating to inequalities in income distribution.

Both economic and noneconomic considerations must be weighed in appraising the quality of any given distribution of wealth and income or any incremental change in it. These considerations are in a measure interrelated. The size of the economic pie affects the possibility of reaching agreement on its equitable distribution. Unfortunately, economists are not yet prepared to broadcast the information that the public and others need regarding the economic import of differences in the distribution of wealth and income. We were able to speak firmly on these matters only when we were not freighted with even the little knowledge that we now possess. Much empirical work is being done and remains to be done before lucid and generally acceptable statements can be broadcast on the economic implications of the distribution of wealth and income.

I conclude that it is primarily the lack of organized data and the unfinished task of applying existing tools of economic analysis to available data, rather than the inadequacy of existing tools, that frustrate our capacities to determine the distributional impact of the tax system and incremental changes in it. Without such information it is not possible to formulate fully informed opinions on whether these distributional impacts are desirable as a matter of over-all tax policy, taking into account economic and equity considerations.

Level of Taxation

Nearly everyone is concerned about the high level of taxation. For years history has been recording the widespread belief that, for a variety of reasons, our country is rapidly approaching the limits of its taxable capacity. Some fear deflationary incentive effects. Some fear inflation. Others fear that mounting taxes to finance growing public expenditures must eventuate in a loss of their cherished economic and political freedoms.

Never more than now, when we are being seriously challenged by powerful enemies and the requirements for defense are so enormous, is it more important to know whether our economy is in such peril that instead of a further increase in taxation it is wiser to expose our military forces and millions of our civilians and their property to the risks of destruction. Here are tax policy issues of major magnitude.

The level of taxation is intimately tied to the level of public expenditures. While it is true that a given tax system will be able to finance growing expenditures as the economy grows, or alternatively, that taxes can be reduced as the economy grows if public expenditures are contained, the basic explanation for the high level of taxation is the high level of public expenditures. Increases or decreases in public expenditures are most likely to bring corresponding changes in the level of taxation. Old-fashioned proponents of fiscal soundness and enthusiastic supporters of functional finance can agree on this, for different reasons. The economist cannot give relevant advice on the desirable level of taxation in a vacuum. He must consider the level of public expenditures. What then has he to offer on expenditure policy?

He can properly point to the total available resources, to the resources engaged in the private sector and to the residual available for the public sector. He can properly warn about the inflationary consequences of efforts to engage over 100 per cent, and even close to 100 per cent, of the available resources. If an emergency, such as war, requires the rapid expansion of the public sector, he is tempted to recommend sufficiently high taxation to curb expenditures in the private sector, so that the additional resources required in the public sector will be released without inflation. He knows full well that inflation is the worst form of tax, yet he does not yield to temptation because in common with the untutored he fears the consequences of his logic. He fears the impact of high taxation on output and, if he is honest, he knows that he has no superior insights into the behavior of the business community and the consumers under the posited extraordinary conditions.

But to return to the present situation. We have experienced a long period of extraordinary conditions. The economist is still no more qualified than formerly to speak out with authority on the optimum level of defense expenditures. If he testifies before the Congress that defense expenditures are too low, and that for this reason taxes should not be reduced, or even that they should be raised, he is testifying as an uninformed citizen, not as an expert economist. For security reasons alone, he cannot be much better informed than, if as well-informed as, a journalist. He is unlikely to have out-distanced the CIA in piercing the security armor of our enemies. We do not know what a large number of able economists operating behind the security curtain in CIA and the other agencies of the government know about the requirements for defense, but it is a safe guess that they play a minor role in the process of establishing over-all expenditure goals, and this indirectly by suggesting more economical ways of adjusting means to ends. Economists, in common with others, know that defense expenditures are an important factor in determining the level of taxation, but none of us can know whether and to what extent faulty concepts of taxable capacity are unduly retarding the build-up of our defenses.

Even without the security curtain, the economist would play a secondary role in establishing desirable levels of defense expenditures, as he does in establishing the over-all level and the priorities of nondefense expenditures. When all levels of government are combined, nondefense expenditures are much higher than defense expenditures. The real or imagined economic consequences of alternative programs influence basic political decisions on the level and structure of government. While the political mechanism can never function ideally, except perhaps in Utopia, every democracy has little choice except to proceed on the assumption that it does. Hence, if taxes are high on account of nondefense expenditures, we must assume that people want the public goods and services more than the additional private goods and services that they could have produced with the same resources. In this sense, taxes can be too high only if the people, by some mysterious standard, make wrong choices. This is, of course, possible, but who has the wisdom to establish a superior standard? I know of nothing in economics that provides this capability.

The economists have given mankind the utility rule as a vague conceptual guide to the determination of the optimum level of public expenditures and taxation. If we knew how to live by this rule, we would attain simultaneously the allocation of resources between the public and private sectors of the economy and the best uses of resources in each sector and the optimum distribution of the tax burden. The price mechanism in the private sector and the voting mechanism in the public sector are the instruments that allegedly guide us to the attainment of the optimum level of public expenditures and taxation. Since neither of these mechanisms functions perfectly, there develops ample room for debate whether the actual level of public expenditures and taxation is optimal. For example, a divergence of marginal social benefits from marginal private benefits, or of marginal social costs from marginal private costs, might justify government intervention in the private sector or the outright taking over of a function in order to increase or decrease the output by comparison with the unfettered operation of the pricing system. Also, monopolies operating in restraint of trade may require government intervention to make the pricing system function more effectively. It is sometimes difficult to determine when government is encroaching upon the spheres of influence that properly belong to the private sector according to the required observance of the utility rule and when it is merely making the rule function more effectively. The regulatory functions of government do not account for a very significant part of total governmental expenditures. It may be, however, that they account for a very significant part of the disagreement with respect to the proper role of government and for the widespread belief that governmental expenditures, and the taxes required to finance them, have mushroomed to unsustainable levels.

Economic tools of analysis cannot prove that government expenditures and taxes are too high. Neither can they establish that they are too low. Yet the economist is tempted or flattered into the untenable position of giving expert testimony now on one side and then on the other side of what is essentially a political issue. It is not sufficient to show that public expenditures, exclusive of national security, are a lower percentage of national income than in some previous period. The change may represent a change in the evaluation of the optimum production mix. At all times, there are many shortages of government facilities. It would be nice to have more and better highways, schools, hospitals, parks, police, purer water and air, and so forth—simultaneously and without higher taxation or inflation. But if these consequences are to be avoided, priorities must be established and the program spread over time. In a sense these shortages are bottlenecks in the path of progress. Any one of us, as citizen rather than as economist, might prefer to expand any of these public facilities instead of dedicating more resources to a further stretch in the length or power of automobiles. But such individual decisions are not a firm basis either for expanding or contracting the level of governmental expenditures. In a democracy these levels are determined essentially by political rather than by economic processes.

But to repeat, the economist's secondary role in establishing desirable levels and priorities of public expenditures is not unimportant. Unlike Univac, he can initiate investigations that offer relevant alternatives to the policy maker and the public. He is *the* expert in analyzing economic consequences of alternative programs. The results of such analyses may provide critically important data for the guidance of the policy maker. Targets that are primarily and initially set without economic guidance may well be reset as the result of the economist's findings. He can point the way to the most efficient routes for the attainment of targets in the public sector as well as in the private sector. The pursuit of economically efficient methods may make possible the release of resources that otherwise would have been engaged, so that projects previously excluded may become feasible.

Effect on Incentives

Some fear a high level of taxation, not because they fear that a high level of public expenditures threatens to dwarf the private sector and to destroy the foundations of economic and political freedom, but because of its impact on economic incentives. They feel that the incentives to work, to save and to invest are adversely affected by high levels of taxation, despite the stimulating effects of high levels of public expenditures. The result is that the rate of growth of the economy is reduced, and, as confidence of businessmen and consumers is weakened, deflationary forces are strengthened. They give tax reduction a high priority.

It is true that the virility of the economy depends in an important way on favorable economic incentives and business confidence. The relevant question is what does the economist know about their operation and their effects on the limits of taxable capacity? In income analysis he can do a respectable job so long as he abstracts from these psychological factors, but the analysis ceases to become respectable when every con-clusion can be reversed by positing an inhospitable climate of confidence and pattern of incentive effects. This makes possible, for example, the view that budgetary deficits result in contraction, not expansion, because the loss in business confidence results in a contraction of private spending that overwhelms the expansionary impact of additional public expenditures, tax cuts, bank borrowing, or any combination of such meddling measures.

If we assume that workers reduce effort or withdraw from the labor force when taxes are raised, output must fall. But if we admit that some workers, particularly low-income work-ers, and many at higher levels, will strive to maintain for themselves and their heirs a given standard of living and wealth status, output may or may not be prejudicially affected, except at extremely high rates. What do workers do at various levels of income and taxation? We do not really know. We do not know how to find out. Some have hit upon the simple idea of asking them. But do they know, and if they know, are their replies conditioned by impure objectives or over-active imaginations which unawarely or consciously guide them away from the truth? It is not a method to be condoned, nor is it one to be condemned because we have no superior alternatives. The external evidence on work incentives is not alarming. Absenteeism is not prevalent, even where the work-ers or professionals are not organizationally tied to a schedule. But external evidence is not good enough. How have high taxes affected the occupational distribution of the labor force? We don't know, and it may prove to be extremely difficult, if not impossible, to find out.

High taxes affect both the ability and the willingness to save. Corporate savings are tied closely to profits, which are highly responsive to changes in business conditions. Com-mitted and institutionalized personal savings tend to be rela-tively unresponsive to temporary and moderate changes in economic conditions and circumstances, including changes in taxation. Another segment of personal savings is fairly automatic, being tied to relatively high incomes. A substantial segment of personal savings responds to forces that we do not fully understand, just as we do not adequately understand the behavior of the consumption function. Some pretend to be able to control both simultaneously with minimal changes in the interest rate. But the precise relationship between the interest rate and the volume of savings, at least in the short run, is even a little more mysterious than its relation to the volume of investment. It takes a long lag to correlate interest rate movements with expected volume of investment. Empirical exploration of theoretical expectations has sometimes been so startling that pending more empirical verifications one can be excused for refusing to believe the facts! The external evidence seems to be that high taxes have not discouraged a satisfactory level of investment in the postwar period.

In a qualitative way, it should be recognized that business and consumer confidence and economic incentives to work, to save, and to invest are highly important, even critically important, in some economic situations, but the quantitative force of these factors, singly or in combination, is extremely difficult to establish. If primary weight is given to such psychological forces, we can discard much of our economic equipment as an aid to the formulation of tax policy.

There is a certain asymmetry in the handling of psychological factors by those who stress them most. Of course it is recognized that low taxes have potentialities to influence incentives and business confidence favorably, and that they can contribute to inflation through overly activated expectations, but on the whole there is relatively little concern about an overdose of confidence and unduly favorable incentives. For the most part, confidence and incentives are big guns in the arsenal of weapons leveled against big government.

Those who fear the effects of high taxation on economic incentives tend to ignore almost completely the expansionary force of the high public expenditures with which the high level of taxation is so intimately linked. Their analysis proceeds largely by assertion, but it should not for that reason be underestimated by comparison with the more complicated income analysis which proceeds over long stretches by assumption.

In a sense those who are preoccupied with economic incentives and business confidence are pessimists, cousins of the stagnationists, who lack confidence in the virility of the free enterprise system. But I hasten to recognize a difference. The stagnationists stand for more and more vigorous government.

The Control of Inflation

Some fear high taxes—the price of higher governmental expenditures—because they fear inflation rather than either deflation or retardation of economic development through the collapse of confidence and economic incentives. According to a popular economic story, whenever in any country taxes reach the level of 25 per cent of national income, businessmen, long subdued by politically potent and oppressive rentiers who held the line on inflation to preserve their economic status and the stability of the economy, arise and overwhelm them, for it profits them to reap the high profits associated with inflation even if they relax their resistance to wage demands and share their gains with the workers. Sometimes, and with greater frequency now, the leading role in this economic drama is assigned to labor. The workers are alleged to recoup higher taxes in higher wages. In such cases, they are supposed to be peculiarly allergic to some varieties of taxes, which by custom or for more profound reasons enter the cost of living index. A peculiarity of this allergy is that the mere exclusion of a tax from the cost of living index is supposed to throw the workers into such convulsions of joy that they are prone to forget and forgive the whole burdensome matter. They no longer try to recoup higher taxes through wage demands.

As an economist, I cannot vouch for the completeness or accuracy of such stories. In fact, I don't believe them at all. But they have gotten into the bloodstream of professional and lay thinking about taxes as anti-inflationary instruments, and they may have an important impact on tax policy.

The implications of these stories are that any further increase in the level of public expenditures and taxation is impossible without inflation; and that payroll taxes, low-bracket-rate income taxes, and sales and excise taxes are as likely to be inflationary as deflationary. Such flimsy findings result not from any inadequacy in the existing tools of economic analysis. The great majority of economists find the truth with these tools—that taxes, all types of taxes, irrespective of shifting and incidence but some more than others always tend to restrain inflation. Their anti-inflationary effectiveness is weaker when the forces of expansion are strong, but it is always significant. The truth is disagreeable, however, so it is extremely difficult to convince those responsible for tax policy, and ultimately the general public, especially when the validity of analyses pointing to the need for higher taxes to fight inflation is called into question by economists, some of whom have built national reputations competing with the fiction writers.

Economists suffer from another handicap when it comes to prescribing tax policy in the context of inflation. They bow briefly to the economic requirements, be it to increase taxes or to hold the line against pressures to reduce them, murmur something to the effect that for political reasons the tax requirements for economic stability may as well be forgotten, then proceed quickly to alternatives—usually inferior alternatives. Why is this practice so universal? There are several reasons—none cogent. Some believe that future Americans may have the political fortitude to apply economically desirable tax policies, but not the present generation. What do we know about future generations of Americans that we don't know about the present generation and which would give us the confidence in the future but not the present? Without experimentation on desirable tax policy future generations will be as ignorant as the present.

Some prefer to cut expenditures, because in their view every such cut is a social gain, a correction in the bias that springs from the voting mechanism, a bias that springs from the eternal hope that somebody else can be made to pay for the social benefits. Some dwell on the viscosity of the legislative process, especially in the matter of raising taxes. I submit that much of the time spent in the tax legislative process is unnecessary. If the economists as experts spoke audibly and with greater unanimity, as they could if they were willing to give up the game of politics and quit angling for favors by persistently flashing their economic statesmanship, their influence on tax legislation would be enhanced enormously. Some, for example, rule out tax policy as an effective weapon against inflation because they feel that this would bind them to a flexible tax policy—taxes would not only be held or increased in prosperity but also be reduced in recession. There is fear that such a flexible policy would result in secular inflation because politically it is easier to reduce taxes than to raise them. The same political objection can be made against every stabilizing instrument—monetary policy, expenditure policy, debt management, and so forth. If any flexible policy is to work, it must be practiced. There is no reason to believe that, if practiced, flexible tax policy would be any less efficacious, because less reversible, than any alternative stabilization instrument.

The case for experimentation with tax policy as an instrument for the control of inflation is strong. Flexible tax policy would take some of the stabilization burden from monetary policy, and it would be a safeguard against the institution of direct controls in peacetime. Perhaps exhortation is inevitable, so let us adjudge it as fine as far as it goes, but it is no substitute either for direct controls or for vigorous flexible monetary and fiscal policies. It may be that experimentation with flexible tax policy in the context of inflationary situations as well as deflationary ones would yield the answer that economists have been groping for as they struggle with the behavior problems of the bad boys—the propensity of labor to push beyond efficiency wages and that of management in its overly acquisitive pricing practices.

Budgetary Policy

This brings me to a discussion of taxation and budgetary policy. Some would readily grant part of the point just made on flexible tax policy. But they would argue that none of the flexible stabilization instruments can be made effective because of human frailties and the backward state of our knowledge of the economic process with its baffling lags and leads, and perhaps also because of the variety of shapes of functional relationships between significant variables which enfeeble our powers of prediction. Humbly, they seek a framework of economic institutions and organization that would eliminate most if not all discretionary fiscal policy.

Nearly everyone is for a balanced budget, but few are agreed on which budget is to be balanced and over what period. The framework approach is as definite on budget balancing as discretionary fiscal policy is vague. Each proceeds on certain assumptions which lead to different tax policy conclusions.

The discipline point plays an important role in the framework approach that seeks to balance the consolidated cash budget. Expenditures must be matched by tax revenues at a given high level of national income. Every incremental program is likewise to be matched by taxes. Extremists would actually earmark the taxes, program by program—so impressed are they with the need to convey to the public that benefits cannot be provided free. Only in this way can the bias for ever-rising public expenditures be corrected. This throws the utility rule and budget comprehensiveness out the window but, for those who weight this simple form of the discipline rule heavily, it is worth it. Under the framework approach the tax system remains fixed irrespective of economic conditions. The level of taxes is determined simultaneously with the level of expenditures, and the structure is determined in terms of other goals—the concept of an equitable distribution of wealth and income, the rate of economic growth, the level of the current standard of living, the need for regulation and controls, and so forth. The level of aggregate demand is controlled by the monetary instrument and the automatic stabilizers built into both sides of the budget. With a bit of surgery that would eliminate fractional reserves and introduce 100 per cent money, both monetary and fiscal policies would function automatically in the direction of stabilization, increasing liquidity in recession and reducing it in expansion.

As economists, we are agreed on the qualitative point, but we know too little about the quantitative responses of spending to changes in liquidity to warrant much confidence in the adequacy of the framework approach to stabilization, whether it be the crude or the refined models. Few, if any, would deny the importance of automatic stabilizers, or fail to be enthusiastic about further structural changes that would strengthen them. However, there is danger in relying excessively on automatic stabilizers. The Employment Act calls for appropriate discretionary action. If a belief were allowed to develop that the Employment Act would be ignored except in extreme emergencies, this would destroy much of the effectiveness of the built-in stabilizers.

Discretionary fiscal and monetary policy is now espoused by both political parties. There may be a little more harmony in principle than in practice. Even if the framework were set to please the opponents of discretionary policy, there would be no escape from flexibility, once the economy became destabilized. Neither Congress nor the Treasury nor the Federal Reserve Board would, could, or should keep hands off if the automatic pilot failed to do a reasonably good job. I fail to see that the discipline point is necessarily lost under discretionary fiscal policy. If the public were to be informed on the rate of public expenditures that is consistent with stabilization, and if it knew that higher taxes would be used along with other stabilization measures to contain inflation, it would be effectively disciplined. It would be unlikely to urge pressing too many public programs into excessively short periods. The reason that there is no discipline in flexible tax policy is that neither economists nor politicians follow through systematically.

A plausible case can be made against flexible tax policy on different grounds—that it would unduly disturb expectations. But on closer examination this is not much of a case. If flexible tax policy is not used, other policies must be varied in response to changing economic conditions or stabilization is lost. If it is inflation, that is as disturbing to expectations as other forms of taxation. If inflation is arrested by tighter monetary policy or shifts in expenditure policy, these, too, disturb expectations. The choice of instrument should depend upon past economic trends and current conditions rather than prejudices with respect to unverified economic repercussions of alternative stabilization instruments.

If economic conditions are made the primary focus of

appropriate budgetary policy, the period over which any concept of the budget is to be balanced becomes necessarily indeterminate. The concept of the budget also affects the level of taxation. Some, for example, have been urging a debt financed capital budget. Clearly the level of taxation will be much lower if only current expenditures are to be covered over some specified period instead of both current and capital expenditures. To achieve something approaching the same stabilization impact as tax financed projects, such borrowing should be outside the banking system. Temptation to invade the banks to facilitate debt financing must be resisted if secular inflation is to be avoided. Only characteristically stagnant economies can indulge in carelessness in the management of a capital budget and still escape inflation. The stabilization burden on monetary policy and debt management would be increased by the adoption of a capital budget.

Some highly industrialized countries have adopted the capital budget without weakening their finances. It merely calls for a different combination of stabilization measures. If they have the sophistication to look to the economic situation instead of some particular subtotal in the budget, there is no reason why the capital budget should prejudice stabilization.

Governments of underdeveloped countries find it increasingly difficult to discipline their financial operations. They frequently employ a capital budget hoping that this might help them control their deficits but the device has not been of much help. These governments embark upon a broad program of capital formation, which includes projects that permanently belong to the public sector as well as projects that are undertaken temporarily in the absence of an economically virile private sector. When tax administration of inequitable tax systems is weak, inflation may not be a much less equitable form of raising money than other taxes. It has the virtue of certainty. In the absence of the voluntary accumulation of savings, or an abundant supply of capital from abroad, the strong-arm methods of inflation are extremely tempting. It requires more than bookkeeping devices to assure adherence to sound fiscal policies.

Tax Structure

So far, I have been concerned for the most part with issues that relate to the level of taxation. I now wish to discuss a few tax policy issues with respect to the structure of the tax system and its administration. There can be substantial relief from high tax rates without imposing unduly severe restrictions on the level of public expenditures. It requires only a satisfactory rate of economic growth and stability, a further broadening of the tax base through the revision of the tax system to eliminate socially undesirable and uneconomic discriminations, and tighter tax administration.

The desirable structure of a tax system is tied to society's economic goals. It can be weighted in favor of savings and investment or alternatively in favor of consumption. If the policy is to speed economic development, the economist can suggest tax revisions and monetary and other economic policy adjustments towards that end. If the policy is to raise the current standard of living, that is, let the future take care of itself, this too can be accommodated by different sets of economic policy adjustments. So with other goals or combinations of goals. These adjustments are particularly, perhaps I should say deceptively, easy to accomplish if the classical full employment model is assumed, if we are permitted to abstract from time, and to make a few simple assumptions about the nature of economic responses to different policies. For example, starting from the full employment level, economic growth can be promoted by reducing or eliminating the federal corporation income tax (assuming that it is not shifted) and by reducing the higher individual income tax rates, but if stability is to be preserved, taxes weighted against consumption must be raised or credit tightened or one of several possible combinations of tax and monetary policy employed. The first alternative—higher consumption taxes—only indirectly affects the rate of economic growth. It should be recognized, however, that the indirect effects of high consumption taxes on investment, and so on growth, can be important. The second alternative—tighter credit—is directly prejudicial to economic development. The net impact on capital formation may turn out to be negative under either alternative policy. Even if the first alternative is adopted, by upsetting the balance which had gradually evolved, it could destabilize the economy unless it were combined with easier rather than tighter monetary policy. A less severe upward adjustment in consumption taxes could, of course, be combined with less tightening of credit than would be needed for stability if it were the exclusive compensatory adjustment to tax cuts primarily affecting savings and investment.

All such adjustments have economic side effects and are extremely difficult to evaluate in advance of experimentation. That is why it is wise to think of revisions in the structure of the tax system in terms of a series of incremental adjustments rather than in terms of major surgery. Uncertainty with respect to the incidence of the corporation income tax, for example, would seem to indicate a policy of moderation and gradualness in its de-emphasis. To the extent it is shifted, substitution of consumption taxes would represent little or no gain in fundamentally changing the structure of the tax system. To some extent, that part of the corporation net income tax which is not shifted forward might have been capitalized, so that windfalls would result from a reduction in the rate. This may not be an undesirable result as regards its impact on capital formation, but it clearly offends against the equity goal. Also, I should note perhaps that there are some methods of reducing the corporation net income tax which, considering the state of our knowledge about its incidence, are preferable to others. To the extent that the corporation net income tax is shifted to consumers, there is no double taxation of stockholders. A dividend paid credit would result in lowering the corporation net income tax, and it has the merit that it would not relieve the stockholder from a burden which he may not have borne.

The higher individual income tax rates are too high. They are uneconomic to the extent that they distort the pattern of occupations and incentives to work, to save, and to invest. They were not planned to be permanent rates, but instead grew as an integral part of the war controls. These rates can be reduced without much revenue loss. For political reasons, this issue probably requires a bipartisan approach for its solution.

The heavy emphasis given to the income tax (corporate and individual) in the federal tax system has made it a target for de-emphasis in speculations about a desirable structural revision of the tax system. Pressures for revenue have repeatedly postponed the operation. More fundamentally, we really do not know whether the economic growth of America can be promoted by a substantial substitution of consumption taxes for the income taxes. Currently there is little discussion of such substitution because payroll taxes are relatively heavy and are scheduled to rise, and the individual income tax, with the aid of inflation, which has effectively lowered exemptions, now reaches down to low income levels. The recent suggestions for a general federal sales tax were to substitute it for the system of federal selective excise taxes. By itself, this would have relatively little economic repercussion. I doubt that anyone could show convincingly that the growth and stability of the economy would be materially affected by such a change. I also doubt whether much could be made of this issue in terms of other goals. If the sales tax were at the retail level, it would be a uniform percentage of consumer expenditures. If it were at the manufacturer's level, considering variations in mark-ups in the process of distribution, it is not at all clear that the desired result, for what it is worth, would be attained. The degree of distortion in the allocation of economic resources occasioned by the existing system of federal excise taxes, outside the hard core of liquor, tobacco, and automotive taxes, not involved in the suggestions, is nothing to get excited about, and I am far from certain that anybody really is. The merit of a uniform rate general sales tax is that it can be made to respond readily to revenue requirements and to required stabilization impacts on the economy. At the same time, this is its political weakness. Those who seem to oppose the low-rate federal manufacturer's sales tax that would be required to replace the fringe excise tax system outside the hard core of federal excises are really opposing the potentially much higher rate that they fear may be levied in the future, and this time in partial replacement of income tax. The objection to such substitution rests on economic as well as equity considerations—the fear that America will be able to produce more than it could consume.

I have already indicated that tax changes should be in the arsenal of stabilization weapons. We do not need a general federal sales tax to utilize tax policy effectively for stabilization purposes. We have in the payroll taxes and the first bracket of the individual income tax the type of broad based taxes that can be moved speedily and with economic effectiveness in response to either inflationary or deflationary developments in the economy. The idea that this should be done is not new, and recently it has been receiving some attention. It merits full exploration by the appropriate congressional committees and favorable legislative action.

The major type of revision in the structure of the federal tax system that is urgently required in the interests of growth and stability is not so much a substitution of one kind of tax for all or a part of another, but a substantial broadening of the individual income tax and the estate and gift taxes with a view to achieving a sharp reduction in the marginal individual income tax rates. Uneconomic tax concessions should also be eliminated under these taxes, as well as under the corporation income tax, for a variety of taxpayer groups. For example, under the income tax we should re-examine the economic case for the retention of each of the nonbusiness deductions, the special treatment of capital gains and losses, percentage depletion, the treatment of deferred compensation including the fringe benefits under private pension plans, the liberal treatment of expense accounts and advertising expenses. Under the gift and estate taxes, the bases could be substantially broadened by a drastic downward revision in the exclusions and exemptions, including a tightening up on the treatment of life insurance, powers of appointment, and life estates. The entire estate and gift tax system is badly in need of reconstruction.

Tools of economic analysis are available to accomplish the suggested reconstruction of progressive taxes in the federal system, the better to serve the objectives of growth and stability. The task involves assembling the relevant data and subjecting them to relatively simple analyses to facilitate a revaluation of those provisions that have punched enormous holes in these tax bases. Some desirable structural changes in these taxes would result in revenue losses, for example, if it were found desirable to institute an income-averaging system or to permit a once-for-all write-off of depreciable property at discounted rates that took into account the variations in risk and the length of life of the assets. Both of these suggestions would require careful exploration to permit an adequate weighing of their implications for the closely interrelated objectives of economic stability and growth.

Finally, a full-scale exploration of administrative efficiency with respect to major taxes at each level of government could yield improvements and additional revenues that again would permit a reduction in the rates. Periodic review of administrative procedures would undoubtedly strengthen tax compliance and tax morale, just as surely as would shutting the door on tax avoidance devices by appropriate legislative action. There has been too long a period of wheel spinning both in tax legislation and tax administration, due primarily to an unduly partisan approach to tax policy.

I am hopeful that the American tax system will soon be reviewed in its entirety in the same spirit as the monetary system is now being studied. Then it may be possible to bear with greater ease and less prejudice to the future, the enormous tax burdens that have been forced upon us by a divided and unhappy world.

5

Monetary and Credit Policy

ROBERT V. ROOSA[1]

HOW SATISFIED SHOULD ONE BE with the tools of economic analysis upon which monetary and credit policy depend? My part in this series is to look at this problem from the doorstep of the central bank. But to find a meaningful answer to this or any other question about economic life, it is not enough to take an inventory of the tools. The starting point has to be with the first principles of our kind of economic society, taken as a whole, in order to have some standards for judgment. This means that my paper must begin quite some distance away from the detailed reality of my own field.

It may be useful for us as professional economists to focus for a moment on some implications of a very humbling thought: the dominant theme of any historians among our descendants, in describing the twentieth century, will probably be that of *economic* rivalry among great powers, representing conflicting *economic* ideologies, and competing for the allegiance of other nations obsessed with a drive for *economic* development. I suppose the sponsors of these lectures are really asking whether economic analysis—disciplined, systematic thought about economic processes and problems—

---

[1] Vice President, Federal Reserve Bank of New York.

has grown up to the needs of a civilization that has become so consciously dependent upon economic forces. And more specifically, they are asking me for some observations on how well we as economists have assessed the essential conditions for economic progress in our own, as contrasted with a regimented, society; whether we can be satisfied with the place now occupied by monetary and credit control in the structure of public policy appropriate to a market economy; and how effectively we have developed the economics of monetary and credit policy, as to diagnosis, methods, and results. The heroic proportions of these questions would, if my own limitations had not already done so, make it essential to state clearly at the start that my approach must be selective, not comprehensive, and inquisitive rather than definitive.

Fundamentals of a Market Economy

At the risk of gross oversimplification, I ought to begin by listing some of the more important conditions for economic progress that we can probably all endorse.

A System of Checks and Balances

The essence of a market economy, it seems to me, is reliance upon a wide variety of checks and balances to assure the greatest possible freedom for each of us to choose among meaningful alternatives, in our capacities as work-seekers, spenders, savers, investors, and producers. Thus competition and rivalry, as contrasted with monopoly, have become the typical form of economic activity (even though at any one given time, for a given purpose, with given technology, a monolithic single operation might appear to avoid duplication and minimize waste and costs). Resources are allocated among alternative uses as the result of a continuous expression of a consensus among individual preferences, through the facilities of markets, usually reflected in market prices. There is no independent source of final and absolute authority. Every process, every group, is in some degree acting as a check upon other processes, or other groups.

The role of the state is not dominant, but only a part of the system of checks and balances, and even within the state, other checks and balances curb the emergence of one person or group as all-controlling. While setting boundaries in a constitutional sense on the scope of individual initiative, the state cannot exercise unrestrained domination because it cannot command labor (except in national emergency) nor directly manage the large sector of resources that is privately owned. In some degree, if only by providing civil order and a law of contracts, the state has always been engaged in assisting the effective working of markets. But gradually the state's role in assuring the general welfare has been expanding, with the result that a public, governmental interest is now generally recognized not only in creating the legal framework and common facilities required for the functioning of the market economy, but also in assuring that a reasonable minimum of economic security is available to all, in promoting growth, and in minimizing economic cycles.

Even so, with all of the detailed intrusion that has ensued, the propelling force of economic vitality and expansion still comes from individual initiative, imagination, inventiveness, enterprise, and managerial skill, functioning within an essentially competitive market economy. The dynamics of our system must rest basically upon freedom and spontaneity. For all the shadings of view among us, the fundamental assumption of democratic economics is that under these conditions the instinctive desire of human beings to improve their lot will generate, year by year, a larger, more diversified, and more thoroughly satisfying national product than could be conceived, produced, or distributed in any other way.

The Place of Planning

By contrast, any attempt by the state to pursue a comprehensive national plan must necessarily stifle the conditions that are essential for optimum progress. There is room, to be sure, for projections or forecasts of the kinds of prospects for various sectors that seem consistent with each other, and with recent developments. There is a place, too, for setting goals, though in broad, general, and flexible terms. The state can make good use of such broad sketches—at times by focusing attention on obvious gaps that have not yet become visible on the narrower horizons of individual firms; at other times by detecting at an early stage some major imbalance that is emerging among interdependent sectors of the economy, before it has gone too far. And whenever there are clear and serious gaps, or if movements in major sectors appear to be getting out of balance with each other—in a manner seriously disturbing to over-all stability, or detrimental to general growth—the state is now expected to exert an offsetting influence at the margins. But there is not, and cannot in the nature of a reasonably well-developed market economy, be any attempt in ordinary times to fix quotas in advance for the output of each sector and the flow of product among sectors.

Any state attempt to guarantee a predetermined total of sales for any producer or industry, for example, or to guarantee permanence of employment to any particular individual or group, removes the uncertainty which is essential for the spontaneity and flexibility that enable a market economy to produce so much, so efficiently. Nor would the state, except in quite unusual circumstances, presume the competence even to determine in advance the appropriate division of national product between such broad categories as consumption and investment, or spending and saving. At any given time there may be good reason to guide the state's influence toward inducing somewhat more consumption, say, rather than investment, or perhaps toward inducing more saving and less spending, just to cite crude examples. But the judgments involved are usually those of the "little more" or the "little less," and they are made in terms of direction and degree of emphasis, in the light of all that is already going on, not in terms of any settled blueprint for the whole.

This is not to deny that an economy can function under the rigidity of detailed planning, but the price in loss of freedom, and ultimately in loss of economic potential, is higher than those who know a free economy would be willing to pay. It is challenging to speculate on how much greater the capacity and output of the Soviet Union might now be if the potentialities of individual initiative had been released to develop the vast resources with which that country is endowed.

The Need for a New General Theory

When put as vaguely as I have just done here, these primary conditions for economic progress in a market economy would, I should hope, find concurrence among virtually all Western economists. But to anyone contrasting these premises with the elegant formulations underlying most of the physical sciences, this is discouragingly thin. Perhaps that is inevitable in economics. In any case, as matters now stand, so much has been happening within each of the separate specialties of our profession over the past generation or two that it has been impossible for any synthesizer to succeed in evolving a new and intuitively satisfying General Theory: to bind together the principles I have mentioned and the essentials of all of the separate parts of modern economics, as they have now developed, into a coherent and unified body of modern doctrine. One promising path toward such an eventual synthesis, that of model building, has regrettably deteriorated into an escape route. Many who started out in that way to study the interrelations among all the parts of a modern economy have instead taken refuge under layers and layers of assumptions that separate them from the reality of a dynamic process. Another kind of effort, of which Professor Galbraith's *Affluent Society* provides a delightful recent example, exposes the foibles and paradoxes among many of the patterns of economic behavior that "our science" and the American public have now produced, but then takes another kind of escape: into a set of assumptions about "what ought to be" sufficiently set apart from "what can be" to make the author's position quite safe—stimulating in the extreme, but hardly usable. Even more regrettably, most of the rest of us do not venture far outside the shells of our own specialties, and when we do, are scarcely distinguishable from laymen.

What this means is that our generation of economists now has no comprehensive, unifying theory—clearly stated and widely accepted—that extends through the performance of individual spenders, savers, and producers to the aggregative behavior of the national economy, domestically and externally. The consequence, it seems to me, is that each of us, in his own area of economics, is dealing with conditions of partial equilibrium that have not been fully rationalized with the events or the theory emerging in other fields. Without a more fully articulated general theory, to expose the inconsistencies among the varied aims and methods of different specializations and, to indicate the path of resolution, a sober modesty befits us all. That is the spirit in which I shall venture a few comments on the economics of monetary and credit policy in a market economy.

The Place of Monetary and Credit Control

Any growing, diversified economy needs a flexible money supply. To provide it, each economy, whether guided by a plan or by the action of markets, must have some kind of accepted apparatus for monetizing credit. Characteristically the market economies have met that need by evolving a fractional reserve, deposit banking system, in which each marginal change in the money supply is inseparably connected with a marginal change in the actual extension of credit. Such an apparatus for money creation thus makes possible a flexible variation in the total of credit availability, because the changeable margin added by created bank credit is superimposed on whatever underlying total of credit has been provided by past savings. This flexible variation at the margin can, in turn, be responsive to the shifting credit needs of a dynamic economy and be reasonably well apportioned among the thousands upon thousands of different centers of initiative within the economy, because the banks that monetize credit are in competition with each other.

It is the automatic linkage between money creation and credit creation, and the desirability of assuring productive use of the new credit which appears as a joint product whenever money is created, that makes fractional reserve banking such a crucial part of the mechanism of a market economy. Yet the mere existence of facilities for furnishing this flexibility embodies a latent potentiality for abuse. This power to create credit, and to decide where it will go, must in a market economy be divided among many competing banks, no one of which can be guided by over-all views of what the changes in the grand total ought to be. More credit might, thus, be created than a nation's physical resources can support, and more money might be created than orderly procedures in making payments and holding cash balances would require at current levels of prices. For any other kind of commodity or service, competition might be relied upon to bring over-all production eventually into line with demand, even though no single firm could know or judge what the total ought to be. But not money, the common denominator for everything else; there is no longer any need to demonstrate that "money will not manage itself." The inherent risk of creating too much, or too little, makes essential some kind of general control by a public body in the public interest. And the inseparable link between bank-created credit and bank-created money is the explanation for the inseparability of monetary policy and credit policy, though, of course, each side of this single shield does face out upon many different, and separable, kinds of problems.

Responsibilities of the Central Bank

The task of central banks in the market economies, even before getting around to limiting the aggregative changes in bank money and bank credit, is ordinarily to see to it that the banking system is in fact organized effectively. Is it able to provide a flexible financial counterpart for the spring and elasticity that dynamic physical production requires? Beyond that, though, it is the task of central banks and monetary authorities to see to it, if they can, that neither "unsound" conditions within the banks nor undue aggregative changes in total money and credit should themselves be the initiating cause of a financial crisis and cyclical downturn. However, once a cyclical swing is already under way, downward or upward, as a result of other forces in the economy, the central bank must also use its influence to avoid a disruptive cumulative impetus to that swing from the banking sector. And in addition, to the extent practicable, the central bank is expected to do what it can, through its influence upon incremental changes in money and credit, to offset other forces that may be causing or aggravating cyclical distortions. Moreover, it is the responsibility of the central bank, year in and year out, to encourage and stimulate growth. To help keep that growth steady, real, and continuous, the central bank must also make a determined effort to limit or avoid attrition in the value of the monetary unit.

This concept of explicit central bank responsibility in a

market economy has grown considerably in recent decades, and the tools of general analysis have developed along with it. At one earlier stage, provision of an automatic link that would assure flexible response to the *credit* demands of the *private* economy was regarded as the determining factor. Analytical tools at that time were developed mainly in terms of acceptable commercial paper and the automatic linkage of bank credit to the "needs of trade." The by-product of that approach during phases of expanding business was, of course, a circular validation of larger and larger quantities of money. Conversely, contraction in business might bring about an unwanted reduction of the money supply. Emphasis consequently then shifted to the other side of the shield, the supply of money. Starting with the statement of identity in the equation of exchange, the quantity theory of money emerged, conveying the implication that the central bank should focus its attention on bringing about changes in that quantity, without regard for the possible uses of the credit that is inevitably created for someone (if not in the private economy then for the state itself) whenever an addition to the money supply occurs.

That emphasis upon "M" alone also proved incomplete, and analysis moved forward along two lines: one taking the general form of income analysis, the other a more particularized analysis of velocity. The income analysis tended to relegate monetary and credit policy to a subordinate or servicing role, and to elevate fiscal policy to a dominant position. The study of velocity in turn fanned out along two broad paths: that of transactions velocity with its emphasis on the analysis of bank debits, and that of income velocity, with its emphasis on the causal interrelations between the total money supply and one concept or another of national product. Both of these paths have in recent years been tending to converge again, in the general form of the analysis of the demand for money. That, in turn, has been joined by renewed emphasis upon the analysis of liquidity, with liquidity viewed as a spectrum consisting of many different degrees of liquidity, represented by a sequence of substitutes among different kinds of money and debt instruments.

Relations Between Fiscal and Monetary Policy

Meanwhile, the preoccupation of many of the macroeconomists among us with fiscal policy passed through several stages, as we became more fully aware of the intricacies of revenue analysis, expenditures analysis, and debt management. Since World War II, there has been general disillusionment with the various arms of fiscal policy as panaceas. At present perhaps one could say that the special analytical tools of fiscal policy, at least on the revenue side, as well as those of debt management, are less well-developed than the analytical tools of monetary policy, which I shall soon briefly mention. At any rate, attempts to analyze the incidence and impact of tax changes, or the consequences of various steps in debt management, seem to me to be at least as imprecise and uncertain as anything we encounter in monetary and credit policy.

With somewhat fuller recognition now of the innumerable direct effects of fiscal activities upon incentives, as well as upon the flow of income, and with the scope of monetary and credit policy now broadened to include some concern with the liquidity of the economy as a whole, the functioning of both of these arms of governmental policy is now recognized as mutually reinforcing. They are not rival methods, nor is one a substitute for the other. Both have a significant place in a market economy, and their interrelations should be given a thorough re-examination. Happily, it is not for me to push deeper into fiscal policy, nor can I pretend to make more than a beginning in the zone of monetary and credit policy. But I do think there is much to be learned from the various stages of development just mentioned, particularly when combined with further study of the thinking and performance of the various central banks of the Western world.

Objectives of Central Bank Policy

My own opportunity for reasonably close observation of central banking, here and abroad, extends back only to the close of World War II. But my more experienced associates assure me that the distinction I want to make among the ultimate, the intermediate, and the operational objectives of monetary and credit policy has been valid for much longer than my own experience can confirm. With respect to their *ultimate* objectives—output, employment, income, and prices, as well as with respect to the even broader kinds of responsibilities that have already been mentioned—there is a high degree of uniformity among central banks. The tools of economic analysis for use in formulating or in appraising central bank policy aimed at these objectives may well be close to universal throughout the market economies. What I should call the *intermediate* objectives—the general financial conditions sought as a means of contributing toward fulfillment of the ultimate objectives—may differ in some important ways from country to country, but for the most part these too may be stated and appraised in terms of a common body of economic analysis. By contrast, the *operational* objectives—the specific guides for use with specific tools in day-by-day central banking operations—are necessarily determined by the particular market arrangements of each country. For these, there must correspondingly be similarly specialized tools of economic analysis, which have to be individually developed and continually improved for each country. Though a fascinating study, and certainly embraced

FUND FOR ADULT EDUCATION
LIBRARY

within the boundaries assigned to me in this series of lectures, I am not going to try to include these operational objectives in my discussion here.[2]

Ultimate Objectives

The central bank is generally regarded, in some sense, as the conscience or the guardian of a nation's financial responsibility, so that a unique position is found for it within each governmental structure. Perhaps that helps to explain why central bankers everywhere, almost without exception, feel that they have much in common and tend to see their ultimate objectives in the same terms. They must use what powers they have, within the framework of each country's financial markets, to keep the flow of money and credit adequate for the productive use and expansion of resources, capacity, and employment opportunities. They must also give full practicable assistance to the necessitous financing of government. But they must keep the total of money and credit generated for all of these purposes within limits. They may differ somewhat in the weights given to various criteria in setting the limits, but they all consider the same array of criteria; they all realize the necessity of demonstrating that they can and will actually set limits; and they all act through a process of successive approximation, setting limits by changing marginal increments, and not by meeting a target for the total (or its many parts) that has been set in advance by a national plan. They all know, too, that theirs is only a partial role within the whole of governmental economic policy, that they cannot expect to produce alone the results toward which they aim, but that unless they take aim on the basis of a full

[2] A colleague of mine has recently prepared a very useful summary of the similarities and differences among the operating techniques of the principal central banks of the world. See Peter G. Fousek, *Foreign Central Banking: The Instruments of Monetary Policy*, Federal Reserve Bank of New York (November 1957).

view of the ultimate objectives, any constructive force which they might exert will be scattered and wasted.

While the ultimate objectives include maximum growth with minimum fluctuation in real output and in real income, I am going to skip over these in order to concentrate on employment and prices. For it is through a closer look at the supposed conflict between optimum employment and reasonably stable prices that the key issues confronting any central bank, in deciding where to set the limits on money and credit, are most readily clarified.

The starting point must be to recognize that some unemployment is virtually inevitable in any growing economy—so long as successive innovation adds new products and new methods, so long as the users of products are free to change their preferences, and so long as there is neither direction of labor nor commandeering of plant and materials by some higher authority. Yet more often than not, a vigorous market economy will also have within it more individually worthy ventures reaching out for more credit and resources than could possibly be satisfied, in total, by its presently existing mix of immediately available facilities and labor skills. That is why, even though reliable statistical measures show that there is unemployment of men, or capacity, or materials, central banks may often find themselves, at the same time, unable to open wide the valves for releasing more money and credit. It would be too much to hope that each innovation, or each important shift in patterns of demand, would need just the manpower, or plant, or materials that may currently be available, or that the aggregate of all new ventures could physically be undertaken at once.

Surely one of the conditions for diversification, expansion, and the optimum fulfillment of consumer preference, is that there must continually be some shifting about of capital and labor. In a market economy that redistribution is accomplished through market processes. Thus any attempt to flush out more money and credit, in the hope of re-employing idle men or materials right where they are, may only prevent or impede the kinds of shifts upon which further growth depends. And simply to put funds at the disposal of every venture would lead to a run-up of prices and costs that would jeopardize the new ventures and generate speculative distortions for all. That is why no central bank can take responsibility for assuring *full* employment.

Yet because of some of these same considerations, there may also be times when a further release of money and credit could usefully help to expand employment and production even though average prices might have been rising— perhaps because of bottleneck situations or seasonal shortages in particular sectors. That is why no central bank is likely to assert that constant prices, or even price stability, will always be its overriding objective. To be sure, if a market economy worked without frictions, movements in employment and prices might never seem in conflict. Unemployment would consist only of people en route from one job to another, or en route into or out of the labor force. Individual prices would move up or down as guides to the flow of resources, but there would be no persistent pull or push upon the averages in an upward direction, and repeated rounds of innovation and quickened productivity might over time generate a gradually declining level of prices as a whole. But it is because these ideal conditions are never fulfilled that any policy, which is related to the performance of the economy as a whole, must instead work within a "band of compromise"—where there are no absolutes, and each objective is weighed against the others, in the existing circumstances, to find a balance of optimum utility for the kinds of influences that marginal changes in the availability of money and credit can exert.

Though the historical result may not be price stability, the essential condition, it seems to me, is that the central bank should be able to maintain genuine uncertainty, at any given time, as to the path of over-all price changes that may lie ahead. Let me illustrate by going to an extreme. Any effort through general measures to stimulate complete employment of men and resources, in an economy characterized by dynamic change and flexibility, inevitably creates strains that produce continued increases in prices. There must, if demand is to be kept large enough to assure the employment of everyone all the time, be sellers' markets everywhere, with a resulting deterioration of efficiency and loss of cost discipline. Confronted with the resulting evidence of steadily rising prices, the members of a market economy will certainly make use of their basic freedoms—the same freedoms which they must have to assure the dynamic flexibility of the system—in order to protect themselves against the implied erosion in the value of the monetary unit. They hoard materials, step up capital programs, and delay payments. Thus it is inescapable, given the essential conditions of a market economy, that inflation, once it has persisted long enough to become fixed in the expectations of individuals and business firms, accelerates. To break the circle, before it becomes vicious, public policy must, it seems to me, give paramountcy to creating uncertainty regarding the path that the general level of prices may follow. Without the "certainty of uncertainty," the freedom that is essential to a market economy will also lead to a fusion of mass expectations that, quite paradoxically, produces the kind of inflation that destroys the orderly procedures upon which the continuous performance of a market economy depends.

Thus it seems to me inherent in a market economy that price objectives must, over the sort of range of variation that has been observed in much of the postwar period, be given a leading place alongside employment objectives. That is why policy aims with respect to employment, as well as prices, must be viewed in terms of variability within a band, with the degree of relative emphasis between them continually reappraised. That is why no central bank should ever be expected to adhere to fixed guides, whether set in terms of a percentage of unemployment, or a percentage change in prices, or any comparable formulation intended to "take the judgment out of central banking" by relying upon mechanical symbols. In their very nature, these ultimate objectives of monetary and credit policy need the continuous resolution among alternatives that can only be provided by informed, responsible judgment. Perhaps that is one of the reasons why, despite the urgings of distinguished economists, for many years, no country has yet tried any of the devices that have been proposed for automatic regulation of the money supply.

Intermediate Objectives

When finding the best balance from month to month among their ultimate objectives, the monetary authorities rely upon all of the tools for analysis of current economic conditions that are well known to economists in most other fields. Since there are no unique strengths or shortcomings of these tools that only become visible inside the central bank, I will not linger over them here, but instead turn to the formulation of intermediate objectives—the translation of any decisions made with respect to ultimate objectives into meaningful general terms, applicable in the financial, and more particularly the banking, sector of the economy. Here, it seems to me, there is a notable gap in the published literature, although I think I see a unifying concept running through the actual performance of most of the central banks of the Western economies—a concept of "pressure." Within the special institutional arrangements of each country, central banks everywhere are using, or looking for, those techniques that will make it possible to alter the degree of pressure, either inducive or restrictive, being exerted upon the performance of the economy as a whole by changes in the quantity of money and in the credit creation related to it.

To help clarify that, let me review the structural fundamentals of fractional reserve banking. In bare outline, these consist of a block of resources upon which the commercial banks can erect a multiple volume of credit and money. The outer limits of this expansion are determined by a reserve ratio that has been set by custom, or law, or regulation in all of the developed Western countries. A number of commercial banks compete with each other to attract a share in the totals of bank credit and bank money that these arrangements allow. In their actual granting of credits, these competing banks reach out into different parts of the entire credit market in different countries, but in every country there is enough possible substitution between the credit supplied by banks and the credit supplied by the other sources of savings, to make the bank credit an integral influence upon the supply conditions of the credit market as a whole. Users of credit, at the same time, have sufficient flexibility in meeting some part of their needs either at the banks or from other sources to make it reasonably certain that a process of market allocation will occur. The banks have some choice among users of their credit; the users have some choice among sources. In the end, with differing degrees of imperfection at different times and in different countries, what happens to bank credit affects all credit.

At the base of this structure is the central bank, controlling the supply of reserves, and thereby determining whether or not there can be marginal increases, or whether or not there shall be marginal decreases, in this total supply of credit, and in the volume of money available for the transactions and balance needs of a money-using economy. In determining whether changes shall be made, and if so by how much, and through which of its own techniques to bring that about, the central bank must start by using whatever gauges it can devise to measure the degree of pressure generated by the push of demand upon the available supply of credit. It must in turn interpret the significance and possible persistence of this pressure in terms of the general liquidity position of the banks and of the nonbank sectors, both financial and non-financial.

Having gauged and interpreted the prevailing pressure for additional bank credit, the central bank must relate all of this to its appraisal of the economic situation as a whole. If aggregate output and employment are declining, for example, does it appear that general credit pressure is one of the causes, or if not and the decline seems persisting, might a general easing of credit availability be of some help in offsetting the downward thrust of other forces? How much easing? May the money supply side of the shield impose some limit on how far to go in expanding the base for bank credit? Does liquidity already seem redundant, so that little more thrust might be expected from further easing on the credit side, while there might be a risk that further additions to liquidity would only create a source of potential speculative pressures once a turnaround is reached and strong expansion begins? Conversely, if expansion is proceeding rapidly, liquidity is stretched thin with velocity rising to high levels, and all sources of credit are being fully tapped while demand for more at the banks is insistent, the central bank must decide whether to reduce that pressure somewhat by releasing more reserves, or to hold steady and let demand intensify the pressure, or possibly add further to the pressure by actually absorbing reserves. In practice, because of the nature of the pressure situation, central banks rarely effect a net absorption of reserves, except at periods of large seasonal increases in reserves or, in the case of most countries, in the face of substantial accumulations of foreign exchange reserves (which, unless offset, ordinarily produce an equal increase in the volume of domestic bank reserves).

What has been called the "discipline of the exchanges," as a country loses foreign exchange reserves because its internal prices and costs have risen out of line with others, is only another variant of the concept of pressure. Simply stated, the emergence of speculative or inflationary conditions in a country usually produces a decline in that country's sales abroad, and a rise in its imports. The resulting loss of foreign exchange produces a shrinkage in the reserve base and a tightening of internal pressure as surely as if the central bank itself had decided to move against the unhealthy internal developments by deliberately tightening pressure. In that event, if the corrective action occurring through the markets should strike abruptly or with extreme harshness, the central bank may indeed soften its impact—deciding how much of the resulting pressure the economy might reasonably be expected to bear, in order to spur correction of the distorting influences, and then offsetting anything additional which might otherwise, perhaps, set off a cumulative downward spiral of retrenchment or possibly even of depression.

Under almost any circumstances, it seems to me, the general aims of the central bank can be expressed for purposes of current policy in terms of the direction and extent of the change that ought to be permitted, at the margin, in the prevailing degree of pressure on bank reserves. This would lead in some countries to setting detailed operating objectives in terms of the probable direction and range of movements in interest rates of various maturities, in some perhaps to changes in discount rates, in some possibly to the setting of new targets for the size of the total reserve base, or to specifying a likely range for what in the United States would be called "free reserves," or in some countries to a revision in the ceilings established for discounting at the central bank, or possibly even a change in the reserve ratio. There is, of course, in every country, a body of economic analysis surrounding those combinations from among these various alternatives which each country has most frequently employed. But, as noted earlier, I will not try to appraise these operational objectives here. Instead, I would like to discuss another set of problems that all central banks have in common—problems that both illustrate some of the limitations upon the influence which central banking can exert upon economic activity as a whole, and at the same time also illustrate the need for further testing and elaboration of the "uncertainty postulate" that seems to me of crucial importance in the economics of a market economy.

Interest Rates, Wage Rates, and Uncertainty

There are two kinds of criticism that every central bank in a market economy encounters when the limits it imposes on further expansion of money and credit are exerting some effect. One is that the accompanying rise of interest rates is too great, or unnecessary, or causing much more harm than good. The other is that rising wage rates are the primary cause of any general price increases or particular dislocations that are disturbing the balance of the economy, and that restrictions upon the availability of money and credit are futile gestures without any real relevance to the basic problem: that is, the need to limit wages, or the "cost-push."

It is important, but not enough, to point out in reply that the central bank cannot purport to fulfill alone the entire range of ultimate objectives that should be pursued by all economic policy, nor to remind critics that the better criterion probably is "what might have happened" without some monetary limitation rather than "what more should be done" by monetary and credit policy or by other means. What seems to me even more important is to ask whether the criticism has been formulated with a clear view of its implications for the conditions essential to the functioning of a market economy.

To be sure, those conditions themselves are not immutable; they can be, and are, modified by changes in the framework of public economic policy year by year. But it should be the economist's task to sort out the issues for evaluation, and in that respect, I question whether we have done enough during recent years in appraising the role of uncertainty. Can a market economy function with fullest effectiveness, over time, if the scope for uncertainty with respect to interest rates, or wage rates, for example, is narrowed appreciably more than has already occurred? Has the United States or some other countries, perhaps, already gone too far, so that some pulling back may be appropriate?

Flexibility and Uncertainty in Interest Rates

The theory of interest rates and the central bank's concern with them is much too vast and exciting a subject for me to undertake here. I should at least assert, however, on the basis of fairly continuous observation of the experience of most leading central banks since World War II, that flexibility of interest rates, under the play of shifting competitive pressures, has been essential to the performance of the market economies. There were many who attempted, as we did here, to peg, or stabilize, or support some or all segments of the maturity range. In the end, every country that chose to preserve the essence of a market economy gave up the effort to maintain interest rates at what were thought to be "socially tolerable" levels, when these proved in practice to be sustainable only by inflating the rest of the economy with increasing quantities of central bank credit. Some instead forthrightly turned to the full apparatus of a planned economy, and began a proliferation of special devices for insulating parts of the market, and sheltering others. But even these efforts, in economies that were extensively "planned," have now largely broken down because a national plan could not build effective barricades against the forces of competition at work in international trade. The actual or suppressed inflation generated by the effort to hold interest rates down had done more damage to the domestic economy as a whole, in its ability to produce goods that could be sold abroad to pay for essential imports, than could possibly be offset by any supposed advantages in making low-interest credits available to all at home.

The evidence would seem persuasive that so long as a country is heavily dependent upon international trade, or if not, so long as it chooses to have a market economy (which is necessarily responsive to many of the same forces that are conspicuously revealed in international trade), interest rates must be flexible. There must, at any time, be good grounds for uncertainty as to where interest rates will be in the weeks or years ahead. Any attempt to remove or limit uncertainty by establishing pegs, or ceilings, for interest rates is, therefore, certain to collapse in time, unless a country is prepared to shut itself off from the Western world and convert to a planned economy.

It is quite possible, of course, having recognized the need for flexibility and uncertainty, still to argue that particular actions of the central bank, in a particular set of circumstances, have led, among other things, to limitations upon money and credit and increases in interest rates that were unwise. To do so is not to qualify as an advocate of planning, or the outvoted minorities in many central banks would find themselves among the many who might feel quite uncomfortable. To be sure, no central bank is always right. But the issue to be joined with these critics is whether the central bank has found the best balance among its ultimate objectives, and whether it has found the best translation of its policy judgments into intermediate and operational objectives. Once the "right" judgments, whatever they are, have been found for any given situation, there should not be any question that any interest rate changes which emerge should be the result of interaction between the policy action taken and all other market forces—not an arbitrary "given" inserted on the basis of some independent judgment of "what ought to be."

Recently, particularly in the United States, criticism has centered on the level of interest rates, not on the need for rate flexibility or rate uncertainty. Rates are said to be generally higher than they need to be. They have reached such levels, so the argument runs, because the Federal Reserve has let out too little of the marginal supply of money and credit. With more bank credit, interest rates would be lower and users of credit would do more to expand the employment of men and resources. The Federal Reserve has failed to permit this expansion because it is preoccupied with potential inflation. Yet that is misguided quixotry, we are told, since prices have been rising mainly because of wage increases. And the Federal Reserve can do nothing about that. High interest rates, and a slow growth rate, it is argued, are the unnecessary price of an unsuccessful effort to combat wage inflation. Does this mean that a stage has been reached for elevating wage policy to comparable importance with monetary and credit policy?

Are Wage Policy and Credit Policy Complementary?

Most other countries have, indeed, gone much further toward the formulation of a national wage policy, and toward various means of making such policy effective, than has ever been contemplated in this country except in wartime. In some, the traditional patterns of wage bargaining—industry by industry on a national scale—seem to lend themselves more readily to procedures for joining spokesmen for management and labor from a number of industries in consultations, at which the public interest is also represented, to determine the basic conditions of the wage bargain for the country as a whole. In some, long-established procedures of arbitration provide a basis for giving effect to nation-wide "norms" worked out by consultative groups, or by cabinet ministers. In some, strong national labor confederations and employer groups respond to appeals of "national interest," particularly with a view to maintaining exports, and voluntarily establish restraints of their own upon the general pace of advance in wage rates. And at the other extreme, there are instances of legal authorization for ministerial intervention to set wage rates, as well as prices and profits, although little use has apparently been made of such powers.

Enough has happened in the other market economies to justify a question whether some method may be needed, and appropriate, for reflecting national considerations with respect to economic stability and growth in the wage bargaining process, year by year. But this question, too, should be referred back to the essential elements of a market economy, as outlined early in this paper and as further elaborated in appraising the concept of uncertainty as it relates to price stability and interest rate flexibility. Though quite unqualified to say, I should think that any independently determined pegs, or arbitrary increments, for wage rates or other labor benefits would be as contrary to the conditions needed for the functioning of a market economy as fixed prices, or pegged interest rates, or arbitrary profit margins. The risk even in any search for "norms" is that they then become universal minima, with most contracts set at the "norm" or higher. And yet it may be important for the vitality of a market economy that the range of variable wage demands and settlements be kept uncertain—both as a spur to the introduction of newer techniques of higher productivity, and as a spur to labor mobility and exertion.

Perhaps it is when single contracts become so important as to exert a general and notable influence upon wages and prices throughout the country that any consideration of new approaches is justified. That seems to have been the case abroad. But even then, the various formalized approaches to a national policy for wages do not appear to have been successful, either in noticeably limiting the actual averages of wage increases or in reducing the burden still to be carried by the central bank through limiting the availability of money and credit. The outstanding instance of governmentally imposed cost-of-living factors in wage contracts, for example, has been abandoned after many years of trial. And although wide differences in national conditions make generalization dangerous, there does seem to be some basis for a conclusion that the best results have been achieved in those countries where the government's role has been to provide improved data and emphasize the relevance of certain broad criteria, with the wage bargain left to contending forces in the market.

Actual experience in dealing with "cost-push" on the wage side has, at the least, provided another stern reminder that there are no easy choices between absolute solutions for the causes of instability. It appears doubtful that a national wage policy could be developed and implemented, within the framework of a market economy, that could achieve a degree of general effectiveness, or of general acceptability, comparable to that of monetary and credit policy. The most effective corrective for distortions among the various parts of the price mechanism, so long as the elements of a market economy are preserved, is to be found in the functioning of the price mechanism itself. In time, any industry that prices itself out of its market will find its own correction, and the same may apply to labor, so long as no artificial props are erected to support or perpetuate a distorted situation.

That proviso brings me back to monetary and credit policy. For it does have a responsibility to avoid being used as one of the props. Can it, should it, when unemployment seems large but wage rates are rising, add to the supply of money and credit in the hope of providing quick employment opportunities? If existing credit is already fully used, what are the chances that new increments will result mainly in general price increases, in an accentuation of cyclical instability, and in stunting longer-range projects that could otherwise provide part of the basis for sustained growth? These are the questions that a responsible central bank must try to resolve, when confronted by a "cost-push" situation. It does not, in practice, have the choice of merely deciding that, because "cost-push" forces are operating, it can give up the effort to find that limit for money and credit which will provide the best balance among all objectives, in the light of all the existing circumstances. It cannot simply open the valve and step aside.

Conclusion

In attempting to keep this paper on a plane of general applicability to central banking in the various market economies of the Western world, I may have left many misconceptions. One is that there may be, down underneath the surface, differences in institutional arrangements, a substantial body of settled and unchanging economic "laws." To be sure, I have been trying to show that there are similarities in approach among countries, which also persist through time within each country; but the essence of effective central banking is still responsive adaptation to changing phenomena. There are very few constants, in analysis, or in methodology, or in the problems themselves. The central bank must not only reappraise continually the current significance of its various ultimate objectives, but it must also be alert to take advantage of changes in financial behavior as they occur, in order to bring about most effectively those changes in pressure that epitomize the general nature of central banking influence.

Another misconception may be that I consider the performance of central banks as the only reliable source of light on the economics of monetary and credit policy. Yet, on the contrary, the tools of economic analysis most needed in the formulation of general policy with respect to ultimate objectives are, indeed, largely the same tools that are relied upon by all economists in appraising business conditions and projecting the implications of current developments. My effort has been to emphasize the nature and limitations of the use made of such tools by the central bank, rather than to catalogue or criticize the tools themselves. I have tacitly, however, also suggested that there is a need for fuller communication of the facts of central banking experience to the economists who study monetary and credit policy from a distance.

There may also be some implication that my principal purpose has been to write a defense of the kind of central banking practiced in the United States. I have, of course, been concerned to point out aspects in the appraisal of Federal Reserve performance that have seemed to me to be relatively neglected. And I have thought it particularly important, in this attempt, to stress the basic conditions that a market economy requires for its continued, effective operation. Many of the criticisms, or notable shortcomings, of Federal Reserve action, or indeed of central banking throughout the Western world, seem to me to neglect the implications that a different course of action would have for the essentials of a market economy.

Yet many current issues do seem to me clearly open for serious debate. Moreover, such debate should contribute further toward illuminating the use of existing tools of economic analysis for purposes of present policy. Is it inherent, for example, in setting limits upon the total expansion of money and credit, that there will be a form of discrimination against the private sector of the economy because the government "always gets through"? Or, on the contrary, does the placing of limits upon increases in total credit interfere with fulfillment of essential services, such as the building of schools? Is it "wrong" that government should have to pay a rate of interest determined in part by the strength of the competing pull of the private sector upon the total supply? Is it true, and if so, is it defensible, that any effective limitation imposed by the central bank only has the effect of raising the rate of interest paid by everyone, without affecting the allocation of the total among alternative uses? These are only examples; there are many more. The principal aim of this paper will have been served if, at this stage, any reader is prompted to ask how well one answer, or another, to any of these questions can be reconciled with the degrees of freedom that the optimal functioning of a market economy requires.

6

Economics and Collective Bargaining

SUMNER H. SLICHTER [1]

COLLECTIVE BARGAINING in the United States today represents the application of the monopoly principle in an economy
that is generally committed to the principle of competition.
In the case of collective bargaining, the community is not
merely tolerating an exception to the general principle of
competition, it is giving active encouragement to the formation of powerful monopolies. The central economic question
raised by collective bargaining is whether encouragement of
the monopolistic principle in the selling of labor is desirable
or undesirable. An answer to this question requires a considerably more thorough investigation of the economic consequences of labor monopolies than economic theory has thus
far provided.

Monopoly in the Sale of Labor

Although the United States actively encourages the selling
of labor through monopolies, it never deliberately adopted
the policy that labor should be sold through monopolies. The
sale of labor through monopolies has been the unplanned
and unforeseen result of the policy of encouraging collective

[1] Lamont University Professor, Harvard University.

bargaining. When public policies in support of collective bargaining were adopted, individual employees were at a disadvantage; they had to sell their labor by accepting or rejecting the standing offers of employers; thus, it was widely believed that the terms of employment would be fairer if the employees would organize for the purpose of negotiating the terms of the labor contract. No one argued that the government ought to foster monopolistic organizations capable of depriving the country of its steel supply, its coal supply, or its railroad service. Most unions controlled merely a small part of their craft or industry and were growing only slowly. Hence, the community was more concerned about the difficulties that most unions were having in acquiring members than about the possibility that unions might acquire monopoly power. When the government took its most decisive steps to encourage trade union membership in 1933 (the National Industrial Recovery Act) and in 1935 (the Wagner Act), unemployment was severe and unions were weak.

The transformation of the policy of encouraging collective bargaining into the policy of encouraging labor monopolies was not the result of any decision by the public or the government; it was the natural result of the growth and success of unions. The unions were aided, of course, by the sellers' markets created by the Second World War and the postwar boom. At any rate, in occupation after occupation and in industry after industry unions quickly succeeded in establishing almost complete control of the jobs and the labor supply. Virtually no one works today at production jobs in the coal industry, the steel industry, the automobile industry, the paper industry, the rubber industry, the can industry, the flat glass industry, the men's clothing industry, the women's garment industry, the railroad industry, the over-the-road trucking industry, the stevedoring industry, the airplane industry, the air transport industry, and in many parts of the construction industry, the printing industry, the entertainment industries, and the hotel industry except on terms agreed to by some union. In some industries, the failure of employers and the union to agree on the terms means that the market is temporarily deprived of newly-produced goods. In other industries, however, unions use whipsawing tactics, shutting down only part of the industry at a time. Whipsawing tactics do not completely deprive the public of goods but may increase the ability of unions to raise wages. All in all, labor monopolies are by far the most powerful monopolies to be found anywhere in the economy. Even in industries in which unions fall short of controlling all production jobs, the wage settlements of unions have a substantial effect on the wages of nonunion production workers.[2] Furthermore, the changes negotiated by unions for production workers affect the wages of nonproduction employees. Thus, though only about half of all production employees in private industry are union members, union wage settlements affect the entire wage structure.

How does the monopoly principle work in the selling of labor? Does it have associated with it the abuses and inequities that are customarily associated with monopoly? The principal objection to monopoly has always been that it produces unfair distribution of incomes, enabling the monopolist to get far more than his fair share. Does this objection to monopoly apply to the monopolistic selling of labor?

The answer is "Yes", and it is fairly easy to find examples.

[2] Sometimes it is said that trade unions are not monopolies because most of them do not restrict their membership. Hence, it is argued that trade unions lack an essential attribute of the monopoly, namely the restriction of supply. This reasoning is erroneous. Trade unions restrict supply by enforcing a minimum union rate. This rate limits the number of people whom employers can afford to hire, and the number of jobs limits the number of persons who attach themselves to the craft or the industry. There are, of course, differences in the degree of restrictiveness, and the few unions, such as the Die Sinkers' Conference, that restrict their membership are far more restrictive than the unions that use the indirect method of the minimum union rate.

The outrageous prices charged by barbers are an example. So also are the wages of photo-engravers or the wages, far above the community level, imposed on can manufacturing plants in the south. The rapid rise of wages in recent years in such declining industries as coal and railroading illustrates the ability of monopolistic organizations to limit the normal response of wages to market influences. But there are important restrictions on the ability of unions to influence the wage and price structure. The restrictions stem from four important facts.

The first restriction is the result of the fact that unions seek substantially the same terms for all of their members in each given market. This rough uniformity of terms within the same market is a necessary condition of union solidarity, and it limits the ability of the union to extract the best possible terms from the most prosperous employers. Of course, virtually *all* monopolies are restricted by their inability to take advantage of the differing elasticities of demand among different buyers, but this restriction is particularly great in the case of unions. To unions, the loss of sales from the inability of some buyers to pay the monopoly price may be more than simply the loss of the sales. Unions must reckon with the possibility that the inability of marginal firms to pay the union wage scale will cause them or some of their employees to become sources of nonunion competition.

The second restriction on the ability of trade unions to influence wages is a result of the fact that the wages of different occupations are linked together so that many skilled workers are limited in their ability to take advantage of the scarcity of their skill. The wages of several occupations may be linked together by custom (each occupation expects to get whatever increases any other occupation obtains) or they may be linked because the members of all occupations are in an industrial union. Certainly the railroad engineers are underpaid in relation to the firemen, and the skilled workers in the automobile industry have been held back by the semi-skilled who dominate the union.

The third restriction on the ability of trade unions to gain a monopoly price for labor stems from the fact that stoppages in the labor market can be foreseen and that in most lines of production the customers can protect themselves from lack of goods by accumulating inventories. Thus, imposing large increases in the price of labor may be a fairly costly process to the sellers of labor.

The fourth restriction on the ability of trade unions to influence wages is a result of the broad extent of collective bargaining. In considering the effects of the monopolistic selling of labor we are not thinking of the ability of a single monopoly to extract gain for its owners in a world of competition. Rather we are considering the effects of monopolies in a world of monopolies. In a world of monopolies the inequity is less conspicuous than would be the exploitation by a single monopoly in a world of competition because the fruits of exploitation are so widely distributed. Undoubtedly, the coal miners' union is exploiting the rest of the community by enforcing a monopolistic wage, but in a world of monopolies the coal miners are also being exploited by the steel workers, the automobile workers, the rubber workers, the clothing workers, the barbers, the musicians and all the other monopolistic sellers of labor.

In this process of mutual exploitation some unions fare better than others. The unions that have the least concern over creating nonunion competition are able to push up their wages faster than the unions that must guard against nonunion competition. Thus, the steel workers, the automobile workers, and the rubber workers have been able to raise their wages faster than the clothing workers have been able to push up wages.[3] As between members of different unions,

[3] Between 1947 and 1957 hourly earnings in the steel industry, where the union does not have to worry about creating nonunion competition, rose

however, most of the exploitation cancels out, and the workers, through the process of collective bargaining, are primarily engaged in exploiting one another. The situation would obviously be very different if unionism were less pervasive and if the influence of union wages upon nonunion wages were less pronounced.[4]

Unions and the Creation of Money Incomes

More interesting than the effects of collective bargaining upon the structure of wages is its effect upon the creation of money incomes, a topic that has been largely neglected up to now.[5] When collective bargaining becomes as pervasive as it has become in the United States, it introduces a major change

---

86.1 per cent. In the automobile industry, where also there is no threat of nonunion competition, hourly earnings rose by 67.3 per cent; in the rubber industry, by 62.6 per cent. On the other hand, in the boot and shoe industry, the men's clothing industry, and the women's garment industry, where there is danger of creating nonunion competition, hourly earnings went up far less—24.2 per cent in the boot and shoe industry, 46.0 per cent in the men's clothing industry, and 19.6 per cent in the women's garment industry. Back in the 1920's before unions were established in iron and steel, automobiles, or rubber, the difference between the rise in hourly earnings in these industries and in the boot and shoe industry was much less than in the period 1947 to 1957. Thus, between 1922 and 1929 hourly earnings in the iron and steel industry rose 29.8 per cent, in the automobile industry 17.1 per cent, in the rubber industry 13.1 per cent, and in the boot and shoe industry 3.5 per cent according to the National Industrial Conference Board, *Wages in the United States, 1914 to 1929* (1930), p. 39.

[4] A few unions ignore the effect of their wage scales upon the extent of nonunion competition and, as a result, may virtually destroy themselves. The full-fashioned hosiery workers' union is an example. It recklessly insisted upon extremely high wages in spite of the fact that it was easy to establish nonunion plants that paid considerably less than the union scale and gave their employees considerably more secure employment than the union plants were able to give. As a result of its short-sighted policy, the hosiery workers' union is now virtually out of existence.

[5] A valuable paper dealing with the income-creating aspects of higher wages was presented at the meeting of the American Econometric Society in December 1958 by Jaroslav Vanek of Harvard University under the title of "The Argument for Higher Wages in Depression Revisited." The paper has not yet been published but mimeographed copies may be obtained from Mr. Vanek.

into the institutions of capitalism by giving the economy substantial new capacity to generate money incomes. The increase in the economy's capacity to generate money income, for which collective bargaining is responsible, has two effects of great significance: (1) it substantially diminishes the susceptibility of the economy to temporary contractions, and (2) it re-enforces the tendency for prices to rise in periods of boom. Such changes in the operation of capitalism are obviously of historic importance. Let me first outline in stark fashion how collective bargaining generates money incomes. Then let me fill in the outline with brief comments on the several points.

The results produced by collective bargaining depend upon the conditions under which it operates and the institutions through which it operates. Both the conditions and the institutions vary from country to country. The following description of collective bargaining and the principal conditions apply to the United States but not necessarily to other countries.

1. The bargains that unions make with employers relate almost exclusively to the price of labor (including fringe benefits) and only to a small extent to the number of workers to be employed. The effects of collective bargaining would be substantially modified if unions were to bargain for a given volume of employment. Not only do unions bargain very little over the number of jobs but in most circumstances they bargain on the assumption that the demand for labor is perfectly inelastic.

2. The unit of bargaining is a small part of the total labor market. Usually it is a small part of the industry. At any rate, it is so small that no union feels any responsibility for the effect of its wage bargain upon the price level.

3. Collective bargaining is sufficiently extensive so that the results of union-employer negotiations in most industries strongly affect the compensation of nonunion employees in those industries and even in other industries.

4. There is considerable rivalry among unions. This rivalry means that a few unions seek to take the lead in getting better conditions for their members. It also means that other unions, which elect to be followers, expect to get promptly about what the leaders obtained.

5. The short-run demand for labor is usually inelastic so that wage increases ordinarily have the immediate effect of raising payrolls, and wage cuts have the immediate effect of reducing payrolls.

These characteristics and conditions have produced the following consequences:

1. The bargaining position of employees is made strong, and the unions have a considerable incentive to take full advantage of their strong bargaining position. The result is that the compensation of employees rises faster than output per man-hour and labor costs per unit of output increase.

2. The increased labor costs per unit of output tend to produce smaller output but larger payrolls and larger total expenditures on the part of those enterprises that raise wages.

3. The increased total expenditures by the enterprises raising wages stimulate production in the rest of the economy.

4. The increased production in the part of the economy not raising wages will ordinarily exceed the decreases in production in the firms raising wages so that the net effect of the wage increases induced by collective bargaining is a rise in output.

5. The higher costs and expenditures produced by collective bargaining tend to increase the demand for money and to stimulate the growth of the banking system.

6. The growth of the banking system limits the tendency for the growing demand for money to raise contractual rates of interest.

7. The strong tendency of collective bargaining to raise money incomes limits the tendency for money incomes to

drop when production contracts, but accentuates the rise of incomes in other periods.

8. Since collective bargaining in a closed economy tends to produce rising expenditures and incomes rather than unemployment, the tendency for collective bargaining to push up wages is not self-limiting.

The Theory in Detail

Let us now examine one by one the eight basic propositions that constitute the theory of the effect of collective bargaining upon money incomes.

1. The conditions of collective bargaining make the bargaining position of employees strong, and the unions have a strong incentive to take advantage of their bargaining position. Behind the strong bargaining position of trade unions is the strong bargaining position of unorganized employees. This strong bargaining position of even the unorganized is a result of the fact that employers have only imperfect direct control over how much men produce. This amount is determined by willingness to work and may be affected by the conscious withholding of efficiency. Striking evidence of the bargaining power of even unorganized workers is the fact that the principal effect of technological progress in pre-union days was to raise wages rather than to reduce prices. The explanation is found in the sensitivity of the labor supply curve to changes of demand for labor. The usual assumption of economic theory that shifts of supply curves are independent of shifts in demand curves cannot be applied in explaining the determination of wages. (As a matter of fact, the assumption is erroneous for most markets; it is a convenient simplification that once made needs to be corrected.) Whenever it becomes evident that there is a rise in the demand for labor—a right-ward shift in the demand curve—there is a leftward shift in the labor supply curve.

What happens among unorganized workers when the labor supply curve shifts to the left? A leftward shift in the labor supply curve does not first manifest itself in the form of greater difficulty of recruiting help; the first manifestations occur among workers who are already on the payroll. Let us suppose that the workers feel entitled to more money because the firm is making more. In various ways, the workers in the plant show dissatisfaction—by a generally less cooperative attitude, displays of indifference or carelessness here and there. There may be a small rise in resignations, and among piece workers and bonus workers a greater disposition to complain about equipment, materials, and shop conditions. If nothing is done to alleviate dissatisfaction, labor turnover and absenteeism will grow, there may be slow-downs or wildcat strikes or refusals to work overtime. Some workers may talk of a union.

Even in the days before unions, most of the gain of technological progress went to employees, but the relationship between output, prices, and hourly earnings was less uniform than it has been during recent years when unions have been strong. There were occasional periods, such as the period 1897 to 1907, which, despite the absence of strong unions, were like the present period, with hourly earnings outrunning both productivity and prices. There were other periods, such as 1922 to 1929, when labor got only a part of the increased output per man-hour but in which wages increased faster than prices. Between 1922 and 1929, for example, output per man-hour in manufacturing rose 29.2 per cent, hourly earnings in manufacturing 16.2 per cent, and the consumer price level 2.4 per cent.[6] Finally, there were periods such as

[6] Joint Economic Committee, *Productivity, Prices and Incomes; Materials Prepared for the Joint Economic Committee,* Committee Print, 85 Cong. 1 sess., pp. 89 and 135.

1908 to 1913 or 1914 when both productivity and the consumer price index outran wages.

The era of trade unionism that began in the middle of the 1930's has brought a rather stable relationship between hourly earnings and output per man-hour and between hourly earnings and prices. In 17 out of the 25 years between 1933 and 1958, the percentage increase in the hourly earnings of factory workers exceeded the rise in output per man-hour of factory workers, and in 22 out of the last 25 years the percentage increase in the hourly earnings of factory workers exceeded the rise in the consumer price level. During the last eleven years the hourly compensation of all employees in private industry has without exception risen faster than the consumer price index and with three exceptions faster than real output per man-hour. Furthermore, with the exception of one year in the last eleven, namely 1950-51, the rise in wages has exceeded the rise in the wholesale prices of finished goods.[7] The table on page 128 shows the changes in wages in private industry and in prices during the last eleven years.

2. *The increased labor costs per unit of output tend to produce smaller output but larger payrolls and larger total expenditures by the enterprises raising wages.* The demand for labor by business enterprises is inelastic, especially in the short run, but not usually completely inelastic. Hence wage increases must be expected to produce some drop in output. But since the demand for most kinds of labor in the short run is inelastic,

[7] The difference between the pre-union era and the union era is epitomized by the steel industry. In the 1920's there was virtually no unionism in the steel industry. Between 1922 and 1929, output per man-hour in the basic steel industry increased by 32.0 per cent, and hourly earnings of production workers increased moderately more, by 39.1 per cent, raising unit labor costs in 7 years by 5.6 per cent. By 1948 the steel industry was thoroughly organized. Between that year and 1956, output per man-hour increased by 28.0 per cent, or slightly less than the increase in the twenties. Hourly earnings, however, far outdistanced productivity, rising 60.2 per cent in 8 years and producing a rise of 25.4 per cent in labor costs per unit of output. See *ibid.*, p. 220.

CHANGES IN WAGES AND PRICES, 1947–58[a]

Year	Increases in Average Hourly Compensation of Workers in Total Private Economy (Per Cent)	Change in Consumer Price Index (Per Cent)	Change in Non-farm Wholesale Prices (Per Cent)	Change in Wholesale Prices of Finished Goods (Per Cent)
1947–48.....	8.5	7.6	8.5	7.9
1948–49.....	2.7	−1.0	−2.0	−2.8
1949–50.....	5.7	+1.0	3.7	1.8
1950–51.....	9.3	8.0	10.4	9.5
1951–52.....	5.8	2.3	−2.3	−0.5
1952–53.....	5.9	0.8	0.7	−1.0
1953–54.....	3.5	0.3	0.4	0.3
1954–55.....	2.9	−0.3	2.2	0.2
1955–56.....	6.0	1.5	4.4	2.8
1956–57.....	6.0	3.4	2.8	3.6
1957–58.....	3.0	2.7	0.3	2.3

[a] The changes in the year-to-year compensation of employees are computed from data in *January 1959 Economic Report of the President*, Hearings before the Joint Economic Committee, 86 Cong. 1 sess., p. 782.

payrolls in the wage-increasing firms will rise. Larger payroll expenditures will usually mean some drop in nonpayroll expenditures by the firms raising wages—some deferring of repairs, replacements, improvements, expansion, possibly smaller distribution of profits to business owners. But unless the wage increases seriously impair the credit standing of the firm, the drop in nonpayroll expenditures will not fully offset the rise in payroll outlays. Hence, there will be some rise in the total expenditures of the wage-raising firms.

This conclusion that total outlays of the firms raising wages will usually rise follows from the fact that enterprises must be expected to use their resources so that for every use the ratio of marginal cost to marginal advantage is the same as the ratio for every other use. Hence, when payrolls must be increased, it is advantageous for the enterprise to meet the cost, not solely by cutting other expenditures, but partly by drawing on liquid resources, partly by greater use of credit, and partly by greater reliance on outside sources of funds. In addition, the larger payrolls may force some cuts in disbursements to stockholders or owners or a slower rate of repayment of loans and a slower accumulation of depreciation reserves, producing shifts in the saving function that are favorable to spending. Only in a few extreme cases where wage increases are so large as to force the enterprise out of important markets or to impair its credit will payroll increases reduce the total expenditures of the firm.

Will not the rise of wages in the wage-increasing firm produce an offsetting increase in the prices charged by the firm so that the wage increase exerts no general stimulus on the economy? This result is extremely unlikely because the multiplier effect of the increase in spending by the wage-increasing firms is ordinarily large enough to increase spending in the community by more than the rise in labor costs in the wage-increasing firm. This effect is discussed next.

3. The increased spending by the firms raising wages stimulates spending and production and tends to raise profits in the rest of the economy. The increase in the total outlays by the firms raising wages (payroll plus nonpayroll expenditures) has the same effect on the rest of the economy as any autonomous increase in spending, such as a budget deficit. In this case, however, the increase in autonomous spending is the result of a change in the private sector, of higher expenditures relative to income by the wage-raising firms.

The effect of the increase in spending by the wage-raising firms falls into two parts: the effect on consumption and the effect on investment spending by the firms which do not increase wages. The effect on consumption is determined by the marginal propensity to consume in accordance with the familiar Keynesian multiplier. Thus, if the marginal propensity to consume is three fifths, consumption in the community will ultimately be increased by two and a half times the increase in spending by the wage-raising firms. The effect upon investment in the rest of the economy depends upon the shift in the investment function in the rest of the economy. This function is the result partly of the state of liquidity of business concerns, and partly of appraisals of the business outlook that are constantly being made. Increased sales by nonwage-raising firms will improve their liquidity and stimulate investment by them. In addition, the larger volume of consumption induced by increased spending by the wage-raising firms will tend to create greater profits and optimistic expectations in the firms not increasing wages.

4. *The increased production in the part of the economy not raising wages will ordinarily exceed the decreases in production in the firms raising wages so that, in the absence of full employment, wage increases induced by collective bargaining tend to raise output in the economy as a whole.* These are not necessary relationships, but they are, I believe, the usual ones. They depend upon the drop of employment in the wage-increasing firms being smaller than the gain in employment in the firms which do not increase wages. The outcome depends upon the elasticity of the demand for labor and for output in the wage-increasing firms, upon the size of the marginal propensity to consume in the nonwage-increasing sector of the economy, and upon the sensitivity of investment functions in the nonwage-increasing part of the economy to changes in demand. Only if employment in the wage-increasing firms were barely inelastic with respect to wage changes and only if the marginal propensity to consume were low and the investment function in the nonwage-increasing sector of the economy had a low sensitivity to increases in demand would the net effect of wage increases be to reduce the total volume of employment and production in the economy. In the event that the economy is operating at capacity, the effect of wage increases is solely to raise money incomes.

5. *The higher costs and the higher incomes produced by collective bargaining tend to increase the demand for money.* It is true that the speculative demand for money is reduced,

not raised, by collective bargaining, since the consequences of collective bargaining make the holding of money a poor speculation. But in the United States the productive uses of money are so attractive that the demand for money to be held as a speculation is not large. On the other hand, collective bargaining, by raising costs and prices, does increase the transactions demand for money—the demand for money for working capital purposes.

6. *The effect of the increased demand for money is not primarily to raise the rate of interest but to divert more capital into banking and to enlarge the banking system.* Only slight advantages are needed to attract capital into any given industry, such as banking, rather than into some competing industry. Hence, from the standpoint of any individual industry, the supply of investment-seeking funds is highly elastic. Shifts in the demand produce only small differences in return. Consequently, the principal effect of the greater transactions demand for funds created by collective bargaining is a larger banking system, not higher rates of interest.[8]

7. *The strong tendency of collective bargaining to raise money incomes of the workers limits the tendency for aggregate money incomes to drop when production contracts and accentuates the rise of aggregate incomes at other periods.* Rigorous statistical proof of this proposition cannot be given, but the figures for the recession of 1958, though less than complete proof, are convincing. Total wage and salary payments, seasonally adjusted, reached their low point in April 1958 when they were 2.1 per cent below April 1957. But the hours worked by all wage and salary workers in April 1958,

[8] Between December 31, 1947 and December 31, 1957, the capital and surplus of all insured commercial banks in the United States increased from $7.5 billion to $13.4 billion. Member bank reserves increased somewhat less, from a daily average of $16.5 billion in 1947 to $19.0 billion in 1957.

were 4.2 per cent less than in April 1957, indicating a rise of 2.2 per cent in hourly compensation—a rise that exceeded the increase in transfer payments in the same period. Unfortunately, one does not know the elasticity of the demand for labor, though one has good reason for regarding it as small. Hence, one does not know how much the rise in hourly compensation might have reduced employment. But when account is taken of the effect of larger disbursements in the wage-increasing enterprises upon the rest of the economy, one reaches the conclusion that the total effect of the wage increases upon employment was favorable. In that event wage increases must have been fairly important in mitigating the recession.

8. *Since collective bargaining in a closed economy tends to produce rising expenditures, incomes, and output rather than unemployment, the tendency for collective bargaining to push up wages is not self-limiting.* This is a fact of great importance, It requires radical changes in our conception of trade unions, and drastic rewriting of wage theory and employment theory. It requires that traditional views of the economic role of unions be discarded and that unions be viewed, not simply as redistributors of income, but as important generators of money incomes. The fact that rising labor costs tend to produce rising expenditures and incomes throughout the economy means that much of conventional wage theory must be rewritten. Widely accepted beliefs concerning the alleged bad effects of wage increases upon employment must be abandoned. Those bad effects are revealed by the foregoing analysis to be under most circumstances local effects, not general effects.[9] The wage increases that are not severe enough to

[9] An example of the sort of statement that the foregoing analysis shows to be fallacious is the following excerpt from the *Economic Report of the President* (Jan. 20, 1959), p. 15:

force reductions in total spending by wage-raising firms stimulate spending and the enlargement of employment in the economy as a whole.

Effects on the Distribution of Income

The picture of trade unionism presented in this paper has far-reaching implications for both economic theory and public policy making. It is not my purpose to discuss these implications, but I wish to indicate their general nature. There are two groups of questions awaiting analysis: (1) the effect of trade unions upon the distribution of incomes, and (2) the possibility and the desirability of controlling the effect of trade unions on expenditures and incomes.

The first question arises because not everyone is fortunate enough to belong to a monopolistic trade union or to work in a nonunion plant that matches the union scale. A broad and searching inquiry into the effects of trade union monopoly power upon the community is needed. Trade unions, through their monopoly power, have introduced the equivalent of civil rights into industry and have accelerated the growth of orderly management. But unions also have imposed burdensome and wasteful practices upon industry. Unions have had only limited success in altering the distribution of income to their own advantage. Many nonunion workers, for example, have their wages adjusted to changes in union wage scales,

---

"But this [increasing pay of employed persons] is a factor that works two ways. It may sustain income for the employed; but to the extent that it leads to higher costs and prices, it may induce reductions in the working force and be an obstacle to re-employment."

As a description of the effect of wage increases upon employment in the firms raising wages, this statement is correct but, as a description of the *general* effect of wage increases, the statement is incorrect. It overlooks the effect of larger outlays by the wage-increasing firms upon the rest of the economy.

though the precise extent to which this happens is not known. Hence, union employers are able to pass on wage increases in the form of higher prices so that union workers are to a large extent exploiting each other. The ability of trade unions to alter the distribution of income to their own advantage is further limited by the fact that collective bargaining tends to raise incomes throughout the economy. Thus owners of business concerns on the whole find that collective bargaining tends to enhance their profits because each wage increase usually raises the demand for the goods of nonwage-increasing concerns by more than it increases the costs of the wage-increasing firms.

The class that one would expect to suffer most from the monopoly power of unions are the self-employed. Unions raise the wage and price structure of the industries using employees relative to the price structure of the industries using primarily self-employed persons. As a result, the number of self-employed is greater than it would otherwise have been, and the increase in their numbers tends to reduce their per capita incomes. But just as collective bargaining tends to increase the total incomes of property owners, so it also tends to increase the total income of the self-employed. The effect on per capita incomes is uncertain. It depends upon which effect of collective bargaining is greater—its tendency to increase the numbers of the self-employed or its tendency to increase the total income of the self-employed. A group that probably suffers on balance from collective bargaining is the farmers. The income generating effects of trade unions tend to accelerate the movement of men out of agriculture, but the rise of costs in nonfarm industries for which unions are responsible tends to produce terms of trade between agriculture and nonagricultural industries that are unfavorable to the farmers.[10]

[10] One is tempted to mention the pensioners as a group that suffers from collective bargaining since the effect of collective bargaining on prices re-

Unfortunately, statistical evidence of the influence of collective bargaining upon the distribution of income is lacking. The distribution is affected by changes in technology and in the pattern of demand, and by other influences. All that one can say is the figures appear to indicate that the direct influence of collective bargaining on wages in the unionized firms apparently have been greater than the indirect tendency of collective bargaining to raise profits or to raise the total incomes of the self-employed. For example, if one takes the income originating in all American corporate business and eliminates profits tax liability (to get rid of the effect of greatly increased profits taxes), one finds that the share of profits after taxes and inventory valuation adjustment dropped from 19.9 per cent in 1929 to 10.0 per cent in 1956, and that the share of compensation of employees rose from 77.0 per cent to 89.4 per cent. These changes may be partly the result of shifts in the relative importance of different industries. Comparison of the change in median income of male factory workers (most of whom became union members between 1939 and 1951) with the change in median income of male professional workers (a large proportion of whom are self-employed), and with the change in the median income of workers in finance, insurance, and real estate (who include a large proportion of self-employed as well as workers least influenced by unions) shows a faster rise in the wage or salary income of factory workers. In 1939 the median income of factory workers at $1,141 was less than the median income of professional workers, which was $1,235, or of finance, real estate, and insurance workers, which was $1,487. In 1951, the median income of factory workers at $3,393 was *above* the median of professional

---

duces the purchasing power of pensions. But pensioners are a powerful pressure group and thus far have been able to get the average pension raised much faster than the consumer price index has risen. But the day may come when the pensioners will have to be counted as important sufferers from collective bargaining.

workers at $3,004 and almost as large as the median of finance, insurance, and real estate workers, which was $3,462.[11]

Controlling Union Activities

Does the capacity of trade unions to generate incomes indicate the need for controlling their activities and, if so, how can control be accomplished? The community has long regarded the process of creating purchasing power as affected with a public interest and as properly subject to public control. The principal creators of purchasing power have been the banks, and the Federal Reserve system was set up to regulate the creation of money by the banks. But now the trade unions have become important sources for the creation of income. Is it not necessary to set up arrangements for controlling the creation of income by the trade unions?

This is a new problem with which economics is not yet prepared to deal for the simple reason that economics has not had an adequate conception of the economic nature of trade unions; it has failed to see that trade unions are income-creating organizations. The suggestion has been made that trade unions be broken up, though the idea behind this suggestion seems to have been to weaken the influence of unions on the

[11] Herman P. Miller, *Income of the American People,* Census Monograph Series (1955), p. 99.

Confirming data are obtained from analysis of the median incomes by occupation. The craftsmen, foremen, and kindred workers, and the operatives and kindred workers, groups that became strongly organized between 1939 and 1951, made progress relative to the managers, officials, and proprietors except farmers and farm managers. The following are the median wage or salary incomes of males in the several groups:

	1939	1951
Craftsmen, foremen and kindred workers	$1,309	$1,601
Operatives and kindred workers	1,007	3,064
Managers, officials and proprietors		
except farm	2,136	4,143
Farmers and farm managers	373	482

Ibid., p. 105.

structure of wages rather than to reduce the capacity of unions to generate income. But weakening the monopoly power of trade unions would diminish their power to create incomes by raising wages. Hence, two questions arise: (1) Would breaking up unions diminish rather than increase their monopoly power? (2) Does the community desire that the capacity of trade unions to create incomes be changed and if so, in which direction?

There is good reason to believe that breaking up unions would strengthen rather than weaken the monopolistic principle in the selling of labor. It is true that breaking up unions would lessen the opportunity of a union to strike one employer while the members in other plants worked and contributed part of their wages to support the strike. But breaking up unions would remove an important restraint on wage settlements.

Suppose that there were four or five unions in the automobile industry and the same number in the steel industry and the rubber industry. Each principal employer would still be dealing with a monopoly. If he failed to come to terms, his plant would be shut down and he would be cut off completely from alternative sources of labor. Furthermore, an important restraint on wage increases would be removed. No longer would the desire of unions to preserve their solidarity lead them to make more or less the same settlements with all employers, with the most prosperous and the least prosperous alike. The breaking up of unions would introduce rivalries among unions in the same industry. Thus, the union in General Motors, the most profitable maker of automobiles, could push its demands without regard to the ability of Ford, Chrysler, American Motors, or Studebaker to meet those demands. Hence, the breaking up of unions would give them a better opportunity to practice the monopoly principle than they now possess and would strengthen the tendency of unions to raise wages and to generate increases in money incomes.

Would the public interest be served by reducing the ability of unions to increase incomes? Or should the public seek to increase the ability of unions to raise money incomes? Unions at present do not raise incomes fast enough to prevent occasional recessions, but, by their influence on costs and incomes, they are a principal cause of creeping inflation. By encouraging trade unions to raise wages a little faster than they now do, the public can accelerate the growth of incomes and pretty much get rid of business recessions—provided, of course, that rising prices in periods of boom do not foster speculative accumulation of inventories. In addition, by encouraging the creation of income by trade unions, the public can accelerate the growth of productive capacity and of physical production since the pressure of demand upon resources (at least up to a certain point) stimulates the expansion of the economy. But the price that the public must pay for a faster and steadier growth of money incomes is a slightly faster rise in the price level. Hence, the public must decide whether it wishes faster income creation by trade unions in order to have fewer and milder recessions and faster growth of physical production or slower income creation in order to have a more stable price level.

When the public has made up its mind, will economists be prepared to tell the public what to do? I have said that today economists are not prepared. Certainly one of the first questions to be answered is whether breaking up unions would increase or diminish their monopoly power. Only experience will give reliable answers, and there is little experience that is in point. Nevertheless, careful studies of dual or rival unionism may shed some light on the matter.

The toughest problems for the economists will arise in the event that the public desires to weaken the capacity of the trade unions to generate incomes. Up to the present the economists have little to offer except general policies, such as credit restraint, which are too costly to be feasible, or decentralized action, such as more capital-saving inventions or plant-wide wage incentive systems of the Scanlon type, which are not subject to central control and which come into effect only as individual firms are persuaded to become interested in the general problem of cutting costs. Something less costly than credit restraint and quicker and more effective than a call for more capital-saving inventions is needed. A special tax on all wage settlements, including fringes, in excess of a given percentage, would probably not be feasible. At any rate, since economists do not know whether the community is likely to demand more income creation or less income creation by trade unions, they should be ready to suggest ways of implementing either demand.

One concluding observation of importance alike to trade union members and to all citizens. The discovery that trade unions are income generating organizations means that capitalism is stronger than we had suspected: it has greater capacity for expansion than we had realized. But it also means that trade unions are affected with a public interest to a considerably greater extent than had previously been evident. Union members must expect the community to assert considerable control over union activities, and the community will be well within its rights in exercising such control.

7

Competition and Monopoly

MARK S. MASSEL[1]

OUR DISCUSSION THIS EVENING concerns the use of economic analysis in the field of competition and monopoly. If time were available, we could discuss both the methods of analysis and the problems involved in their application. However, given the time limitations of this lecture, we shall discuss the applications of the analysis and leave the methods for another occasion.

First, it might be useful to indicate the kinds of economic analysis that are applicable in this field. They include definition of a market, analysis of cross-elasticity of demand and of supply, cost behavior and cost structures, measurements of price movements and price structures including differentials, statistical sampling, statistical analysis and inference, measurements of industrial concentration, and such competitive criteria as the structure, the behavior, and the performance of the market.

Next, I should like to advance a general thesis: that the tools of economic analysis will not be utilized adequately in the field of competition and monopoly until economists and lawyers learn how to coordinate their disciplines effectively. The last two or three decades have witnessed some progress in applying economic concepts in the antitrust field.

[1] Senior Staff, The Brookings Institution.

However, the progress has been inadequate, and we have scarcely started to realize the potential usefulness of economic analysis in either the development or the administration of our competitive policies.

As you will see, it is hard to resist the temptation to lay the blame for this under-utilization of economic analysis either on the lawyers or on the economists. However, assessing blame would be an unfruitful task at best, and it would serve only to restrain future progress. Indeed, impartial consideration of the basic reasons for the situation will show that it stems from differences in the methodologies of the two disciplines rather than intellectual provincialism or lack of imagination on the part of either profession.

Law and Economics in Antitrust

Antitrust, the central area in the field of competition, is probably unique among the government areas in which economic analysis can be applied. Since our antitrust laws are forms of business regulation, their application is focused on litigation. In contrast, government activity rarely provides occasions for litigation in such fields as stabilization, monetary and fiscal policy, international trade, and economic growth. Even when broad policy issues are considered in antitrust, the spotlight remains on litigation. The procedures applied in the pertinent administrative agencies, such as the Federal Trade Commission, are patterned after the courts. The emphasis is on litigation and the settlement of controversy, not on affirmative, nonlitigious government administration.

With this focus, it is only natural that lawyers should dominate the administration of our antitrust policies. Lawyers represent the government and private plaintiffs, lawyers represent the defendants or respondents, judges adjudicate the controversies, and lawyers generally run the antitrust agencies and the pertinent congressional committees. Inevitably, lawyers play the central roles in the development and administration of our antitrust laws. Therefore, a prerequisite for the adequate application of economic analysis in antitrust administration is to develop analytical tools that are useful for litigation procedures and that can be effectively adapted to the skills of the lawyer.

Effective application of economic analysis in antitrust requires an appreciation of the differences between legal and economic methodology. The law provides rules that are based on a recognized structure of statutes and court decisions. True, there are many uncertainties in the law. However, they are all capable of resolution, though it may be temporary, by procedures operated within a clear framework.

Our legal system provides an effective mechanism for determining the winner and the loser in a controversy. Since the system is founded upon the technique of adversary proceedings, it requires that all parties accept the decision of the highest court which may be involved. Therefore, during the course of litigation, a lawyer is told whether he is right or wrong.

In contrast, the economist functions within a nebulous operational framework. Though he frequently must make predictions, there can be no clear determinations of his success or failure. Even if his colleagues or superiors—whether in government, business, or the universities—should agree with him, there is no mechanism for a clear, overt determination of the correctness of his findings. In the final reckoning, the test of economic analysis is what takes place in the economy. However, even that test cannot be conclusive because of the effects of forces and circumstances which are not covered by the analysis or which could not have been visualized at the time the analysis was made.

Another distinction between law and economics relates to

differences in the standardization of technical terms. In most fields, the law employs relatively well-defined terms which are accepted by all the participants. Meanings of most words are established through statutes and court decisions and can be proven through precedent. On the other hand, there is no organized procedure for fixing the meaning of economic terms which will be accepted by all members of the profession. Since economic problems are harder to resolve, questions of terminology are especially difficult, and much attention is given to debates on the meaning of words.

Another set of problems in applying economic analysis in antitrust is technical in nature. Litigation, especially in the antitrust field, frequently calls for long drawn-out proceedings, with many technical involvements concerning the nature of the evidence which will be considered in the course of the case. Additionally, there are many subtle rules concerning the burden of proof, the weight of the evidence, and the theory of the case. Therefore, technical legal procedures, rather than straightforward economic analysis, determine what evidence will be heard and how it will be applied.

Cutting across these basic differences between the two disciplines are several factors which influence the relationships between the two professions. Lawyers, on the whole, are not accustomed to working with experts in other disciplines in planning or prosecuting a case. By and large, it seems fair to say that lawyers and judges prefer the free-wheeling of their own understanding and of their own interpretations. Even though they employ experts from other fields as witnesses, they are not accustomed to consulting these experts on equal terms.

Lawyers also prefer working with concepts and techniques that they use regularly. For example, lawyers are much more comfortable when a case involves intent, conspiracy, or good faith than when it turns on such economic issues as a lessening of competition or a tendency to create a monopoly. Given the lawyers' commanding position in this field, it seems only natural that they are not inclined to handle economic problems in a case if they have other alternatives. Therefore, whenever possible, antitrust litigation centers on issues of good faith and conspiracy, rather than on competition.

It would be an exaggeration to say that lawyers never seek help from economists or that economic analysis has made no inroads in law practice. Antitrust lawyers, whether they stand in front of our judicial benches or sit behind them, have exhibited a growing awareness of the economic aspects of antitrust problems. However, because of the lawyers' predilection for issues of intent and good faith, it has not been easy for them to plunge into unknown, imprecise economic analysis when they could handle a case on a theory of good faith or conspiracy. Nor is it easy for them deliberately to forgo filing charges of conspiracy in favor of proceedings which call for complex economic analysis.

On the other hand, economists have overlooked some strategic factors that influence the application of economic analysis in the antitrust field. On the whole, they have tended to neglect operative problems. They have not clearly recognized the need for economic tools that can be applied by the lawyers within a statutory and judicial framework. In general, they have concentrated on methods of analysis that engage the interest of their fellow economists only. They have overlooked, also, the need to develop analytical tools for forward action to help the lawyers to formulate court decrees which will inject competitive forces into a market. Instead, they have concentrated on interpretations of past developments, which are useful primarily in finding a violation of the antitrust laws. Lastly, their frequent failures to distinguish between issues of policy and issues of administration have limited the contributions of economic analysis in the broad field of competition.

This evening I propose to examine some of the problems

involved in the formulation of policy concerning competition and monopoly, and some aspects of the administration of the laws, including the negotiation and the trial of cases. With this background sketched in, we will re-examine the thesis in the light of these operating problems.

Policy Formulation

Policies affecting competition and monopoly are formulated through a number of channels. Some policies are developed directly through legislation—federal, state, and local. Most of them, however, are developed through judicial opinions, interpretations, and activities of administrative agencies, congressional investigations, and congressional pressures.

Dependence upon court-developed law is clearly indicated by the generality of the language used in the antitrust laws. Thus, the key phrases in the Sherman Act, the first of these laws, are "restraint of trade" and "monopolize." The Clayton Act and the Robinson-Patman Act rely upon such clauses as "substantially to lessen competition, or to tend to create a monopoly." The Federal Trade Commission Act strikes at "unfair methods of competition."

In employing such general language, Congress intended that the specific content of the laws would be established through court or agency interpretations. The justification for such judicial development is that the law will evolve slowly, since the courts in moving case-by-case can consider the effects of previous decisions. This evolutionary method should permit orderly consideration of the subject through the process of judging specific controversies which are presented by skilled lawyers who are close to the operating problems.

In the evolution of law through litigation, lawyers play central roles whether they represent the government or private clients. On the government side, the selection of cases to prosecute is strategic. If a government agency decides not to prosecute a given practice, the courts are not afforded the opportunity to consider the question of law which may be involved. On the private side, lawyers for plaintiffs in antitrust actions play a similar role, while lawyers for defendants play a vital part through their formulation and exposition of other theories of the law. The courts cannot determine, on their own, which theories to test or which cases to try.

Congressional investigations and pressures are of substantial import even when they do not lead to new legislation. Administrative agencies must consider congressional reactions even when no statutory changes are in prospect. Congressional pressures and legislative inquiries can exert strong influences on the volume of activity of the agencies, on the vigor behind it, and on the direction it takes.

Over-all, these administrative, legislative, and judicial developments are influenced by the climate of public opinion. Through published analyses of industries and commentaries on judicial and administrative developments, economists and students of the law play increasingly important roles.

Problem of Defining Objectives

The formulation of competitive policies requires consideration of much more than our economic goals. Deep political and social aims also constitute important elements in antitrust policy.

While our most obvious concern is with economic efficiency and higher standards of living, the social and political implications of concentration of power have been major influences in antitrust policy. In fact, there has been substantial support of a militant antitrust policy from people who are interested primarily in broad political and social forces. They believe that an economy run entirely by large companies entails a number of antidemocratic consequences. They fear that the political and social influences of the middle-class in our society would be lost, that the leadership contributed by independent members of the liberal professions would be weakened, and that the loss of these strong influences would damage our democratic institutions. In general, they are not ready to rely on the good will of industrial giants and the newly-heralded "business statesmanship" as the major political forces in our society. They fear concentration of power in any form.

Another facet of these political and social objectives concerns the appropriate areas of governmental regulation. Many feel that a strong democratic society cannot endure under stringent government regulation. This does not imply that they favor a simple, uncomplicated *laissez faire* system. Rather, they are interested in utilizing the smallest practicable amount of government regulation. They believe that, if competitive forces were destroyed, pressure for government supervision of the dominating enterprises would be irresistible, and we would lose our free enterprise system. Consequently they feel that maintenance of active competition is vitally necessary if we are to avoid an economy dominated by government regulation.

Recognition of these political and social objectives does not imply that the economic objectives play a minor role. Nor does it require that economic analysis should be reformulated to encompass all three objectives. Rather, it seems to me that an understanding of the three-way consideration of antitrust policy makes it even more important that the economists produce vigorous economic analyses of the policy problems.

It is assumed in many current discussions that there are many incompatibilities between economic efficiency and these political and social objectives. This assumption is premised on the belief that large companies in concentrated industries produce goods and services with greater efficiency and lower costs than smaller, competitive enterprises and that they will generate more substantial innovations in products and services. Support of this premise does not always imply a willingness to discard the political and the social objectives in order to improve economic efficiency. However, it does imply that we need to weigh the relative importance of the various objectives for a clearer formulation of national policy.

Accordingly, one of the main challenges for economic analysis today is to provide a clear, definitive picture of the influences of the competitive framework on efficiency, innovation, and the volume of production and employment. For, if it were clear that the economic, political, and social objectives are compatible, we would avoid the fuzzy frustrations which beset the formulation of government policies in this field. Conversely, if it were shown that a diminution of competition would raise standards of living, we would have clearer-cut choices to consider. Then, we could weigh the balance among the objectives more effectively. We could decide whether we were willing to pay the price for these social and political objectives or whether we preferred higher economic levels.

If we were to adopt a consistent policy in favor of competition, we could forge clearer criteria for the application of the economic analysis. We could then confine economic analysis of individual markets to the single criterion of whether they are competitive, without having to evaluate social performance on a broader basis. We could begin to develop a more logical pattern of government regulations. We could avoid the serious inconsistencies which generate both rules that encourage competition and regulations that stifle it. For example, in order to strengthen the over-all policy, we might apply a firm policy to promote competition even in those industries which might acquire greater efficiency through monopolistic practices, on the ground that such a consistent policy will produce better total results in our society. Conversely, if an in-between conclusion were reached, we would recognize the need for developing a method to determine those industries which do not require the same degree of competition as others. For example, we might conclude to tolerate anticompetitive trends in certain defense industries.

We need a clearer understanding of the contribution of competition even in the implementation of our economic objectives. In recent years, we have progressed beyond the elemental objectives of higher efficiency in the allocation of resources to the more advanced problems of growth and stability. The contribution of competition to these more advanced objectives is still uncertain. There are some strong indications, fragmentary in nature, that competition contributes to growth. But we need more definitive analyses. The problem of stability has many facets that are still to be uncovered. Perhaps this area will not be ready for exploration until economic stability is itself defined. Does it mean stable employment, stable prices, steadily increasing employment, or some balanced combination of the three?

Boundaries of Competitive Policies

The policy issues concerning competition are not confined to the consideration of antitrust laws. They extend to many other phases of government activity which have strategic influences on the competitive framework. They apply to the many types of government regulation on the federal, state, and local levels. They also cover a number of nonregulatory activities.

Not all federal regulation is based on a clear competitive policy. For example, the protective tariffs, quotas, and "Buy American" regulations discourage foreign competition; tax laws encourage corporate acquisitions and discourage corporate spin-offs; regulation of communications and transportation prevents new business entrants and curtails rate competition. In addition, there is room for reasonable doubt about the competitive effects of some federal regulations which are supposedly dedicated to the protection of the small business-man. Thus, the Robinson-Patman Act and the federal encouragement of resale price maintenance have been criticized on this score.

Two other problems on the federal level concern the competitive effects of the antitrust exemptions allowed for agriculture and for labor unions. These are exceedingly bothersome problems because of their political overtones. Thus, labor unions have been able to charge that some critics of labor's broad exemptions are really anxious to undermine all union power. Objective economic analysis of these two sectors is badly needed if we are to achieve clear competitive policies.

State and local governments provide a host of regulations which limit competition. For example, various farm measures limit production and promote price-setting by agricultural co-operatives. There are many substantial barriers to interstate commerce, such as dairy inspection requirements which limit the geographical areas of milk sheds, trucking regulations, and state labeling requirements for various products. Price competition is dulled by state regulations which permit fair trade as well as by some rules which practically compel control of resale prices. Provisions against selling below cost, or loss-leader limitations, frequently conceal arrangements which boost prices substantially above the level of cutthroat pricing, although they are represented as regulations which will merely raise competition above this level. Many licensing rules limit entry into various businesses and curtail the competitive potential. Such production controls, as those affecting petroleum, add to these forces.

Government purchasing is one of the important non-regulatory activities that can have a profound effect on competition. Because of the size and nature of federal, state, and local government purchases, for both military and civilian purposes, they cannot avoid influencing competition and monopoly. Thus, if the bulk of research and development contracts goes to large companies, the long-run competitive effects may be quite significant. If contracts providing for government assistance in the construction of new facilities or for the purchase of existing government plants are confined to a select few, competition is affected. On the other hand, some federal purchases are so large that they could be used to encourage new entrants in certain industries. If, in addition, means could be found to coordinate federal, state, and local government purchases, it would be possible to exert a profound influence for competition.

Role of Continuing Analysis

A realistic competitive policy requires a continuing diagnosis of competitive conditions in order to assist the Congress, the Executive, the judiciary, and public opinion.

In recent years there have been many conflicting reports about the state of competition. Some have reported a substantial weakening of competitive forces and an increase in concentration. Others have said that competition has increased in recent years and that concentration is no problem. However, flat assertions and the analysis of the deficient data that are available provide uncertain bases for policy formation. We badly need sharpened tools of empirical economic analysis which will provide more profound, continuing evaluations of the state of competition in major industrial sectors and in our society. We need to develop measurements of concentration that adequately portray economic power in the economy, in regions, and in markets.

Similarly, we need to forge better tools to evaluate the effects of our antitrust activity. We must find out whether the sum total of antitrust activity encourages competition, or merely changes some of the forms of business activity. In the latter case, we need to evaluate the desirability of these changes in form.

Unfortunately, current methods of evaluation make it tempting for any national administration to build up the appearance of active enforcement with only nominal accomplishment. The major gauges for measuring antitrust activity are statistics from the Federal Trade Commission and the Antitrust Division on the following: cases instituted; proceedings in court or other process; cases the government has won and lost; consent decrees and orders; and cases appealed. However, we do not have satisfactory evaluations of the significance of these work loads and accomplishments. We do not know what proportion of these cases affect important companies and significant industries, or unimportant companies in insignificant industries. Nor can we judge whether adequate attention is paid to trouble spots in the economy.

Unless we can attain more incisive analyses, it is difficult to see how well-intentioned people in the antitrust agencies can obtain firm support for realistic enforcement of the antitrust laws. Without such analyses, Congress does not have a firm basis for determining what resources are required for the effective application of our antitrust laws. Are larger budgets necessary or will they lead only to that proliferation of bureaucratic empires which would provide further illustrations of Parkinson's law?

Need to Analyze Effects of Types of Decrees

Related to this over-all evaluation is the need for specific analyses of the effects of court decrees and FTC orders. As pointed out earlier, general language is employed in antitrust statutes in order to permit the administrative agencies and the judiciary to develop the law case-by-case. This reason implies an experimental approach which should call for a close examination of results. But we experiment without examining the results. We have no organized program for reviewing the competitive effects of individual decrees and orders. We do not know which types of decree promote competition in what types of business situations.

Let me illustrate the need for such reviews with the Standard Stations case. The Supreme Court held that Standard Oil of California violated the Clayton Act when it entered into agreements which provided that retail gasoline stations would purchase *all* of their gasoline, tires, batteries, and accessories from Standard. Therefore, those agreements had to be canceled. In a dissenting opinion, Justice Douglas raised a troublesome query regarding the effect of such a holding on the objectives of our antitrust policy. He argued that such a decree would induce a large company to establish stations of its own instead of selling to independent retailers. Justice Douglas felt that even though the retailer might have to deal with one producer under such an agreement, he could maintain a degree of independence which is quite important politically. He contrasted this with the dependence of employees of Standard who would run the same gasoline stations. Therefore, he expressed considerable doubt about the majority decision, which was regarded by some as a rather strict interpretation of the Clayton Act.

We have here a strong position taken by a man who is known to be deeply in favor of competition, a man with wide experience in the executive and judicial branches of the government, one whose opinion cannot be lightly dismissed. Nevertheless, we have no mechanism for testing the question he raised since no one bears the responsibility for observing the effects of decrees.

Without a continuing review of the effects of decrees, we have no way of judging what types of decrees will provide constructive remedies for any type of antitrust violation. We have theories, but we have no empirical data. Therefore, though the formulation of a decree calls for forecasts of the effects of various alternatives, we have practically no guide-posts based upon past experience.

This requirement for review calls for a discriminating analysis. It would be fruitless to seek the one type of decree which would be effective in every situation. We need incisive studies that differentiate between various types of market conditions. With such analyses, the antitrust agencies and the courts could perform their tasks more effectively, and we would have firmer policy guides.

Consent Orders and Decrees

The need for broad economic analysis of the effects of antitrust enforcement is enhanced by the extensive use of consent orders and consent decrees. Under the consent procedures, there are no trials of the issues of fact or of law in either the courts or in hearings before trial examiners at the FTC. The consent order or decree is formulated in closed-door negotiations between the lawyers for the defendants and the lawyers for the antitrust agency. There is no public record spelling out the reasons for filing a complaint, nor the basis for the decree. Neither the general public, lawyers, nor economists have an opportunity to examine fully the backgrounds for the consent decrees or orders.

The extent of this practice has not been widely recognized. During the last five years, the consent procedure accounted for approximately 88 per cent of the civil decrees rendered in prosecutions by the Antitrust Division. Roughly three quarters of these consent decrees were negotiated by the parties before the division filed a complaint. During the same period, about 71 per cent of the cease and desist orders issued by the FTC were negotiated, while 4 per cent of the orders were issued when the respondents offered no defense. In effect, roughly 75 per cent of the FTC's cease and desist orders were issued without public hearings.

When the Department of Justice negotiates a consent decree before filing a complaint, the public record probably does not disclose the full reasons for the prosecution. Since the complaint is filed after the consent decree has been agreed upon, the department naturally would not allege any charges which are not covered by the decree. Therefore, there is no public record of any potential charges that are not reflected in the decree.

Without a continuing review of consent orders, their backgrounds and their effects, neither Congress, nor the Executive, nor the public can have a satisfactory basis for evaluating our antitrust administration. Without such a review, the present procedure can tempt the antitrust agencies to play a "numbers game" in response to pressures from Congress and other sources for a militant prosecution of the antitrust laws. The consent procedures make it relatively simple to show a substantial record of prosecutions.

Without an adequate review of consent orders and decrees, there is little assurance that all prosecutions involve substantial issues. There have been prosecutions of small companies, in insignificant industries, which have consented to rigorous decrees and orders simply to avoid the great costs of litigation. A reasonable defense entails not only high court costs and legal fees, but also a great deal of the time and energy of important company executives, not to mention expensive preparation of material in operating departments. Therefore, a small company literally cannot afford to carry on the active defense of an involved case. Hence, without some safeguards, the antitrust agencies can be so busy with unimportant consent orders and decrees that the more important competitive problems in the economy are neglected.

Extensive use of consent procedures can give rise to broad issues of equity in government regulation. Our legal system is designed to provide safeguards against undue prosecution and undue penalties. Among those safeguards are provisions

for public hearings and other procedural restraints on administrative agencies. Since the Antitrust Division is an executive agency, it is not confined by these restraints. Yet, it is
difficult to distinguish between its consent procedures and
those of the Federal Trade Commission. In effect, the Antitrust Division operates as an administrative agency without
the limitations provided by the procedural safeguards erected
around our administrative agencies. Further, because of the
pressures of heavy defense costs and the fear of treble-
damage suits, the defendant is frequently caught in a bad
corner during the closed-door negotiations with either agency.
Meanwhile, the agency's position is often formulated by
lawyers who are overly enthusiastic about the "chase" at
lower levels, and who are not reined-in by a thorough policy
review in the upper levels. This situation has, on occasion,
produced orders and decrees that appear to be considerably
harsher than those which would have been entered by the Commission or by a judge after an open hearing. Since the procedural restraints on administrative agencies are focused on
public proceedings, they have little effect on the consent procedures in the FTC and no influence on the work of the Antitrust Division.

On the other hand, some have felt that there have been
consent decrees and orders which were too soft. It has been
suggested that in some instances a court or hearing examiner
would have imposed a tougher order, and, further, that the
lawyers supporting the complaint would have presented
stronger cases in public proceedings than the consent orders
seem to imply.

These deficiencies do not, it seems to me, make it desirable
to eliminate consent decrees. Consent procedures of some
type are vital in the enforcement of antitrust laws. As we
shall see, public antitrust proceedings are so extended that
requiring such an adversary hearing in each case would place
an intolerable strain on our administrative organization. Such

a burden would force either a substantial enlargement of the antitrust agencies, the courts, and the antitrust bar or a drastic curtailment of antitrust activity.

Here, then, is the dilemma: on the one hand, the consent procedures are necessary for effective enforcement; on the other hand, they can lead to injustice, they can induce an agency to overlook important problems because it is busy building a paper record of accomplishment, they can provide remedies which fall short of the mark, and they provide a curtain which removes the proceedings from public scrutiny. To pose this dilemma is not to deny that we have a number of capable fair-minded men in our agencies, men who are anxious to promote fair, rigorous applications of the antitrust laws. Rather, the issue is: what can be done to assist these men in their goals and to provide more significant policy evaluations of the operations of our antitrust agencies and the effects of our antitrust laws. Until some process is developed to meet this need, a most significant opportunity to apply the tools of economic analysis in policy formation will be foreclosed.

Administration

From a broad institutional view, there are a number of participants in the administration of our antitrust laws. The federal agencies include the Antitrust Division of the Department of Justice and the Federal Trade Commission, as well as a number of other agencies, such as the Department of Agriculture, Federal Reserve Board, Interstate Commerce Commission, and Federal Communications Commission. The Federal District, Appeals, and Supreme courts are important participants. In this context, many lawyers have significant roles in the administration, whether they represent the government, plaintiffs in treble-damage suits, or defendants.

If it is to be effective in the field of competition and

monopoly, economic analysis must fit into the framework of this administrative structure. The mere transfer of methods of economic analysis that are useful in policy formulation will not meet this need. The methods for applying analyses differ, as do the advisory needs.

It seems to me that one of the road-blocks against the practicable use of economic analysis in antitrust administration is a confusion between the roles of the economist in policy making and in administration. During the process of legislative policy formulation, the economist is expected to engage in free-wheeling analysis, free of the fetters of existing regulation. Current laws and their administration are operating data which he must cover in his analysis; they are not restrictions. Indeed, at the legislative level, the economist can use the lawyer to assist in supplying legal interpretations and in legislative drafting.

In contrast, the lawyer runs the administrative show. Here, the economist is the assistant, aiding the lawyer in ideas, preparation of material, and analysis. The economist must accept the limits of the existing law and operate within them.

This distinction has been stated rather baldly here in order to point up the differences in the functions. Obviously, the differences are not black-and-white. They are found in varying shades of gray. Since policy formulation is not confined to the Congress, economists have to advise lawyers on policy on many occasions. Thus, they must be prepared to advise the lawyers who are called on for legislative recommendations.

However, the main point remains. Economists frequently confine their analysis unnecessarily, within the limitations of existing law, when they discuss policy. On the other hand, they frequently fail to recognize the task of the lawyer in the administration of current regulation and overlook pertinent operating problems.

Let me illustrate the differences in the application of economic analysis in policy making and in administration. When the Robinson-Patman Act was under consideration, there was concern lest the act stifle marketing innovations that might lower distribution costs. As you will recall, the Robinson-Patman Act is aimed at price differences that may injure competition. Some members of Congress wanted to be sure that the act would not restrain low-cost methods of distribution even though they might hurt those competitors who followed the older methods. To avoid this danger, the law permitted a seller to pass his cost savings on to his lower-cost customers. For example, if a food packer's costs in selling to supermarket chains were lower than in selling to small retailers, he could sell to the chains at discounts which were as large as his cost savings even though competing small grocers might be hurt.

At the time the act was under congressional scrutiny, most economists working in the field were convinced that the provision for cost justification of lower prices was not practicable. Both the economists and the cost accountants knew that techniques of cost accounting were not definitive enough to make this cost justification a tolerably workable defense. In fact, there was agreement that conventional cost accounting methods produced data on average costs, and not on cost differentials; that costs of distribution and administration, the principal areas in which such cost differences might be found, were regularly treated as average percentages of sales volume; therefore, cost differentials could not be readily measured by ordinary industrial cost accounting. Incidentally, many economists were concerned about this provision because they feared that it might be an opening wedge for a policy of price-setting by cost formulas. At any rate, it seemed clear to these economists that the cost proviso was not a practicable tool to avoid a tendency to freeze methods of distribution if the act were enacted.

Conceivably, if Congress had been given a clear understanding of the impracticability of the cost proviso, many legislators would have been concerned about the effect of the law on lower distribution costs. They might have voted against the bill, and it might not have passed.

Here, then, we have an example of the basic difference between economic analysis in policy making and in administration. When Robinson-Patman was under consideration, the tools of economic analysis relating to cost structures and cost behavior should have been brought to bear on the policy issue. Such analysis would have called for a strong stand regarding the impracticability of the cost defense. However, when the law was passed, the economist's help was needed to develop methods of measuring cost differentials as an aid to the lawyers for the FTC and the respondents, and to the courts. At that stage, preoccupation with the argument against the cost proviso would foreclose the usefulness of economic analysis as an affirmative aid in administration.

If he is to participate in administration, the economist must accept the limits of existing law. Such acceptance by the economist engaged in administration does not, of course, imply that economists generally should overlook the importance of continuing to review the effects of the law and its administration in considering policy issues—such as the continuation or the enforcement of the law.

Making Analytical Tools Operational

The economist's tools must be operational within the legal system to be useful in the field of antitrust. Otherwise, many lawyers will cling to their argument that economists do not offer practical help. In litigation, economic tools of analysis must fit within the context of the lawyer's methods for considering antitrust problems. If they are to be utilized by lawyers, they cannot require direct application of a rounded structure of economic theory. Thus, it does not seem possible, in the near term, to get courts or administrative agencies to use a fully defined model of competition in an industry as a yardstick. I know of no lawyer who would offer a systematic presentation of such a model in order to establish the presence or absence of adequate competition. As a matter of fact, economists have themselves been long on discussing this method in theory and short on applying it in industry studies.

Economists must appreciate the legal setting of a trial in order to understand the evidentiary problems. Otherwise, economic analysis, which may be first-rate, may fall wide of the mark. Similarly, they must recognize that there are cases which do not call for any economic analysis even though the subject matter of the case may have substantial economic effects. For example, in the General Motors Acceptance Corporation case the charge was that General Motors and G.M.A.C. had conspired to restrain trade in violation of the Sherman Act by forcing automobile dealers to finance customers' paper through G.M.A.C.[2] The government produced several dealer-witnesses who testified that they had been coerced. The defendants sought to bring in dealer-witnesses to prove that most dealers had not been coerced and that competition had not been restricted. The court refused to listen to the defense witnesses on the ground that the government's witnesses showed that a conspiracy existed, even though they were the only ones who were coerced. In effect, no economic evidence of effective restraint of trade was required to support the government's charges of conspiracy to restrain trade, though it would have been essential to support a charge that trade had been restrained. Thus, the intent to restrain was the central feature of the case rather than the possible success of the attempt.

Another difficulty in applying economic analysis arises because the economist and the lawyer frequently use the same words but with different meanings. Take, for example, the term *price discrimination*. In economic theory, *price discrimination* covers undue similarities as well as undue differences in price. Thus, a manufacturer who sells to two

[2] 121 F. 2d 376 (1941).

customers at the same price would discriminate if there were differences in his costs of selling to each of them. For, in economic theory any prices which do not reflect cost differences are discriminatory.

In contrast, under such regulations as the Robinson-Patman Act and public utility legislation, a price discrimination occurs when there is a difference in the prices charged to two customers who compete with each other. Thus, if the same price is charged to two customers, there cannot be a price discrimination under the Robinson-Patman Act regardless of what differences there may be in cost.

Here, then, is a basic language problem: some price discrimination, as the economist defines it, will not fit the legal definition; some price discrimination, under the legal regulations, will not meet the economic definition; while some price differences would classify as price discrimination under both definitions.

Opportunities to Apply Economic Analysis

In the administrative process, there are several fairly distinct opportunities to apply the tools of economic analysis.[3] Effective administration of our antitrust laws calls, first, for concentration on those industrial markets which require most attention. Antitrust agencies need to conduct a continuing review of the economy in order to identify those industrial sectors in which competitive influences seem to be inadequate. In this review, measurements of concentration and criteria

[3] It might be noted, parenthetically, that this discussion is confined to equity procedures which lead to an order governing future activity. We are not covering criminal procedures, with or without a jury, or private treble-damage actions. Though there are a number of differences between the equity procedures and the criminal or damage cases, the role of economic analysis is roughly the same in all three types of legal actions except for the determination of a remedy. In treble-damage actions, the proof of damages calls for another economic analysis. After a criminal conviction, the judge may set a fine, or in very rare instances, a prison sentence; neither penalty calls for economic analysis.

for gauging competitive conditions would be applicable. However, there are few public indications that our antitrust agencies have employed economic analysis to that end. By and large, except for merger cases, the antitrust agencies seem to institute their investigations only after they receive protests from the public.

After a decision has been made to investigate a market, economic analysis can be applied to find out whether there may be a violation of the antitrust laws. Such a review calls for a determination of what are the anticompetitive influences, what antitrust statute has been violated, how good a case can be made, and what practical means there may be for stimulating competition.

During the negotiations of a consent decree or order, the lawyers for each side can use economic analysis to evaluate the strength of the government's case and the probable effects of a proposed decree.

During the course of the trial, as we shall see, economic analysis can help to determine whether there has been an antitrust violation and to formulate a decree which will stimulate competition within a market.

Lastly, on the government side, economic analysis could be profitably employed to review the effects of past antitrust proceedings. Such analysis would enable the agencies and the courts to evaluate the relative merits of various types of decrees.

Trial Procedures

We shall take a quick look at the mechanics of the trial of antitrust cases for an illustration of the nature of these general observations about administration. It seems to me that an appreciation of these trial procedures is a prerequisite to an understanding of the size, scope, and nature of economic analysis as a realistic aid in antitrust administration.

To begin with, one must consider the conceptual framework of the judicial process. This process is essentially one of selection. The judge's primary function is to make choices, regarding facts and law, on the basis of the evidence and the legal arguments presented to him in open court. It is presumed that each adversary before the court will present the strongest evidence and arguments on his side. The judge is expected to base his decision solely on the presentations made by the adversaries. He does not strike out, on his own, to investigate other data or other legal theories.

This procedure puts each adversary on notice of the evidence and the legal arguments that the judge has under his consideration. Therefore, if A hears B present evidence or legal arguments which are unfavorable to A, he has full opportunity to present evidence or arguments to counter the unfavorable material. Such an opportunity would not be available if the judge were to conduct his own private investigation. This open procedure is so firmly imbedded in our judicial traditions that many legal scholars feel that our respect for the courts depends on it.

This theory of the judicial process is implemented by the various stages of an antitrust trial: first, the definition of the issues of the trial; second, the collection of data; third, the presentation of the data, within the rules of evidence and court procedure; fourth, the presentation of arguments by the lawyers analyzing the data and the law in the light of the issues presented; fifth, the judicial sifting and determination of conclusions regarding the violation; finally, the formulation of the decree if a violation has been found. In some instances, and these are becoming more common, decrees call for continuing judicial supervision of certain behavior of the defendants after the trial. At each stage, there are definite opportunities to employ economic analysis effectively.

The starting point for an antitrust trial is, of course, the definition of the issues. During this phase the pleadings are presented. In some instances, trial briefs outline the evidence which will be presented. Pre-trial conferences may be held between the judge and the counsel for both sides to review the types of evidence which will be introduced at the trial, and agreements may be developed regarding specific evidence which will be acceptable to both sides. On occasion, both sides will stipulate certain evidence so that the length of the trial may be shortened. This phase of the trial frequently is of major import for an adequate consideration of the economic issues. Many cases are lost by the plaintiff or defendant primarily because the economic issues were not clearly defined before the trial began.

Before the start of the trial proper, the collection of data is the task at hand. During this stage, economic analysis can be used profitably for collecting data, handling problems of sampling, and developing statistical inference from the data. Important decisions have to be made regarding sources of information, both quantitative and nonquantitative, what published material can be used, how internal operating information can be employed, what special studies should be undertaken and what information should be obtained through inquiry from the other side. Here, as in the definition of the economic issues, economic analysis can help to plan the strategy of the case.

After the data have been developed, determining how best to present them can involve some interesting problems. As we all know, the presentation of complex economic data for easy understanding is an art in itself. It calls for such a combination of testimony, explanation, and visual aids that the judge, who is not skilled in economic analysis, can grasp the economic situation—or overlook it, depending on what the lawyer's strategy may be.

When one side knows how the other will present its evidence, the economist can suggest ways and means for disproving or counteracting it. Sometimes, the other side's presentation is known before the trial proper starts; on other occasions, it is learned only in open court.

Needless to say, in the presentation of the case the economist can be used as an expert witness. However, many lawyers think of the economist solely as an expert witness, and they overlook the significant help that the economist can offer in planning the strategy of the case.

Circumstantial Evidence

The trial of economic issues in an antitrust case almost always turns on indirect or circumstantial evidence. Rarely is an antitrust case tried on the basis of direct evidence alone.

Direct evidence is useful mainly in a trial which turns on simple, uncomplicated issues of fact. Consider, for example, the testimony in a murder trial of an eye-witness who saw the shooting. Here, it is possible to prove that a specific crime took place, through the direct testimony. Similarly, if a suit concerns a written agreement which was signed by the parties, the presentation of the contract and direct evidence that it was signed may be sufficient to establish the facts of the case.

However, antitrust cases are rarely tried on such direct evidence. If the complaint charges that there is a price-fixing agreement, a written contract signed by each party would be presented as direct evidence. But the government lawyer who finds such a written agreement is fortunate, indeed. Usually, he can prove a price conspiracy only by presenting circumstantial evidence which supports an inference that there has been a price agreement. Further, if his case requires proof that competition has been lessened (which proof is not necessary if the charge is price fixing), he cannot find any direct evidence of this phenomena, since the lessening of competition is an analytical conclusion.

The treatment of circumstantial evidence involves a rather interesting methodology, based upon the testing of a hypothesis. The plaintiff presents his hypothesis, for example, that competition has been lessened because of certain market practices of the defendant. He then offers his factual evidence, through testimony and exhibits. In some instances, he offers opinions of expert witnesses regarding the validity of the information presented and its implications. On completing his evidence, his position is: (a) that his information is clearly compatible with his hypothesis; and (b) that this evidence is not compatible with any other hypothesis; or (c) that, while it might conceivably be compatible with another hypothesis, the possibilities are so remote that his hypothesis is the only reasonable one.

Now, consider the position of the defense. The defendant's counsel seeks to knock down the plaintiff's hypothesis. He may, in the unusual case, persuade the court that the plaintiff's evidence is not compatible with the hypothesis, without presenting any further evidence. More frequently, the defendant does produce evidence. He may undertake to disprove some of the evidence presented by the plaintiff by cross-examining the plaintiff's witnesses or producing other information which directly controverts the plaintiff's evidence; at that point the defendant may argue that the believable part of the plaintiff's evidence is not compatible with his hypothesis. Or, the defendant may introduce additional evidence and argue that the total evidence is not compatible with the plaintiff's hypothesis. In some instances, in order to defeat the plaintiff's case, the defendant may argue that the evidence at hand is more compatible with a new hypothesis which would wreck the plaintiff's case.

It may be useful to illustrate this procedure. Suppose that the Department of Justice has alleged that several competitors conspired to fix prices in violation of the Sherman Act. It does not have a written contract and cannot produce direct oral testimony that there was a price agreement. It shows that several competitors, located at widely separated points, submitted identical bids for "widgets" on a government contract at a price of $8.73445 per gross, delivered in Washington, D.C. It shows further, that over a period of several years the prices of each of these competitors were changed at approximately the same time. It argues that these events could not have taken place unless there had been an agreement.

The defendants deny the charge. They prove that the peculiar price of $8.73445 is the mathematical result of applying a series of percentage discounts to list prices. They show that these are the largest discounts they allow to any customer; further, the industry has sold to the government at its lowest prices since 1932 when a government purchasing agent induced a wholesaler to make a purchase for the government with no mark-up. They prove that the industry has always sold its products at delivered prices which are uniform in every state east of the Rockies; that, while the prices of each company did move together, the first company to cut a price was not always the same; and that there were occasions when one company raised its prices but had to cancel the increase because other competitors did not follow suit. Further, the defendants account for less than 75 per cent of the volume of the industry. Therefore, they did not and could not control prices or enter into an effective price conspiracy. Hence they argue that the evidence presented, taken as a whole, is compatible only with the hypothesis that competition set the industry's prices.

The judge must consider on the one hand the plaintiff's hypothesis that there was a price conspiracy, and on the other the defendant's that prices were set by the free operation of a competitive market. He must test them by sifting through the evidence, considering what is more plausible and deciding which hypothesis is more compatible with this evidence. However, he cannot make a field investigation himself. He must base his decision on what has been presented in open court.

It might be noted, parenthetically, that the hypothesis-and-test method of considering circumstantial evidence is not unique. This essentially is the methodology used in empirical economic analysis. It rests on the same foundation as the methodology followed in the physical, the natural, and the social sciences.

Since the treatment of circumstantial evidence requires formulating and testing hypotheses, the trial of economic issues in antitrust cases calls for the clear application of the methodology of economics. The stages of an antitrust trial, outlined above, with the definition of issues, presentation of data, and the analysis of the data in the light of the issues, are similar to the prosecution of empirical economic analysis. The formulation of a theoretical framework for the empirical investigation closely resembles the formulation of the theory of the case. The trial of the issues calls for adversary proceedings. However, the over-all shape of the trial presents an interesting parallel to economic studies of the same types of problems.

Before leaving this discussion of evidentiary procedures, it may be interesting to consider its connection with recent debates on the nature of antitrust rules of law. You will recall that there have been a number of complaints recently that the courts are applying too many *per se* rules in antitrust cases and too few "rule of reason" rules. Roughly differentiating, a *per se* rule does not require a court to inquire into the economic effects of a practice, while the rule of reason does so require. For example, if a price conspiracy is proved, one of the *per se* rules applies and the government does not have to show that the price agreement may lessen competition. In contrast, if there is an attack on a corporate merger, the government must introduce evidence to show that it may tend substantially to lessen competition or to create a monopoly.

Because of the reliance on circumstantial evidence in most antitrust proceedings, it seems to me that the contrast between *per se* and rule of reason has been somewhat exaggerated. Differences do exist, but they are not in the day-or-night category. Thus, in our illustration of a price-fixing case there was no direct evidence; circumstantial evidence involved the structure of the market and the behavior of competition; in fact it did not fall far short of the evidence needed to *prove* that competition was lessened. Proof of some *per se* violations can delve as deeply into economic analysis as proof of some "rule of reason" violations. This feature is not a complete negation of the differences between *per se* and "rule of reason." It merely suggests that the contrast may have been overdrawn.

The Judicial Burden

The task of sifting evidence and relating it to the hypotheses constitutes a key element in the judicial function. Considerations of the arguments about the law is the other part. Frequently, economic analysis affects the interpretation of both statutes and judicial precedents. The distinctions between issues of law and fact are frequently fuzzy, especially when economic interpretations are involved. However, we are considering only issues of "fact" here, as if the distinction were clear.

To appreciate the judicial burden in an antitrust trial, one must recognize the tremendous size of the task. Many proceedings pose such complex problems of economic analysis that the judge's task would be formidable even for an able, experienced economist. To illustrate the physical size of this task, here are some extreme examples.

The trial of the case against the Aluminum Corporation of America lasted over a period of two years and two months. During that period the judge heard 153 witnesses fill up 58,000 pages of testimony. In addition, he had to consider 15,000 pages of documentary evidence. Similarly, in the recent Pillsbury case before the FTC, the hearing examiner had to contend with 31,000 pages of testimony.

Compare the size of these records with the material covered

in a respectable industry study. Remember, however, that it is the rare judge who has had the benefit of an education in economic analysis. Further, in keeping with the general framework of the judicial function, the judge does not enjoy the economist's opportunity to discuss his ideas with other economists during the course of his study.

To develop more effective use of economic tools of analysis in such trials, we urgently need to devise ways to help our judges to develop skills of their own or to provide them with skilled assistance. Yet, this task is formidable.

Use of a Judge's Economist

What would seem to be an obvious solution for this problem will not fit the needs of the situation. At first blush, it would seem reasonable to supply the trial judge with an economist who would review the evidence and consult with him. However, such a practice would run counter to the basic premises of the judicial trial since it fails to give each adversary an opportunity to counteract any argument or evidence which has been presented to the judge.

During the trial of the United Shoe Machinery case, Judge Wyzanski, a jurist of outstanding ability, decided that he needed help on the complex economic issues of the case. Accordingly, he appointed Professor Carl Kaysen of Harvard University as his law clerk to advise him. There is no clear record of what happened between the judge and his "law clerk." However, one can only presume that the judge relied heavily upon the interpretations offered by a "clerk" of such capacity.

Unfortunately, this procedure overlooked a conflict with strategic elements in the judicial process. As pointed out before, the premise of our trial procedure is that the judge will base his decision entirely on the evidence and arguments presented to him in open court. Within narrow technical limits, he may take "judicial notice" of certain public information, available to anyone. However, he is not supposed to base his decision on any of his own library or field research, nor is he supposed to act on any advice which he has received outside the presence of the lawyers for both parties.

The basis for this rule is a keystone in the structure of our legal system with its many protections against Star Chamber proceedings. It is based upon the premise that all judicial decisions should be openly made on the basis of open evidence. It is intended to afford each party a full opportunity to counter evidence or opinions which may hurt his cause.

If the trial judge takes under consideration some information or expert opinion which is not known to the adversaries before him, the party who may suffer has no opportunity to counteract that evidence or opinion. If the injured party had been aware of the opinion or evidence, he might have presented other data or arguments against it. Such an opportunity is not available to either party if the judge engages in private discussion with an economist.

Here, then, is another dilemma. Our judges, able though they may be as lawyers, do not have the background for effective use of these tools of economic analysis, with few exceptions. Nevertheless, we ask them to analyze long records of highly-involved economic data. On the one hand, we assume that they do need help. On the other hand, the considered advice of economists, that would be most helpful to them, does not easily fit into the framework of our judicial system.

It is interesting to note a lecture given by Judge Wyzanski just about the time he had the United Shoe Machinery case under consideration.[4] In this lecture he raised some questions regarding a judge's use of research which was not made available to the parties before the court. He suggested one possible solution which merits consideration: that, if a court

[4] "A Trial Judge's Freedom and Responsibility," *Harvard Law Review*, Vol. 65 (June 1952), pp. 1281-1304.

uses material based upon outside work, the "better course may be to submit the material [to the parties] for examination, cross-examination and rebuttal evidence."

The difficulties of this problem are matched by its importance. Until practicable solutions are found, the effective utilization of tools of economic analysis in antitrust as well as other trials will be sharply limited.

Formulating Decrees

After a judge has decided that the antitrust laws have been violated, his next problem is to formulate a decree. At this stage, he should be able to consider economic evidence regarding the competitive effects of various alternative decrees. The trial is not a sporting contest governed by an umpire whose sole task is to name the winner. The goal of an equity case is not how to punish a violator, but how to inject more competition into a market.

On the whole, it seems fair to say that the courts have had even less economic guidance in formulating decrees than in finding violations. Similarly, lawyers for the antitrust agencies have had little economic advice in formulating consent decrees or orders.

An indication of the importance of economic analysis in formulating orders can be found in three recent decrees which were issued after successful antitrust attacks on collusive pricing.[5] In substance, each of these ordered individual companies to set prices on the basis of their costs, plus the margin of profit they desired, and "other lawful considerations." Economists generally associate this method of cost-plus pricing with monopolistic conditions. You will recall that similar formula pricing was written into many NRA codes.

[5] *U.S.* v. *N. E. Concrete Pipe Corp.*, C.C.H., *Trade Cases 1958*, Par. 68, 925; *U.S.* v. *L. A. Young*, C.C.H., *Trade Cases 1950-51*, Par. 62, 908; *U.S.* v. *Gold Filled Mfrs. Assn.*, C.C.H., *Trade Cases 1957*, Par. 68, 760.

The most serious deficiency involved in the promulgation of such decrees is the fact that there is no agency to study their effects. In theory, such decrees are deficient since they appear to foster monopolistic, rather than competitive, forces. However, it is possible that in practice they may provide effective bases for promoting competitive pricing. Remember that these competitors had agreed on prices. If they were told merely to discontinue the agreement, each company might continue its old prices "without agreement." The cost-plus order might jar the price situation enough to start a new pricing pattern in motion. Then, if "other lawful business considerations" were taken to mean that prices could be reduced to meet competition, a competitive situation might develop. It might be observed, parenthetically, that fears of Robinson-Patman prosecution might reduce the testing and probing of the market which seems to be the hallmark of competition in an oligopolistic industry.

The essential point here is that we should not continue to depend upon theoretical evaluations of these decrees. We require a mechanism for employing empirical economic tools to give us some analytical predictions of the effects of various types of decrees.

An increasing number of antitrust decrees require some judicial supervision over a period of time. For example, we have the cost-plus decrees discussed above. Similarly, there are a number of orders providing that patents should be licensed at reasonable royalties and allowing prospective licensees to petition the court to set the royalties. Again, in several recent cases defendants were ordered to sell, as well as lease, certain types of machinery; the decrees specified the relationships between the sales prices and the rental rates charged for the same machines. In each such case, the affirmative action required of the defendant presupposes that the court will be available to supervise the action.

No mechanism has been established to aid the judges in

this supervision. In some instances, private petitioners can be expected to police the decrees by demanding patent licenses and complaining to the court if the royalties charged are unreasonable. In others, the Antitrust Division may keep tabs on the industry and petition the court to enforce its orders. However, there are few public signs that the division has organized itself for such a surveillance. When the new petitions are filed, lawyers will "battle it out" before the courts in the same manner as in any trial. But, whatever may be the occasion for the new court proceedings, we are back to the basic need for making economic advice available to the courts.

Summary

If economic analysis is to be applied widely in the field of competition and monopoly, its methods must be operational. While there has been some progress, these methods are not operational today.

In order to improve the utilization of economic analysis in antitrust, lawyers and economists will have to develop a clearer understanding of each other's methodology. The economist will have to acquire a more precise grasp of the judicial system and of the operational framework of the law. On the other hand, the lawyer will have to realize that the economist will not learn to operate within the legal framework unless he feels some pressure to do so because he is called upon for affirmative assistance. The lawyer must reach out for help before he gets it. Just as the economist has to improve his understanding of the legal framework, the lawyer has to work with the economist on a more realistic basis if he expects progress.

The economist must recognize that in the administrative arena his analytical methods will be used by lawyers who have not been brought up on technical economic analysis. Lawyers are not skilled in the economic jargon, nor do they have much patience with economic models. Further, in their daily work they must operate within the bounds of the current state of the law—the statutes, the judicial opinions, the legal definitions of terms, and the judicial system.

The economist needs to differentiate more precisely between the use of his analysis in policy making and in administration. In the broad development of public policy, the economist does not operate within the limitations of the current laws or of the judicial system. He has an opportunity to consider economic issues on a wider base, recognizing the present state of the law and the judicial system as data in his analysis. However, he is not bound by them.

It is within the economist's province to challenge the statutes and decisions as well as government policies and procedures which do not focus on litigation. He can look into government action which dulls the edge of competition as well as policies which sharpen it. He can make recommendations about the use of nonjudicial government action to inject competitive forces. For example, he can suggest the removal of a protective tariff to increase competition or the use of government purchases to induce other companies to enter into an industry.

To repeat, it seems to me that it would be fruitless to assign fault to the lawyers or to the economists for the inadequate utilization of economic analysis in the field of competition and monopoly. The task is much greater than either profession has recognized. Neither can expect the other to tackle the task alone. The process must be developed cooperatively.

In order to promote such coordination, it seems to me, several activities would have to be undertaken. The legal and the economic professions would have to make organized efforts at cooperation. In this program, government agencies could make a forward contribution. Since the government agencies are the active instigators in antitrust litigation, they provide the setting for most cases. If they were to make wider use of economic analysis, they could exert a profound influence on their application in litigation. At the same time, their employment of economic analysis in deciding which industrial sectors need attention and in reviewing the effects of past decrees would give further impetus to the practical application of the tools of economic analysis.

Another substantial contribution could be made by the universities. Graduate students of economics can be given an appreciation of the function of economic analysis within this legal framework, and law students can be shown the uses and advantages of economic analysis. Various research agencies can contribute to a better understanding and a testing of the methods of analysis in an effort to make them operational. I trust that Brookings' program in the field of competition and monopoly will help to make some modest contribution to this development.

8

Economics and Economic Development

EVERETT E. HAGEN[1]

I AM ASKED TO DISCUSS Economics and Economic Development in a brief essay. I do not find the limitation objectionable. After all, when the king asked his adviser to give him a philosophy of history in five words, the adviser, as you may remember, bettered the target length by 20 per cent, and did it in four. I found it stimulating to attempt in brief compass a profile of the landscape whose watersheds I have been following for eight years.

My task, however, is not the straightforward one of summarizing the consensus of economic thinking about the process of economic development. This is not because there is no consensus. On a number of aspects of economic growth, there is a fair degree of agreement among students of economic theory. But in my judgment a large part of it is wrong, for reasons I shall indicate. At some points my analysis will therefore have a personal tone.

First, let me define the problem I shall be discussing. Aggregate production in a country may increase merely because the labor force increases, without any increase in output per

[1] Center for International Studies, Massachusetts Institute of Technology.

worker. Few countries find much satisfaction in this process, though a few national leaders seeking greater national power may do so. But one of the goals of every low-income country of the world, and indeed of every high-income country as well, is continually rising output, and therefore income, per person. This is the process referred to as economic development or economic growth.

How Economic Growth Begins

Low-income countries want higher income. But there is no magic known to man, except perhaps the discovery of large oil deposits, by which a low-income country can become a high-income country overnight. Increase in per capita income is achieved only by a process of starting where you are and improving methods of production, step by step—or, to use the technical phrase, by continuing technological progress. In many countries today, methods improve and income rises decade after decade, generation after generation, and there is no reason why it may not continue to do so indefinitely in the future. In many other countries, changes in methods are few and sporadic, and the level of income is about what it was 100 years ago, and indeed 500 years ago. One crucial question in the theory of economic growth is: How does the change from technological stagnancy to continuing technological progress occur?

At the heart of technological progress is invention—that is, creativity. The rise in per capita income in the West during the past 175 years has occurred because of an ever-widening stream of inventions. Among the spectacular ones are new methods of spinning and weaving; new sources of power: the steam engine, the internal combustion engine, the electric generator and motor, and—too recent yet to be of much use in production—atomic fission and fusion; new methods of

refining steel, copper, aluminum, and other metals; the creation of synthetic metals and materials; new methods of communication and transportation; new methods in agriculture;
new methods in medicine. Along with the spectacular improvements have been thousands of unspectacular ones.
Steady change has occurred at one time or another, not only
in large plants, or in key places, but in virtually every occupation in every industry.

Creativity, of course, is not enough. In addition, technological progress requires the devotion of productive resources
to making machinery and equipment embodying the new
methods—capital formation, to use the economists' term. But
the emphasis should be on creativity, not on capital formation. One of my colleagues, Professor Robert Solow, has
estimated that of the increase in output per man-hour in the
United States from 1909 to 1949, not more than 13 per cent
was due to increase in capital. Eighty-seven per cent or more
was due to technological progress.[2] If creativity ceased, and
capital formation in the United States were limited to producing additional machinery and equipment embodying methods
already known, increase in output per capita would probably
decline almost to zero within two decades. For a few minutes, therefore, let me center attention on the problem of
creativity.

It is sometimes stated that while creativity was necessary in
the initial discovery of new methods, it is not necessary in
present low-income countries, since they can merely imitate

[2] If net capital formation is used in the calculation, the share of increase
in productivity attributed to increase in capital is 10 per cent. If gross
capital formation is used (equivalent in this calculation to assuming that
capital retains its efficiency to the end of its useful life and then all wears
out at once), the share attributed to capital is 10 per cent. Robert M.
Solow, "Technical Change and the Aggregate Production Function," *Review of Economics and Statistics,* Vol. 39 (August 1957), pp. 312-20;
but note correction of an arithmetical error in a "Note" by Warren P.
Hogan in the November 1958 issue, and a further comment by Solow
in the same issue.

the methods of advanced countries. However, this turns out to be incorrect.

If a "traditional" society is to enter upon a continuing rise in per capita income, the construction of a few large manufacturing plants, including the steel mill that every country desires to symbolize power, is not enough. Construction of such large plants will raise the income only of the fortunate few workers who find employment there. Other persons will not benefit, for typically such plants can produce goods only at a higher cost than the previous cost of importing them. If per capita income is to rise steadily throughout the economy, steady technological progress must be widespread throughout the economy, in small shops as well as large ones, in petty ways as well as grand ones, diffusing new methods throughout the economy as well as introducing them in large-scale industry.

This widespread progress cannot occur, and indeed even progress in a few central places cannot occur, merely by importation of ready-made methods from abroad. Ready-made methods fit less often than ready-made suits. Let me cite two examples. In Burma and India, and no doubt elsewhere in South Asia, the digging spade is virtually unknown. Digging is done with a broad-bladed hoe. Though this is done with dexterity it remains an awkward process in many circumstances. Surely, it would seem, the simple substitution of the spade would greatly increase productivity. But it turns out that the ordinary digging spade cannot be used with sandals or bare feet, and that if the spade is constructed with a broad plate across the top, upon which the bare foot can press, then dirt sticks to it and it will not release its load. It requires creativity to adapt even the simple spade to a barefoot or sandaled society. The problem, incidentally, has been solved in Turkey, by a real act of creativity. But so far as I know, the solution has not yet reached Asia.

To cite a complex example that contrasts with this simple

one, when Japan came to develop a factory system, it was impossible for her to adopt Western managerial or personnel relationships, because in the Japanese culture Western relationships are cruel, irresponsible, and immoral. She solved the problem by devising management methods and personnel relationships which to a Western executive would seem to guarantee bankruptcy of any organization within a year.[3] Yet in her culture these practices—which for lack of time I cannot summarize—have worked so well that during the past 75 years productivity in the Japanese economy as a whole has risen at a faster rate than in the United States.

Even where low-income countries can use Western methods in virtually their original form, it is often inefficient for them to do so, because they have available a large amount of labor and little equipment, whereas our methods of production are deliberately devised for a situation with scarce labor and an abundance of equipment. Where they blindly follow our methods, they leave many workers idle and raise total output in the country less than if they creatively modified our methods.

There remain, of course, many technical processes that can and must be adopted intact to attain the necessary precision or quality of product. And where methods must be modified, technical advance is easier because they are there to modify, rather than being invented anew. But with due allowance for this, it remains true that in present low-income countries as elsewhere, continuing economic growth will require widespread continuing creativity, innovation, and invention in methods of production.

A basic question therefore is: Why was there little creativity in technology anywhere in the world until a few hundred years ago? Why is there still little in many societies? What circumstances will cause it to appear?

[3] See James C. Abegglen, *The Japanese Factory* (1958).

The first modern economist, Adam Smith, who was a practical man, appreciated the importance of technological creativity, and concerned himself with it. But his successors gradually turned their attention away from it, for a thoroughly justifiable reason. By limiting the scope of their thinking somewhat, they sought to think more clearly about the remaining problems, just as a physical scientist excludes various complexities from his laboratory experiments or his statement of physical laws in order to be sure of the cause and effect relationships among the remaining variables. In virtually every book of neoclassical economic theory, from Alfred Marshall to J. M. Keynes, one will find the careful explicit statement, "Assuming for simplicity a constant state of the arts, let us see. . . ." A constant state of the arts: that is, absence of any advance in technological knowledge. By this simplification, more penetrating thinking about the remaining problems was possible. Those problems included questions of prices, competition and monopoly in the production and marketing of goods and services, international economic relations, the distribution of income, and the level of employment. Concerning them, economic theorists have formulated increasingly keen analytical tools, and have contributed importantly to policy decisions. In doing so, as a practical matter they have taken into account the effects of technological change; but in their formal theory, technological change is absent.

Nevertheless, many of them have assumed that economic theory provides clues concerning how economic growth begins. They rely on the fact—which is a fact—that one of the desires of people everywhere is to increase their income. Further, people everywhere know about the higher levels of income in the West. Many economic theorists therefore have assumed that if the people of any given low-income country do not adopt Western methods of production, it must be because some economic barrier prevents them from doing so, and the theorists have studied low-income countries, or have sat in their studies in Western countries and pondered, to find the peculiar barrier. The resulting doctrines of peculiar barriers are the main contribution of conventional economic theory to the problem of why economic growth does or does not begin.

One of these doctrines is that income is so low in the low-income countries that they cannot save, and therefore have no resources with which to construct capital for the improvement of methods.[4] Another is that because of low income the market in underdeveloped countries is very small, whereas, machine methods must produce a certain minimum output to be efficient. The market will not absorb this volume of output; hence there is no incentive to introduce improved methods.[5] A third is that economic growth can go forward only after a certain foundation of basic utilities has been laid—notably transportation facilities, power facilities, and urban utilities.[6] These are known as social overhead capital,

[4] The doctrine is neatly stated in R. Nurkse, *Problems of Capital Formation in Underdeveloped Countries* (1953), Chap. 1.

[5] See Nurkse, *idem.*

[6] This thesis is most closely associated with the name of Professor Paul N. Rosenstein-Rodan. He has stated it in a paper which will be included in a forthcoming volume to be published by the Macmillan Co. in London, that will present the proceedings of the 1956 conference at Rio de Janeiro of the International Economic Association. It is by far the most plausible of the economic doctrines of peculiar barriers. Certainly it is true that much investment in social overhead capital often takes place in an early stage of economic growth, and is of great advantage at that time. But both history and logic seem to me to argue against giving the thesis quite as much importance as a number of economists do. While in some countries investment in social overhead capital seems to have formed a larger share of total investment in the early stage of growth than at later stages (historical statistics are not good enough to permit us to be entirely sure how much larger), it continues to be important later. Witness the present road-building program of the United States. And in other countries it does not seem to have had any special early pre-eminence. If they did not have the resources for social overhead capital, they turned to other enterprises which in time produced the necessary resources. Colombia is a conspicuous example.

Further, the theory is called in question by the general principle of the continuity of nature. That at a certain stage this one type of invest-

or the infrastructure. Because these can be built only in large units—ten miles of railroad is of little use and one fourth of a dam of none—low-income countries cannot finance them, and without them they do not have the foundation on which to introduce improved methods in other types of production. A fourth such doctrine is that a "big push" throughout the economy is necessary to introduce growth.[7] Insofar as this is an economic rather than a psychological proposition, in large part it is based on the first three. If the process of growth is to start, income must be raised throughout the economy, and social overhead capital constructed, in one big effort, so that thereafter the level of income necessary if there is to be saving, adequate markets, and a technical base for continuing advance will all exist.

In criticizing these doctrines, let me be categorical in order to be brief. Each of them is entirely sound in a theoretical model—and neither singly nor in combination do they seem of sufficient importance in the real world to explain the failure of economic growth to begin. Even the lowest income agricultural economies do in fact use a significant share of their incomes for purposes other than providing the necessities of life, and could allocate enough resources to investment to improve methods. The markets of small low-income countries are not large enough to support a steel mill, an aluminum plant, or a light-bulb factory, but they are more than large enough to support improved rice or wheat mills, sugar, textile, and shoe or sandal factories, improved methods in agriculture, and so on. And big units of social overhead capital, while they are undoubtedly advantageous at an early

---

ment should be a peculiar barrier, as if in the nature of the world a country was doomed never to progress further without outside help, implies a model of the economic world of a sort that is repugnant at least to my sense of the nature of historical development.

[7] The theory of the "big push" is also associated with Professor Rodan. See the reference cited in the preceding note. A somewhat different version of the thesis has been stated by Harvey Leibenstein in his book, *Economic Backwardness and Economic Growth* (1957), Chaps. 8 and 9.

stage of growth do not on historical examination seem to have been a *sine qua non* of growth. Social overhead capital seems often to have developed in a hen-and-egg sequence with other types of capital. Finally, economic growth may in some societies burst through some social barrier with a rush, but in others it may appear gradually. A "big push" rather than gradual change may occur, but it is not a necessary element.

Conventional economic theory, in short, has little to contribute to the question how growth begins. When we economists are shocked into a realization that this is true and free ourselves from our economic preconceptions, we realize that the part of the problem we have been neglecting is precisely the element which our theory has neglected by design, namely, why technological creativity does or does not appear in a society.

We are therefore forced to look outside of economics for explanations of the appearance or nonappearance of technological creativity. This is not surprising, for so great a change in the way of life as that involved in the transition from traditional life to life which focuses on technology, obviously involves motives and values broader than merely economic ones. Indeed, the assumption that economic theory alone can explain such a change evidences the sort of parochial arrogance that seems to appear in every science at some point in its development.

It would be inappropriate to discuss noneconomic factors at any length in a talk on the relationship of economics to economic growth, but I should like to suggest one such factor, in order to illustrate their nature.[8]

In a traditional society, labor involving dirty or mechanical work with the hands is done by peasants, artisans, and menial laborers. Of course, technological change cannot begin with these classes, because they have neither the education, the breadth of experience, nor the access to capital that are necessary. It must begin in other classes of the society. But it is an important part of the self-image of other classes— the land-owners, the bureaucracy, the professionals, the military, and, by and large, the religious functionaries—that they are different from these menial groups; an important part of their sense of identity is that they are not-peasants. Their attitude is analogous to the compulsive need of Southern whites to separate and distinguish themselves from Negroes; to be, in their way of life, not-Negro. As a result of this identity problem, no matter how fervently the elite of a traditional society desire economic development, they themselves are not interested in manual-technical or (by extension) business or industrial occupations. They are no more apt to be psychologically free to use their energies creatively in technology than a respectable businessman in a small midwestern United States temperance town would be to increase his income by becoming a saloonkeeper, or his daughter to increase her income by becoming a chorus girl.

The society is not apt to enter upon continuing technological progress until some group within the elite develops antipathy to the old values and acquires new ones, that is, until the members of some groups become social rebels. Such social rebellion, historical research and research in contemporary low-income societies suggest, is not apt to occur merely because of exposure to foreign ways. A group is not apt to be attracted to foreign ways—even ones including higher levels of living—so long as it feels properly appreciated at home. The social rebellion necessary for technological creativity is apt to occur only if a group has been pushed out of its traditional and appropriate place in its society—is looked down upon by other groups who have no right to feel themselves superior—and is unable to regain its "proper" status by traditional means. Feeling denied its due, or discriminated against, a group may reject the values of the society that is in some sense rejecting it, and may enter new paths. In England, the religious Dissenters and the lowland Scots, both scorned or condescended to by the Church-of-England gentry, provided the nucleus of innovators. In Japan, the new men came from the so-called outside clans and from samurai, merchants, and so-called wealthy peasants who had strong reason to be bitter about their social status. In Colombia, the innovators are predominantly from one of the three major valleys, whose inhabitants for historical reason were looked down upon during the eighteenth and nineteenth centuries by the residents of the other two valleys.

If social tension appears, it does not necessarily lead to economic growth, however. The men of rebellious spirit may migrate, or enter upon military rebellion. If the pressure on them is too strong for effective overt action, they may become apathetic, like many American Negroes, or may turn to philosophy or science, in an attempt to gain mastery and understanding in the realm of the intellect, or may go into a religious retreat. But if the availability of technical knowledge and conditions of resources and markets and capital are even moderately favorable, so that economic prowess seems a better way out of their dilemma than armed rebellion, migration, or some other channel, they may turn to economic prowess to gain economic power and regain their dignity and social status. Thus the economic variables are important determinants of the channels that deviations from the traditional society will take; but to understand the likelihood of economic innovation and growth, we must take into account a group of other variables as well.

I have discussed this one noneconomic factor, among several that might be discussed, only to make the point that these factors are important.

Can Economic Aid Help?

In this situation, what is the function of economic aid? Can it be effective, if noneconomic determinants are so important? Several things can be said about it. It will not automatically bring economic progress. But even where the society is still deeply traditional, aid can provide such bases of progress as schools, which may bring glimmerings of possible change as well as increased individual capability, and roads, which permit mobility that widens horizons while it markets goods. And where some rebellion against traditional ways has begun, economic aid may open channels in the direction of economic growth rather than in some other direction. The opportunities it provides may cause leaders to channel into an effort for economic growth energies that might otherwise go into international aggression, political revolution, or be dissipated in frustration. In these and other ways, though the availability of capital is not the only factor determining the success of economic growth, it has direct and indirect influences which make it an important factor.

My reference above to economic aid is to *governmental* aid. Governmental aid will of course serve functions that private investment cannot be expected to serve. Even granted political stability in the low-income country, private investors do not invest in schools, or in roads, or in agricultural credit or land reform. In the present era they would not invest in public utilities even if such investment were welcomed, which it is not apt to be. And for fairly obvious reasons, they need not be expected to invest in bonds which low-income governments might issue to finance these activities. The sale of Japanese bonds in the New York market early in 1959 is the exception that draws attention to the rule.

Even in such ventures as manufacturing enterprises, the

local government may be unwilling to permit private foreign ownership, or at least may not grant conditions necessary to attract it. Although such an attitude is usually economically illogical, it is possible to understand its historical roots. Pressure by the United States government on the local government to relax its restrictions on private investment would strengthen the claim made in the low-income country by persons hostile to us or suspicious that we are imperialistic; frequently it would result in refusal of our aid. To forward our own national interest, we shall probably do well to accept the nationalist attitudes of low-income countries as they are, and to deal with them and provide them economic aid, on that basis.

But an important point to be made here is that, even if the low-income countries welcomed private foreign investment in all fields, in the early stages of development there would undoubtedly be little of it. For a United States firm, difficult new problems must be solved in producing successfully in a foreign country. Management practices may have to be changed, labor relations will certainly be different, and many local laws and customs, restrictive in American eyes, will have to be adapted to.

A small American firm is not apt to have either the capital or management ability it can spare, sufficient for such a venture. Investment abroad is apt to be done by large companies. But for the large American company, a project in a low-income country may not justify the risks involved and the considerable trouble of overcoming the difficulties mentioned above, when considered in comparison with the prospects for expansion in the growing American economy.

Exploration of ways of increasing the incentives to American enterprises to invest abroad is now going on both in the executive department of the federal government and in Congress. This is highly desirable, since an increase in private American investment in low-income countries is highly desirable. But to be realistic we should recognize that in the early stages of development the amount of private investment will be limited.

However, if government aid stimulates economic growth, we should regard it as providing the basis for a greatly increased flow of private investment in the future. For an expanding market is one of the most powerful incentives to private investment. At the same time, economic progress is apt to give the government of the low-income country self-confidence and lead to relaxation of its suspicion of foreign investment. American companies that are now investing in an increasing volume in the expanding economy of Mexico hardly remember the expropriation of American oil companies a generation ago.

So much for the question of economic aid. Let me return to the process of economic growth.

The Allocation of Resources in Economic Growth

I have suggested that economic theory alone cannot explain the beginnings of economic growth. It does, however, have a great deal of sound advice to contribute concerning the most fruitful course of economic development, once it has begun. That is, economic theory has useful suggestions to make concerning the types of expenditures that will bring the most effective progress in economic development. Unfortunately, economic theory has not as yet been much more successful in influencing the world here than with respect to the problem of how economic growth begins. While its advice concerning the beginnings of growth is largely wrong, that concerning the allocation of developmental expenditures is largely disregarded, at least in the low-income countries to which it is addressed.

Most economic propositions concerning allocation, while important, are rather technical, and I shall not discuss them here.[9] One, however, which need not be stated in technical terms, merits discussion.

One of the important conclusions concerning economic development drawn from economic theory is that the methods of production adopted by a country attempting to get development under way should be ones which use all of the productive resources the country has. A country with much labor and little capital, and where much of the labor is partly idle or ineffectively employed, may devise projects which put this underemployed labor to work with simple equipment, or it may concentrate its development efforts on obtaining Western machinery and equipment for a small fraction of its workers, meanwhile neglecting the vast pool of underemployed labor until eventually, in the long run, it may get enough equipment for them also.

It is a curse of many low-income countries that through imitation of envied Western methods, or through lack of imagination, they are following the latter course. It is a clear

[9] Conventional theory indicates, for example, that a country does not benefit by a policy of autarky. For a low-income country, producing an industrial product within the country does not become directly advantageous until the country's quantity and types of capital, techniques, labor skills, and organizational abilities have reached such a stage that the factors required to produce the industrial product will create more value when used for that purpose than they will in the production of the raw materials whose export may be used to pay for it. For a number of products, this is true only at an advanced stage of development, and for other products it is never true.

Economic theory also suggests a number of propositions concerning the desirability of concentrating on "growing points" in development, and concerning the need for "balanced growth" throughout the economy. The two are not contradictory when properly stated. It also indicates that the usual marginal considerations are not sufficient to determine the economic desirability of a project in a developing country. One project cannot be considered in isolation when the entire system is changing. The system must be considered as a whole. Mathematical methods of doing so, known as programing techniques (of which input-output analysis is an elementary forerunner), are being developed. As yet, however, they are of limited practical use.

and sound corollary of economic theory that to obtain the greatest increase in per capita income, enough resources should be diverted from investment in Western methods to plan projects and provide simple improvements in equipment with which all underemployed workers can be put at work in productive jobs. Highly mechanized methods should be used only if their products cannot be imported and substitution of simpler methods of production is technically absolutely impossible, or if resources are available after putting all at productive work. Indeed there may be little conflict between the two efforts, for the types of resources required to put the underemployed at work differ from those required for the construction of Western-type plants. But there will be some conflict of effort, and where there is, it should be resolved in favor of projects using much labor. When all of the underemployed are at work, the amount of equipment per worker should be increased steadily as more becomes available.

There is considerable dispute among economists concerning a fact assumed above, namely whether a significant amount of surplus or underemployed labor exists in low-income countries.

I think that the dispute is not a serious substantive one. If underemployed labor exists, the largest pool is in agriculture. By a strict definition, the term underemployment refers (in agriculture) to a condition in which, if some workers were removed from agriculture, the same total output could be produced by the remaining workers without any change in methods. I think it probable that this situation, strictly defined in this way, is fairly rare. Methods are in effect that make some use of all available labor. But if we modify the definition to what might be termed a practical one, namely that if some agricultural workers were withdrawn, the same total output could be produced by the remaining workers after a relatively simple adaptation of methods, then I think there can be little question that there is a large amount of agricultural underemployment in China, Japan, India, Ceylon, Malaya, Indonesia, Egypt, countries of southern and eastern Europe, and a number of other countries.

Even granted that the underemployed labor exists, it is said by academicians and administrators in some low-income countries that methods which will increase the efficiency of production while using much labor with little equipment do not exist, since the inventions of the past 175 years have been in the West, where labor was scarce and all of the inventions were deliberately designed to economize on labor by substituting capital. This observation is correct, and so long as the development effort consists merely of imitating Western methods as closely as possible, few ways of employing underemployed workers will be found. Of course Western industrial methods, using much capital equipment, must be adopted in many cases; one probably cannot bore an efficient cylinder by hand, no matter how much labor one uses, or produce high-grade steel except in a very expensive steel mill. But where real creativity is at work, capital-saving methods appear in surprising number. Witness the device recently developed for India—by an American engineer— by which oxen turning a generator that costs $200 create enough electricity to light a village.

The example par excellence no doubt is the primitive blast furnaces of Communist China. Constructed with virtually no materials except indigenous ones and labor, almost literally in back yards on the edges of cities and also throughout the countryside, they produce small amounts per day of crude pig iron high in sulphur content and perhaps also in phosphorus. Iron ore of low grade is plentiful throughout China, but coal is not, and no doubt in many places coal or other fuel, and in some places iron ore and scrap, must be carried on human backs for a long distance. As a result, output per person directly and indirectly employed is low. It may be

100 pounds per day, or 25, or perhaps only 10. But even assuming that it is ten, one million persons working 300 days per year will have produced 1,500,000 tons of iron, and two million persons, 3 million tons.

Some American periodicals have made much of the sulphur content of this iron, claiming that the iron is useless as a result, and that the entire program is a stunt whose only or primary usefulness is psychological. But this overlooks the fact that high-sulphur iron, while not usable for modern industrial purposes, is entirely adequate for crude farm tools and equipment. Thus there is a net addition to China's production, at no social cost whatever—for the persons involved would otherwise have been producing nothing.

It is pertinent to note that the Chinese apparently overdid their allocation of effort to such labor-intensive production.[10] It is reported that the authorities are now ordering the closing down of some of the furnaces, and the conversion of others from primitive to Western methods, and also that in the zeal to obtain much pig iron and also bumper agricultural crops, by labor-intensive methods, transportation, storage, and other problems of supply and marketing were neglected. As a result food has become scarcer in some major cities. The recent sharp decline in exports may also be due to this fact, though it may also be due to diversion of exports to the Soviet Union. These failures of over-all organization illustrate the difficulties involved, but they do not detract from the economic desirability of putting underemployed labor at productive work.

In general, it is a reasonably safe assertion that high-grade dams, small and large, durable highways, irrigation, drainage, and water-supply systems, structures of many sorts, and many simple industrial products, can with imaginative devising of the necessary techniques be constructed by highly labor-inten-

[10] Information available as this goes to press indicates that the furnaces have now been closed down completely.

sive methods. The densely populated low-income countries of the world, for example India, are the poorer because their native genius is not energized to solving the necessary technical and managerial problems.

Methods using much labor typically require a great deal of organization—that is, a great deal of entrepreneurship, administration, management. At least they require the solution of problems of management different from those of conventional Western methods. Where they are not used to put underemployed workers at work in low-income countries, one reason no doubt is that the management energies involved are not available. That is, they are not used for the same reason that other technological creativity is absent, namely because national and community leaders are not psychologically free to devote their energies to these unconventional tasks. Even with great administrative efforts and resourcefulness, there would be errors—as the example of Communist China perhaps proves. But the absence of any serious effort may be ascribed in large part to the unconscious psychological bonds which hamper the imagination.

It is also true that there are institutional barriers. The underemployed cannot be put at work except by totalitarian methods, it is said. Obviously to do so is easier with totalitarian methods, but the statement that it is not possible otherwise is a reflecion of the condition just mentioned, insufficiency of creative leadership.

If a farm family member is moved from his family to perform such work elsewhere, the remaining members of the family, having more food available per person, may eat more, and it will be necessary to provide additional food, by import or otherwise, in order to execute the labor-using projects. Foreign aid may be required to help meet this increase in food consumption. Since, however, the change in consumption involved constitutes a rise in the level of living of the lowest-income section of the population, and since aid in the form of food supplies is a type of aid that the United States is uniquely suited and willing to provide, this problem seems to be of the sort which a low-income country should be exceedingly delighted to face.

The Population Problem

Early in this talk I defined economic growth as increase in per capita income. The faster the population is growing, the more difficult it is to achieve this, for an increase in output resulting from improvement in methods may be offset by an increase in population.[11] It is no doubt proper that before I conclude I should summarize what seems to be known about the population problem.

There is a fairly commonly held view that economic growth will be, if not impossible, at least extremely difficult, in low-income countries in which the population density is already high. There is such a curious mixture of truth and fallacy in this view that it deserves careful examination.

Much of our thinking on population today is dominated by a simple version of Malthusian doctrine. Because this is true, it is sometimes difficult for us to appreciate the significance of obvious facts concerning population, if they seem to contradict the conventional version of Malthusianism. With this warning, let me state some obvious facts.

[11] Even though the labor force increases by the same percentage as does the population, this does not solve the problem, for the quantity of natural resources remains fixed (in the absence of technological progress), and the problem of providing the added workers with productive equipment also remains. Further, during the first fifteen years of accelerated population increase, the labor force increases only slightly, for the population increase is primarily in the younger age groups. For a technical discussion of the facts concerning population presented here, including proof of some propositions presented here without proof, see my article, "Population and Economic Growth," in the *American Economic Review,* Vol. 49 (June 1959), pp. 310-27.

First, where continuing technological progress has appeared, population growth has nowhere in the world prevented it from producing a continuing rise in per capita income. Let me consider for a moment every case in which technological creativity—a tendency to "think up" successive improvements in methods of production—appeared before 1900, so that enough time has elapsed to note the results. There are less than twenty such cases: England, a number of countries in Western Europe, the United States, Canada, Australia, New Zealand, Japan, and Russia. In each of these countries, when income rose the death rate declined and the rate of population growth increased, but in none of them did it reach the maximum rate forecast by Malthus, and in none did it equal even a moderate rate of increase in output due to continuing technological progress. Per capita income continued to rise. Later the birth rate fell and population growth slowed down.

Population has also grown in the low-income countries of the world, where income is not rising, but this population increase has not, as many persons assume, been a result of an initial rise in income which was then foiled by population growth. There is no historical evidence of any such initial increase in income in these countries. On the contrary, there is good evidence that there was none. Rather, population growth has resulted from improvements in health and medical measures introduced two and three generations ago under colonial administration, and further ones introduced since the second World War by international technical assistance teams at the request of newly independent countries. The recent experience has been dramatic. Rapid and spectacular improvement in public health measures, by bringing rapid and spectacular declines in death rates, have caused population growth at a rate of 2½ to 3 per cent per year in Ceylon, in Malaya, in some Central American and Caribbean areas, in Egypt, and elsewhere. At 2½ per cent per year the population will double in 28 years; at 3 per cent in $23\frac{1}{2}$ years.

From these two simple sets of facts, let me make some predictions about the future. First, if technological creativity takes hold in a low-income area, it can bring a rate of increase in output sufficient to more than match even a $2\frac{1}{2}$ or 3 per cent per year rate of population growth. Per capita income will hold its own or slowly rise, in spite of increasing population, and then after a period, as birth rates fall, the rate of increase in per capita income will accelerate and the society will enter upon a course of steadily rising income per capita. Some persons worry about food supply. But empirical study indicates that there are no fundamental barriers to an increase in food production sufficient to feed the increasing population.

This is true in densely populated countries as well as in sparsely populated ones. The present level of income is maintained with present crude production methods, in spite of population density; with a moderate rate of improvement in methods per capita output can be increased even though population density increases. It is true that in densely populated countries the problem is somewhat more difficult than elsewhere because the type of technological progress needed is one that devises labor-intensive methods to a greater extent than elsewhere. And it is also true that income in densely populated countries will always be lower at any given time in the future than it could be if the population were smaller— but this fact is consistent with the fact that per capita income can continue to rise without any definite limit.

Second, where improved health methods have brought accelerated population growth, but technological progress does not occur—and there is no reason why it should occur merely because health methods have improved—there per capital income will fall steadily and a truly catastrophic population problem may be faced. On the assumption that India will escape this fate through continuing increase in production, the areas where this danger is great are all fairly small ones, except for Java—but this fact does not minimize the gravity of the problem where it exists. Misery can be as great in a small country as in a large one. In some of the Latin American countries where population is increasing rapidly, no such problem yet exists, for there is still plenty of land. In others, notably Mexico, Colombia, and Brazil, the problem has been conquered, for technological progress has taken hold and production has increased faster than population.

Third, there seems no basis for the assumption that the population of the world as a whole, if it continues to increase, must reach a volume at which there is universal starvation, "standing room only," and no "road to survival." When we project population growth indefinitely into the future, we should also project technological progress. Projection of population growth for a thousand years—or even for 100 or 200 years, yields staggering numbers. But projection of technological progress for even 50 or 100 years suggests the possibility of advance in human productive power so great that it is hard to visualize it. There is no reason to project population growth forever; human habits may change. But if we project it, there is equal reason to project technological progress; and if we project both it is plausible to visualize a time when emigration from the earth will equal the rate of natural increase on the earth. In such a situation, the population problem is obvious in balance.

Let me be clear. This is not a forecast, but only an indication of the kind of thinking we ought to do if we choose to play games about the far distant future. The population problem may appear, for man's anxieties may cause him at some time in the future to turn his energies away from technological progress, so that it falters, while population growth continues. But it seems reasonable to be more concerned with any of a dozen other world problems than with the population problem of "standing room only."

At the beginning of this essay, I refrained from stating how the king's adviser summarized a philosophy of history in four words. The true philosophy of history, he said, is simple. "This too will pass." But this dictum was criticized. Some learned persons said that it had a pessimistic bias. On further thought, the adviser agreed. He solved the problem by further simplification. The true philosophy of history, he said, can be summarized in one word: "Maybe."

Since we are hardly yet in a position to be dogmatic about the process of economic growth, that seems a good note on which to end.

Index

Abegglen, James C., 182n
Aggregate demand, 51, 80
Agriculture
  competitive effects of antitrust exemption, 150
  Department of, 157
Air Force, 22
Aluminum Corporation of America, 170
Analogy method of forecasting, 9
Antimonopoly policy, needed reforms, 53-54
Antitrust
  administration: lawyer-economist relationship in, 157-59, need for continuing review, 155
  areas of government regulation, 147
  decrees, need to analyze effects of, 152-54
  Division, 154, 156, 157, 175
  exemptions, competitive effects, 150
  law and economics in, 141-45
  laws, 53, 157-63
  opportunities to apply economic analysis, 162-63
  policy, political and social aims in, 146
  trials: formulating decrees, 173-74; judicial burden, 170-71; procedures, mechanics of, 163-75
Autarky, 192n

Bank, central. See Central Bank
Bank reserves, 106, 107
Banks. See Central bank; Commercial banks; Deposit banking system; Federal Reserve; Fractional reserve
Bierce, Ambrose, 6
Budget
  balanced, 80
  capital, 14, 82
  considered in forecasting, 34
  effects of surplus or deficit, 39
  procedure, use in forecasting, 5

Budgetary policy, 79, 80
Bureau of Labor Statistics, 2, 4
Burns, Arthur F., 6
Business cycle
  analysis, 35
  feedback effects, 34
  forecasters, 6
  short-term forecasting of, 3
  turning points, 9, 11
  See also Economic cycle

Capital formation
  barriers to, 184
  requirement in technological progress, 180
Capitalism, strength of, 139
Central bank
  criticism of U.S. interest rate level, 111
  money and credit limitations, 108
  objectives of policy, 99-108
  questions to be resolved by, 114
  responsibilities, 96
Central Intelligence Agency, 70
Chamberlin, E. H., 53
Checks and balances, economic, 90
CIA. See Central Intelligence Agency
Clayton Act, 145, 153
Collective bargaining
  central economic question of, 117
  conditions of, 125
  description, 123-24
  effect on money demand, 130-31
  effect on money incomes, 122, 125-33
  See also Labor; Unions; Wage
Colm, Gerhard, 8
Commercial banks
  capital, surplus and reserves, 1947-1957, 131n
  in public debt financing, 82
  use of economists, 3
  See also Federal Reserve
Commerce, Department of, 4
Commission on Money and Credit, 61